Intaglio

MYCHAEL BARRATT

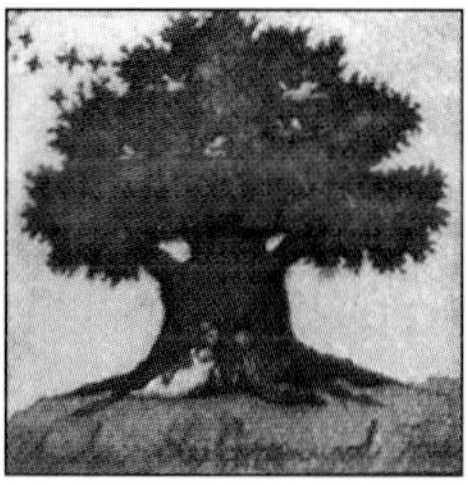

A & C BLACK ▪ LONDON

Dedication

To Amanda, Matilda and Freya as is everything I do and to Madeleine and Jon who gave me such a vibrant place to sit and write.

First published in Great Britain in 2008
A & C Black Publishers Limited
38 Soho Square
London W1D 3HB
www.acblack.com

ISBN-13: 978-07136-7388-3

CIP Catalogue records for this book are available from the British Library and the U.S. Library of Congress.

Typeset in 10.5 on 12.5pt Minion

Photography by Nigel Swift
Book design by Susan McIntyre
Cover design by Sutchinda Rangsi Thompson
Project Manager: Susan Kelly
Assistant Editor: Sophie Page

Printed and bound in China

A & C Black uses paper produced with elemental chlorine-free pulp, harvested from managed sustainable forests.

Publisher's note: Printmaking can sometimes involve the use of dangerous substances and sharp tools. Always follow the manufacturer's instructions and store chemicals and inks (clearly labelled) out of the reach of children. All information herein is believed to be accurate; however, neither the author nor the publisher can accept any legal liability for errors or omissions.

Cover image by Mychael Barratt
Frontispiece by Freya Payne – *King of carrion (T.H.)*. (See p.105).

Intaglio

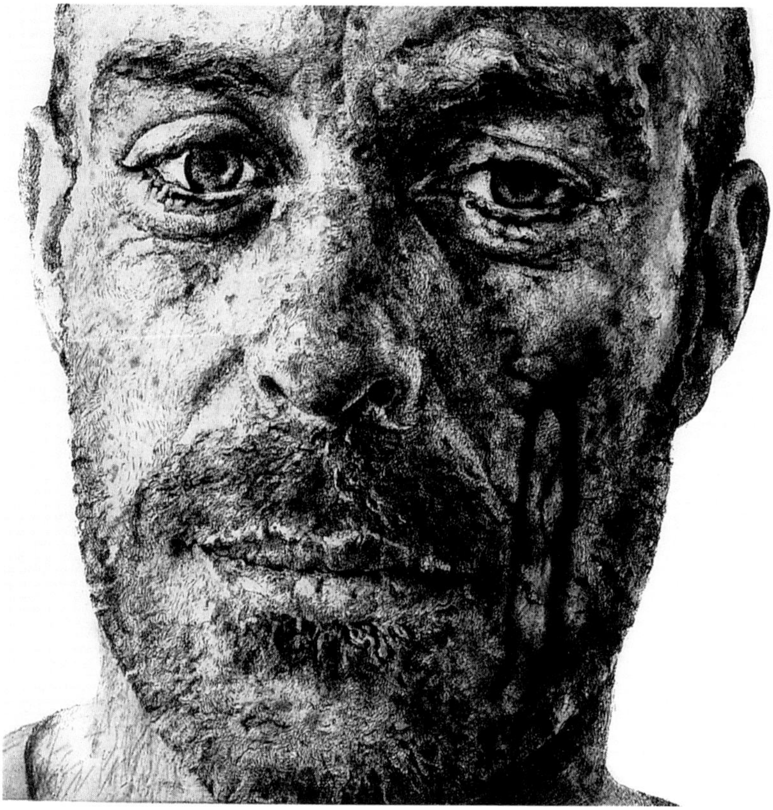

CONTENTS

Acknowledgements

I would like to thank all of the people included in this book who spoke to me at length about their work and were generous when discussing their techniques. In particular, I would like to single out Chris Orr, Norman Ackroyd, Martin Langford, Willow Winston, Trevor Price, Anita Klein and Brenda Hartill. I would also like to thank Colin Moore for his invaluable encouragement and proofreading.

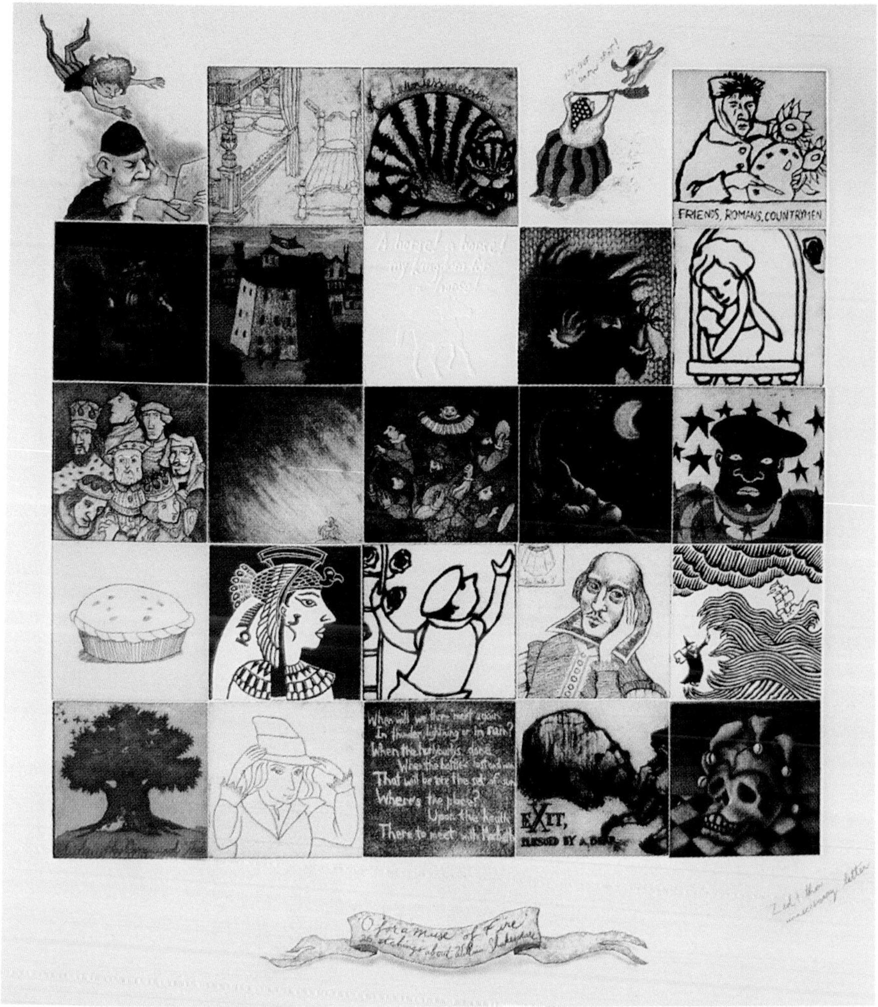

Mychael Barratt – *O for a muse of fire*. Drypoint, hard and soft ground, aquatint , sugar lift, counterproofing, blind embossing, mezzotint, engraving, spit-biting and photocopy transfer etching. 70 x 60 cm (24 x 27½ in.). This piece is an A-Z of William Shakespeare and became the vehicle through which I sampled all of the techniques that I learned and wrote about in this book. When she first saw it, Susan Kelly referred to it as an 'intaglio quilt'.

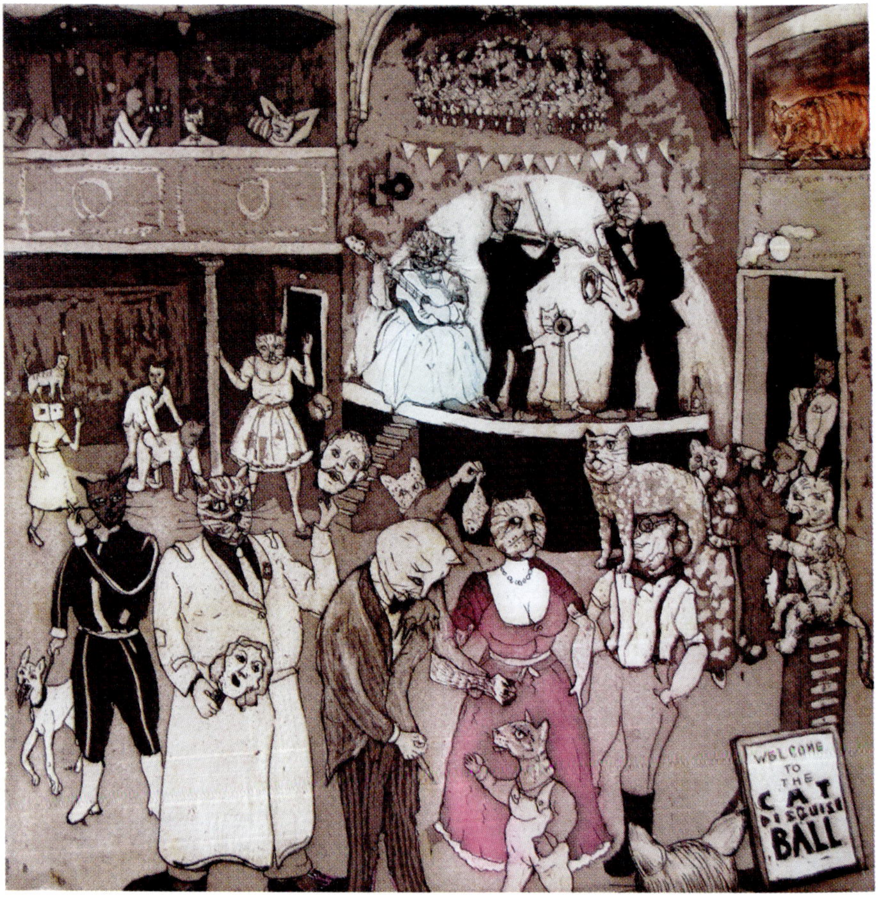

Chris Orr, *The Cat Disguise Ball*. Hard ground and aquatint. 30 × 30 cm (11⅘ × 11⅘ in.)

INTRODUCTION

When I first started this project I began by looking up the dictionary definition of intaglio. I was informed that it meant 'a printing technique in which the design is cut into the metal plate rather than protruding from it' and also 'a printing plate into which the design is cut or incised'.
I already knew enough to recognise that these definitions, although loosely accurate, are inadequate to describe the nuances of intaglio. The word in fact covers a vast number of hugely diverse printmaking techniques ranging from practices where the artist uses quite simple tools to directly draw into the surface of the metal to those where acids and chemicals are used to alter the metal. The presence of these techniques and tools between the artist and the metal do not distance him from his creation: they fuse and connect him to it in a way that is totally different to working on any other two-dimensional art form. He is not merely laying marks on the surface of paper or canvas but is manipulating sheets of metal to create his images. There is a tangible physicality about intaglio and this is apparent in many of the terms we use to describe our processes: we *bite* our etching plates, *rock* our mezzotints and *pull* our prints.

I decided that the best way to learn enough to write about intaglio was to meet artists who practice the full range of techniques and to try them out myself. As a printmaker, there are clearly some processes with which I am very familiar but others that are entirely foreign.

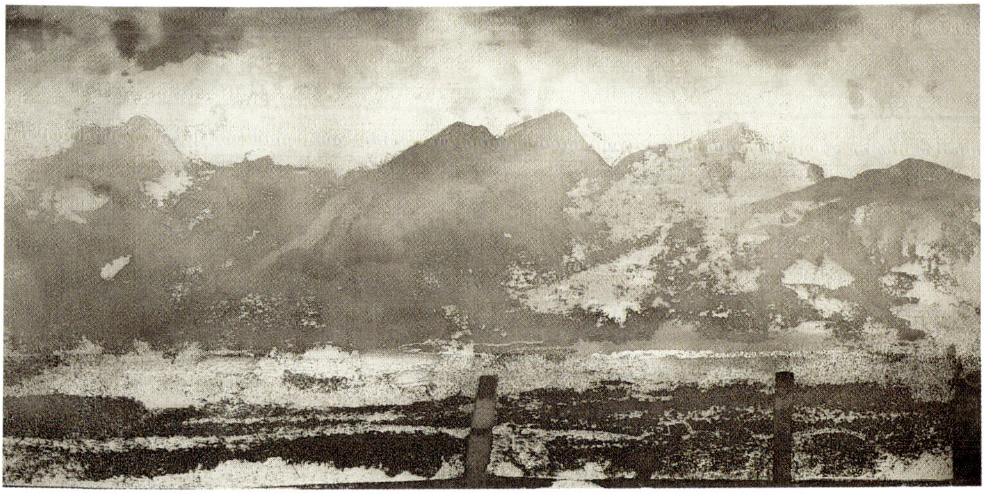

Norman Ackroyd – *Connemarra Pins from Roundstone Bay*. 20 x 41.5 cm (8 x 16½ in.)
Aquatint: sugar lift and spit bite

I have divided up the various processes under the two broad headings of 'Direct Intaglio' and 'Indirect Intaglio'. The section covering 'Direct Intaglio' will deal with all techniques in which the artist uses tools to physically incise the lines or alter the surface of the plate and will include drypoint, engraving and mezzotint. The section entitled 'Indirect Intaglio' will include all techniques that involve the use of acids to etch the plate and will include hard-ground etching, soft-ground etching and all variant uses of aquatint. I have followed this with a section of profiles of various artists whose work exemplifies the use of one or more of the techniques described, complete with relevant examples of their work.

A brief history

The intaglio process was first used as a method of decorating metal items such as suits of armour, cups and plates. Goldsmiths and armourers were using metal engraving at the start of the 15th century. Initially, craftsmen cut engraved lines into the metal, a very labour intensive process. They then discovered that by protectively coating the metal, then selectively exposing lines and immersing it in acid they could incise similar patterns in a fraction of the time. Historians have speculated that armourers would lay ink into the incised lines and press paper onto the metal in order to keep a recorded catalogue of their work. It is easy to imagine that an artist seeing one of these armour indexes would have quickly realised the potential.

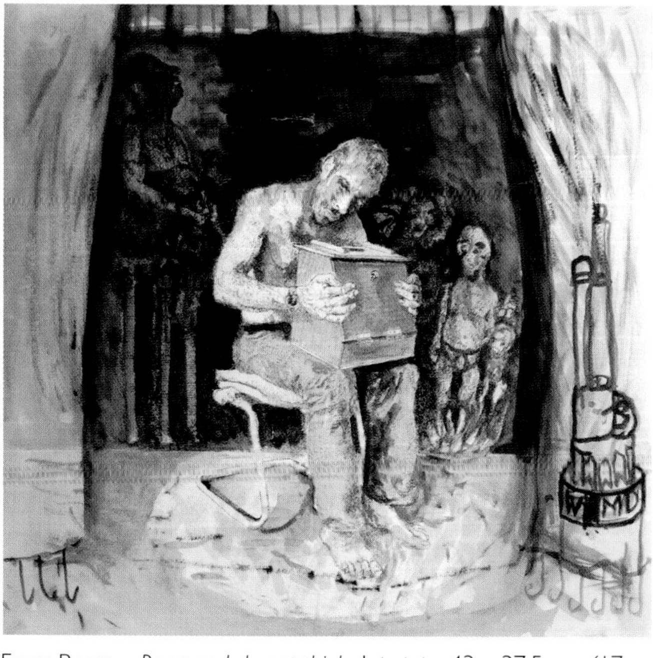

Freya Payne – *Because I do not think*; 1st state. 43 × 37.5 cm. (17 × 14¾ in.). Hard ground and ink

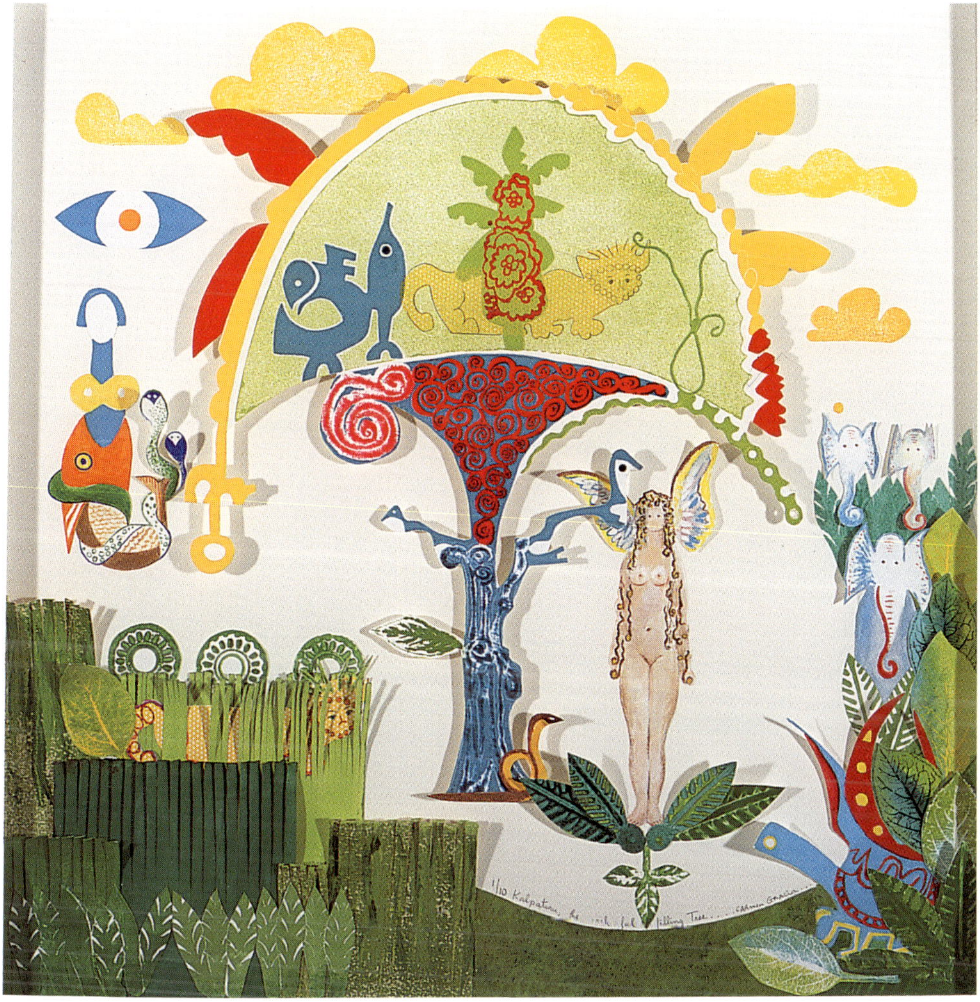

Carmen Gracia – *Kalpaturu, The wish fulfilling tree.* Deep bite etching, relief etching and mixed media, 60 × 60 cm ($23\frac{1}{2}$ × $23\frac{1}{2}$ in.). In the etched areas of this image, the lines have been deeply bitten, inked up in one colour and then rolled over with contrasting inks. The intricate shapes of the metal plates were cut using an electric jeweller's band saw.

The first recorded engraving on paper was a German print made in 1446, entitled *The Flagellation*. The first etchings appeared about 100 years later. Initially, both engravings and mezzotints were primarily used as techniques for copying or imitating paintings in order that they could be made available to a wider public. Drypoint and etching were more consistently used as art forms in themselves than simply as methods of reproduction. The notion of editioning (printing multiples from a single plate to make them more widely available) is a constant amongst all intaglio techniques. Ultimately the activity of creating the plate is what attracts the artist, rather than simply the potential to create more than one original.

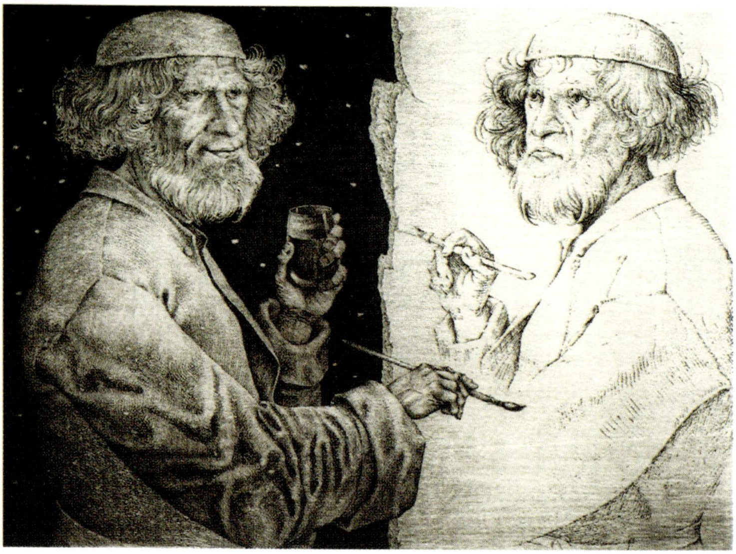

Konstantin Kalinovich, *Living Bruegel*. Hard ground and aquatint etching, 9 × 12.5 cm (3½ × 5 in.)

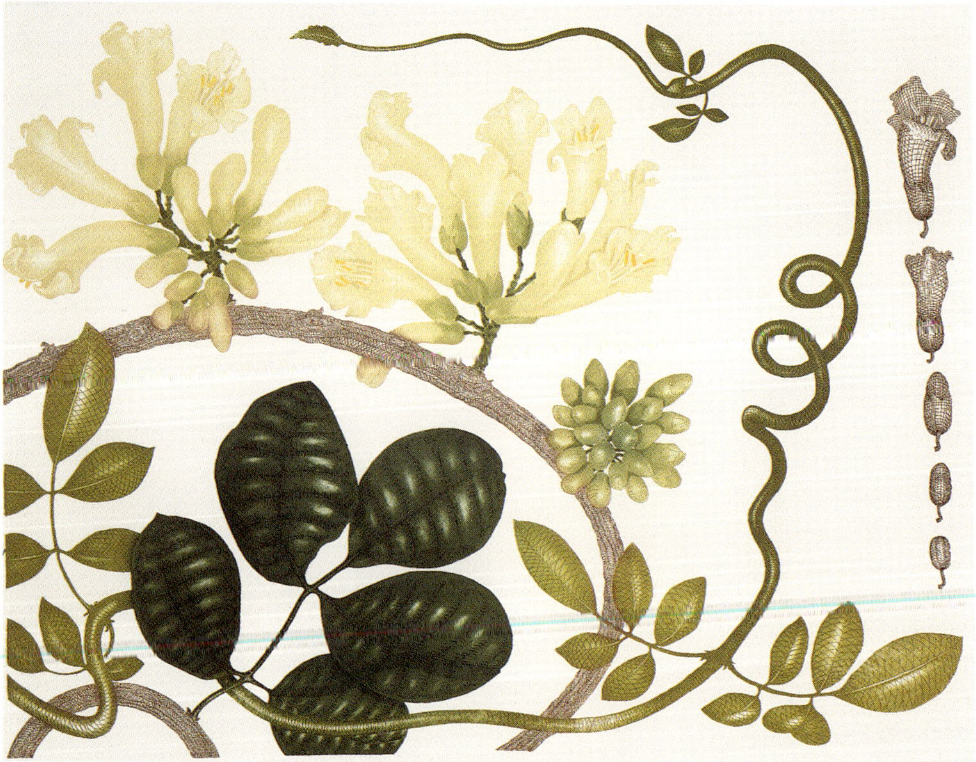

Bryan Poole, *Tecomanthe speciosa – Three Kings Climber*. Etching and aquatint, 38 × 51 cm (15 × 20 in.). This is a single copper plate inked up *a la poupée* in six colours. Some details on the print are hand coloured once the print is dry.

1 BEFORE YOU START – THE BASICS

Filing the plate

All metal or Perspex® plates that you intend to put through an etching press must have filed edges. This prevents the paper tearing and, more importantly, prevents damage to the blankets. How thoroughly you file your edges and what level of perfection you achieve is not prescribed; this is largely a matter of personal taste.

If your polished plate has a protective coating of plastic do not remove it until you have finished filing. Clamp the plate face up so that it overhangs your worktop or table. Protect the plate from damage by inserting a small piece of etching blanket or a scrap of printing paper folded to make a thickness of approximately 3 mm ($^{1}/_{10}$ in.) between the plate and the clamp. Holding the file at a 45-degree angle, evenly file the edge of the plate until you have achieved a uniform angle along the entire length. A roughly filed edge will print as a tone and can be quite effective. If you want the edge to print more cleanly, use a finer file to smooth this edge down and then repeat on the other three edges and slightly round the corners. Sandpaper and wet and dry paper are useful if you want a very smooth edge. If you want a completely smooth, clean edge that will print white then you can polish it with a burnisher also held at a 45-degree angle. If you are using a curved burnisher be careful not to scratch the plate.

Protecting the back of the plate

If you are planning to etch the plate in acid and the plate does not have a coating on the back then you must protect it. Parcel tape is often used but can prove hellishly difficult to remove after the plate is etched. Fablon is a sticky-back plastic used in the home for covering shelves, walls and work surfaces and it is available at most hardware stores. Fablon is exceptionally useful for protecting plates, as it is easy to apply, waterproof and even relatively heat resistant. It comes on a roll and should be cut to a size slightly larger than the plate. It is self-adhesive and has a paper coating covering the sticky side. Remove the paper coating from one edge and place the Fablon along one edge of the back of the plate. Work your way across the plate, simultaneously pulling off the paper with one hand and pressing along the length of the Fablon with the other to prevent air bubbles. When you have finished, turn the plate over and cut off the excess with a Stanley knife (Kraft knife). I leave this covering on the plate throughout all of the subsequent etching procedures, although you must make sure that it is still intact after baking on an aquatint. Any holes must be filled with stop out or they will etch, and any areas that have melted or bubbled must be sanded flat and filled prior to proofing or they will damage the front of the plate when they go through the press. Remove the Fablon when you are completely finished with the plate making. Fablon is also very effective if you are printing from Perspex®. Coating the plate stops the back from becoming too dirty during the inking up and allows you to more clearly see the image when you are wiping.

Degreasing the plate

Degreasing is absolutely essential for all indirect intaglio techniques such as soft and hard ground etching, spit-bite, sugar lift and aquatint. Any grease that remains on the plate will prevent the ground from properly adhering to the plate.

There are many ways to degrease a plate and I know printmakers who swear by washing-up liquid or other household cleansers. I have found nothing that compares with a very simple technique used by Norman Ackroyd so that is what I will describe. Sprinkle a small pile of whiting, a calcium carbonate powder, onto the middle of your plate. Add to that a small amount of ammonia diluted with approximately five parts water and mix up into a paste with a fresh piece of paper towel. Spread over the entire surface of the plate with a gentle polishing action. Take a fresh paper towel and wipe off the paste completely. Use a third fresh piece of paper towel if necessary to dry the plate. It will then be grease free. I must confess that I find it impossible not to check that the plate is grease free by running water over it. If a thin layer of water covers the entire plate then it is ready but if any area obviously repels the water you must repeat the process on those areas. Some artists use rolled scraps of etching blanket to make a permanent degreasing pad, but I avoid these as they seem to hold grease and unnecessarily prolong the procedure. Remember to handle the plate only by the edges from this moment onwards, to prevent contamination.

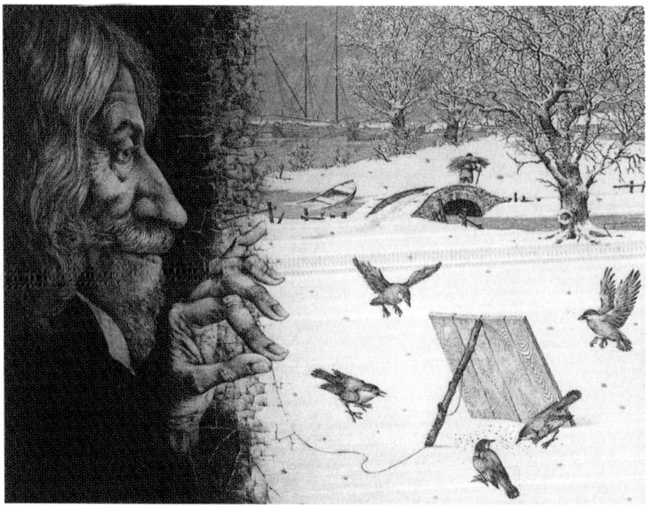

Konstantin Kalinovich, *Big Bird Catcher*, 12 x 15 cm (4¾ x 6 in.)

2 PRINTING

Although there are subtle variations, essentially all intaglio techniques (with the exception of relief prints) are printed in the same manner. In all cases you cover the plate in ink and then wipe it off, leaving the intaglio marks holding enough ink to print accurately on dampened paper when rolled through a printing press.

Inking

Lay out your ink on a stone slab – an old lithographic stone is ideal – or a heavy piece of glass; I use the glass from an old full-length mirror. You can use various tools to apply ink to the plate. A dabber is a tool comprising a leather-covered pad attached to a handle. The dabber should be rocked back and forth in the ink to pick up a good supply and then the same action repeated on the plate to drive ink into the intaglio lines. Continue until the plate is covered with ink.

You can also use a section of rubber squeegee blade cut to a length of between 5-8 cm (2-3 in.). Pick up a bit of ink on the squeegee and then, with

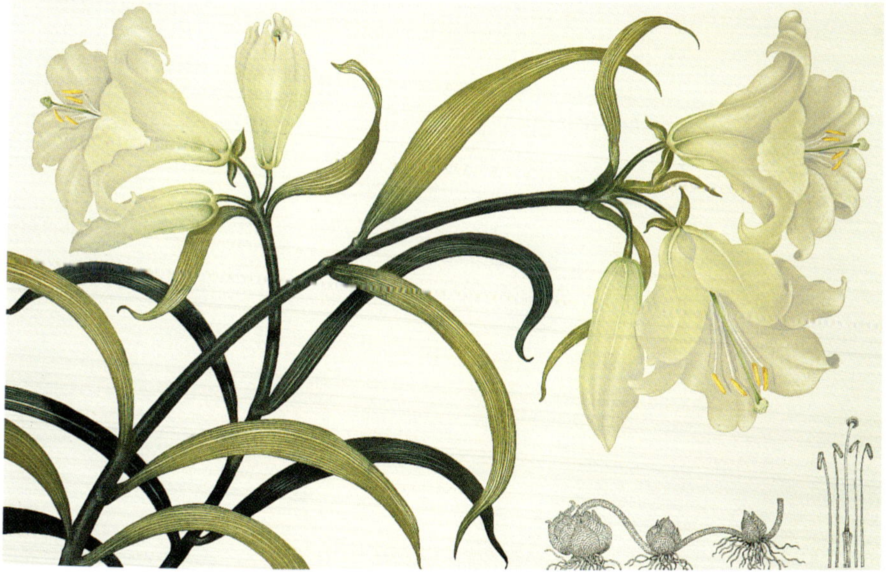

Bryan Poole – *Madonna Lily – Lilium candidum*. Hard ground and aquatint, 41 × 65 cm (16 × 25½ in.). Inked up in four colours *a la poupée* on one plate. The flowers are a mixture of white and very light grey ink with the green of the stems bleeding in from the bottom. The crucial thing about printing such a subtle, light colour is that the aquatint must be very strong. The aquatint on these flowers would print black.

the edge of the rubber, pull ink over the surface of the plate. Apply a bit of pressure to the squeegee to push ink into the lines. Art schools will often use small pieces of mountboard for this purpose, but although they do work well they are more likely to scratch your plate.

Finally, you can also use a small roller to spread ink over the plate but this technique is only suitable for plates that are not too deeply bitten, as it will not push enough ink into deeply incised lines. If ink is rolled over the surface of the plate and then printed, the intaglio lines will print white as a negative image. This is called a *relief print* and for this to work well it is best to use a hard roller.

Ink should be spread over the surface of the plate thoroughly but in a thin layer. All different metals have an inherent plate tone, so it is important that you ink up every area of the plate whether there are any intaglio marks there or not; plate tone which ends where you have stopped inking will spoil the look of open areas on the finished print.

Scrim wiping

The most common material used to wipe your plates is called scrim. This is a starched material sold on rolls measuring 1 x 50m (3 x 164 ft) but is generally cut to be used in one-metre (3-ft) square sections. Scrim comes in three grades – fine, medium and coarse – and all of these have their uses, however, the medium grade is best for most intaglio printing. Scrim is supplied heavily starched and it must be made pliable prior to use. This can be done by bunching the material into a loose roll and placing it round a square table leg or the wheel of your press. Holding onto one end of the roll with your left hand and the other with your right pull it tightly back and forth for about 30 seconds. Flatten out the scrim, bunch it into a loose roll in the opposite direction to the previous roll and repeat the pulling action. It should then be soft enough to use.

Ideally you want three pieces of scrim. They should be used in order so that the first one takes off the bulk of the ink, with the second and third progressively wiping the plate to a state where it is ready to be printed. Ideally, the first scrim should have been used previously for ink of the same colour but if it is new then you should dirty it up with some ink before using it so that it does not suck up too much ink from your plate. The scrim should be folded and bunched into a ball that fits your hand. It is crucial that the surface of the scrim ball is smooth and uncreased or you will not be able to properly wipe the plate. The first scrim should be pushed into the plate and twisted to drive ink into all of the etched areas until you have dealt with the entire surface of the plate. Then take up the second scrim, which should be considerably cleaner than the first but not necessarily as clean as the third. Quickly move the scrim in a circular motion over the entire surface of the plate until you begin to see the image appear. Imagine the plate to be larger than it is and continue your movements beyond the edges of the plate to avoid the tendency to over wipe

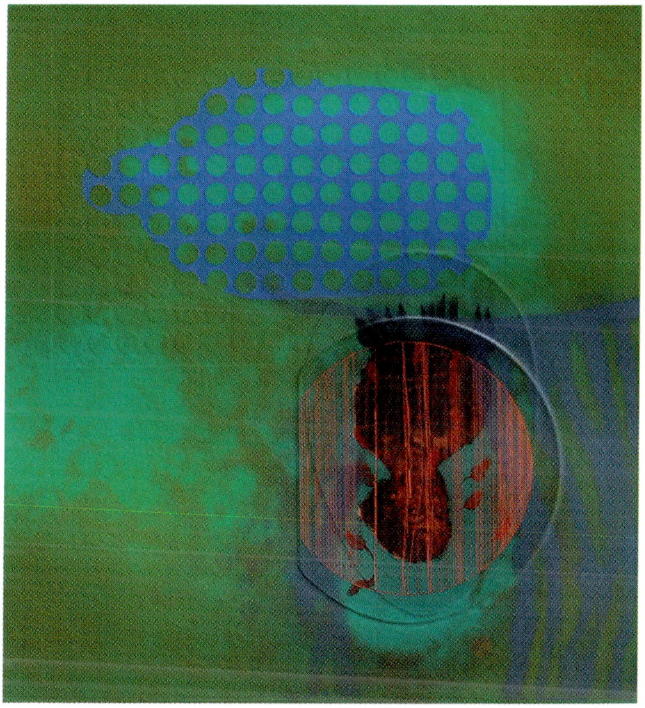

Freya Payne – *Unmoored.* Hard ground, aquatint, spit bite and *chine collé* 23.5 x 22 cm (9 x 8½ in.). In *chine-collé*, a thin layer of glue is applied to the back of a piece of delicate paper or tissue paper which is generally the same size or smaller than the plate and it is then laid glue side up onto the plate. The heavier printmaking paper is then placed over the surface of the plate and when it is run through the press the image is transferred to the delicate paper that is fused to the heavier printmaking paper.

the middle and leave too much ink around the edges. When the image is quite clearly visible move to the third piece of scrim and repeat the process. Whenever the scrim becomes too saturated with ink, refold and bunch it to expose a fresh, clean area. Continue to wipe until there is just a thin layer of ink on the surface. You can then either print or carry on with the clean scrim until the unetched areas start to appear shiny. Over-wiping is the most common mistake in this process, but with practice you will learn how best to print your own work and to recognise when it is time to stop wiping.

A la poupée

If you want to ink a single plate in a variety of ink colours, you will need to use a technique called '*a la poupée*'. This name literally translates as 'with the doll', and in English we still refer to the small ink dabbers as 'dollies'. A dolly is made by taking a small piece of de-starched scrim and rolling it into a pencil shape, then taping it along the side to strengthen it. You will need one dolly for every colour you plan to use. Rub the end of the dolly, which should be clean scrim with no tape, into the ink until you have picked up an ample supply; then use the dolly to ink up specific areas of the plate as required. If you want to keep the separate coloured areas bright, it is essential that you wipe carefully so as not to mix the inks with the surrounding colours. If you want a certain amount of colour bleeding, allow the colours to touch while you are wiping. You can also use *a la poupée* on a plate that is already inked, wiped and ready to print. This will give the introduced colours a subtle common hue and stop the delineations of colours becoming too clumsy or obvious, which is a potential problem to be aware of when using this technique.

Hand-wiping

At the point where there is still a thin layer of ink on the plate you may decide to either hand-wipe or tissue-wipe to further expose the highlights. To hand-wipe you need to smear a little ink from the first scrim on the side of the palm of your drawing hand. Rub whiting over the ink with your other hand and dust it off on your apron. You should have no visible traces of ink or loose whiting on your hand. Then pass your palm quickly and lightly over the plate to bring out the highlighted areas and remove the plate tone. You can selectively spot-wipe small areas using the same process but with the ink and whiting on your fingertip.

Tissue-wiping

Tissue wiping is a far easier technique to master than hand wiping. Tear a stack of clean tissue paper to a size larger than your outstretched palm. Lay the tissue on the inked plate and gently move the tissue around the surface with the flat of your palm. As with hand wiping, you can be selective by using your fingertip on the tissue. You can also use newsprint or pages from old phonebooks for this, but it is a good idea to wear rubber gloves as the paper does tend to stick to the ink more. In all cases try to avoid your hand slipping off the paper as it will mark the plate.

Printing

Once you are satisfied that the plate is ready then prepare the press and paper for printing. The press bed should be rolled to one end and the blankets placed in the middle of the bed. Roll the press back in enough to trap the end of the blankets and then flick them back over the top roller, making certain that there are no creases or folds in them. Place a piece of tissue paper larger than the size of the printing paper on the press bed. This will stop the bed from marking and possibly spoiling further prints. Place the plate face up onto the tissue paper.

The rules for paper soaking vary from brand to brand but in general paper should have been soaked for at least 30 minutes prior to printing. Make little hinged paper 'grips' from folded off-cuts of printing paper and use them to grab the paper out of the bath, to protect the paper from your fingers. Drain the paper until no excess water drips from it, then place it between sheets of blotting paper and rub thoroughly over the entire surface of the top piece of blotting paper. The paper should be damp to the touch but with no visible surface moisture. Place the paper printing side down onto the plate. All paper

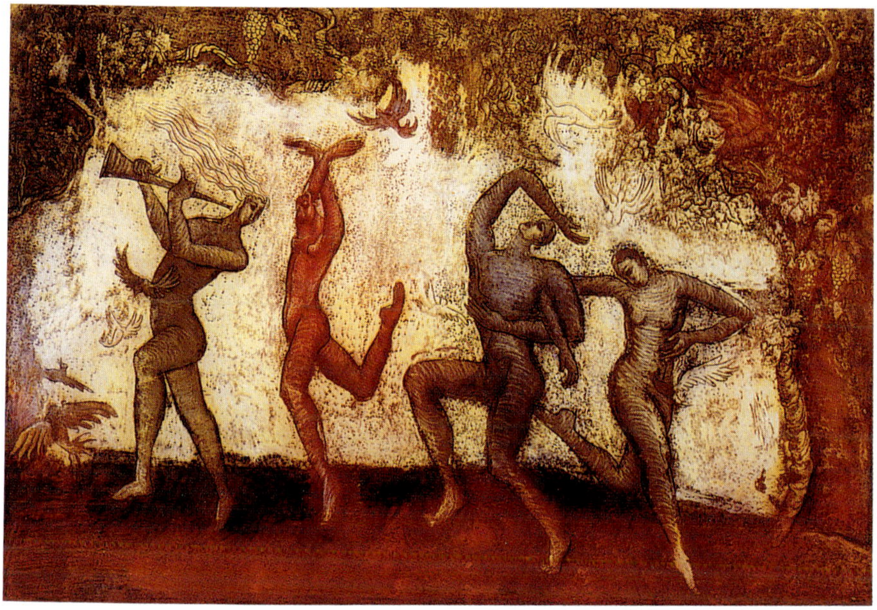

Aimee Birnbaum – *Primavera*. Hard ground and aquatint, 41 × 61 cm (16 × 24 in.). This print is unusual in that it is a 2-plate etching where both of the printings have been pulled from the same plate. The first inking is in diarylide yellow that has been used neat around the edges of the image but mixed with extender in the middle. Some areas have almost been wiped clean. Once the plate has been through the press the first time, keep the paper trapped in the press and sandwich it between pieces of acetate to keep it wet. Use registration blocks to mark the exact placement of the plate and then remove and clean the plate. The plate is then inked up with neat violet and dark red inks applied *a la poupée*. When the second inking is run through the press the inks blend to form a rich variety of colours. In the plate making, Aimee has placed sandpaper over the plate at the hard ground stage and rubbed on it with a spoon. This creates irregular marks that resemble foul biting or a very coarse aquatint.

has a 'printing side' and with experience you will be able to tell which side is which. A general rule of thumb is that if the manufacturer's watermark is the right way around you have the paper printing side up. Marking the back of the paper with a pencil prior to soaking makes life easier. Then slowly but steadily wind the plate through the press.

Although there are no rules about placement of the image on the paper some things are imperative: the border at the bottom should be larger than the border at the top; the borders at the side should be equal; and whatever decisions you make should be consistent throughout the edition. The easiest way to register the prints is to mark up a piece of plastic acetate so that it clearly shows the placement of the plate and the paper. Lay this on the press bed before the tissue paper and plate are placed down. Once you lay the plate down, if it is not perfectly in place, move the tissue paper until the plate lines up with the marks on the acetate.

Drying the prints

To dry the prints you will need: a good supply of blotting paper; firm boards the same size as the blotting paper made of plywood or MDF and varnished so that they are waterproof; and a couple of weights (ideally about 20kg/44lb each). On a flat, stable surface lay down one of your boards and then two pieces of blotting paper. Place your print in the middle and cover with two more pieces of blotting paper. You can repeat this process twice more before you need to place another board on top. If you have been editioning, you can make quite large stacks providing you do not exceed three layers of prints between boards. After you have added the last board, place the weights on top. The blotting paper will need to be changed for dry sheets the next day and then again the day after that. It takes approximately one week for prints to completely dry. When you have removed the blotters, hang them from a drying rack (this should be high enough that they clear the ground). Drying racks can be purchased from printmaking suppliers but if you are even a little bit handy you can easily make your own. Take a piece of 5 x 5 cm (2 x 2 in.) wood at least 1.8 m (6 ft) long and nail wooden-spring clothes pegs to it at approximately 4 cm (1½ in.) intervals so that the bottom of each peg hangs down clear of the wood. This can be hung from the ceiling or suspended between solid objects in your studio, such as the press and your workbench. Hang one piece of blotter from each clothes peg and leave for as long as you are able – 12 hours is usually ample.

Safe printmaking

All of the techniques in this book can be used relatively safely, but the conditions must be right and some simple precautions must be followed. If you are etching using nitric acid, then you need an etching cabinet fitted with a good extractor fan. Aquatint requires a well-ventilated area, ideally isolated from the rest of the studio although if this is not practical then covering it with a plastic sheet when it is not in use also works well. If you are using an extractor fan with your aquatint box, it should be placed close to the ground, as high level extraction will remove dust from your plate. Low level extraction is also useful for etching with ferric chloride as the fumes settle to ground level before dispersing. In all cases, even with good ventilation you should wear a gas mask while you are working with mordants, solvents, or aquatint.

Where solvents are concerned, paraffin is preferable to white spirit and turpentine should be avoided. Furthermore, remember that your skin is porous so always wear gloves if you are working with acid, solvents or ammonia. You can use washing-up liquid to wash your hands.

Water first!

When mixing any mordant such as nitric acid or ferric chloride it is imperative that you always add the mordant to the water. Always mix in a well-ventilated place, preferably a purpose-built fume cupboard with an extractor fan or in the open air. Always wear a fume mask, goggles, a plasticized apron and heavy-duty rubber gloves.

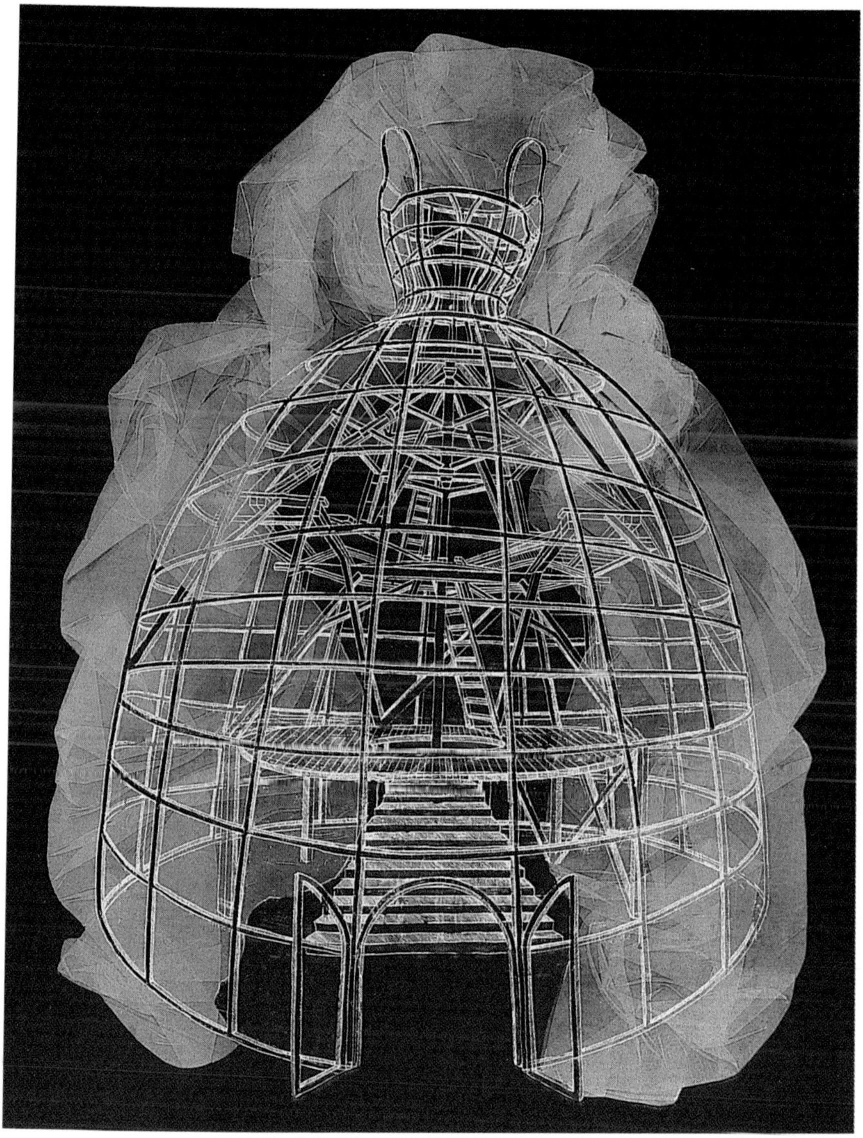

Mila Judge Furstova – *Ontogenesis*. Hard ground and aquatint, 60 x 90 cm (23½ x 35½ in.). This traditionally etched plate has been altered dramatically by being printed with white ink on black paper.

3 DIRECT INTAGLIO

This chapter incorporates all intaglio techniques in which the artist is using tools to directly alter or incise the plate. The tools are used as drawing mediums and consequently these techniques are especially appropriate for the artist whose work relies heavily on draughtsmanship. They are difficult to master but the marks made are unique, autographic and wonderfully immediate.

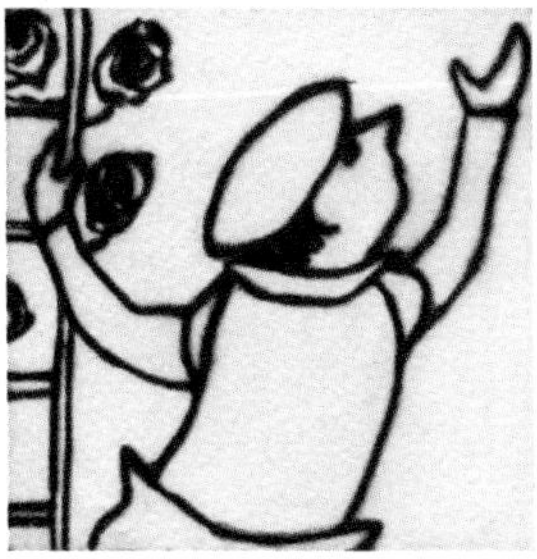

■ DRYPOINT

Drypoint is the direct technique that most closely resembles drawing. It is a perfect introductory intaglio technique, as it requires very little in the way of materials or preparation. The mark making on the metal plate is created by directly scratching or incising lines with tools that can be as basic as nails or scribes. The incised lines displace the metal creating a burr, which holds the ink and prints as a characteristic softened, velvety line. The burr has the disadvantage of being quite delicate and will wear down with the abrasive act of wiping ink from the plate. When it has worn away the look of the drypoint is dramatically altered, so drypoints tend to be very small editions of generally 30 or fewer; even still, throughout the course of the edition there is an unavoidable lack of uniformity. If you wish to print larger editions then you should probably work on copper and have the plate steel-faced or refer to the section covering using a soldering iron on Perspex® (p.26).

You will need:

- Filed metal (aluminium, zinc, copper or steel) or Perspex® plate
- Drypoint scribe or Hayden Point (or any other fine pointed drawing tool)
- Roulette (optional).

Drypoint tools

The choice of tool has as much of an impact as the choice of metal. As mentioned earlier, a drypoint can be created using any implement to make marks, but while this is true, it is slightly misleading. It is advisable to invest in proper drypoint tools as they are not hugely expensive and they will make the experience so much more enjoyable that you are more likely to pursue it further. The tool that I use is a drypoint scribe or Hayden point with a fine steel point; the difference between this and an etching needle made of a softer metal is enormous. Diamond-tipped drypoint tools are expensive as well as being more difficult to control and prone to breaking.

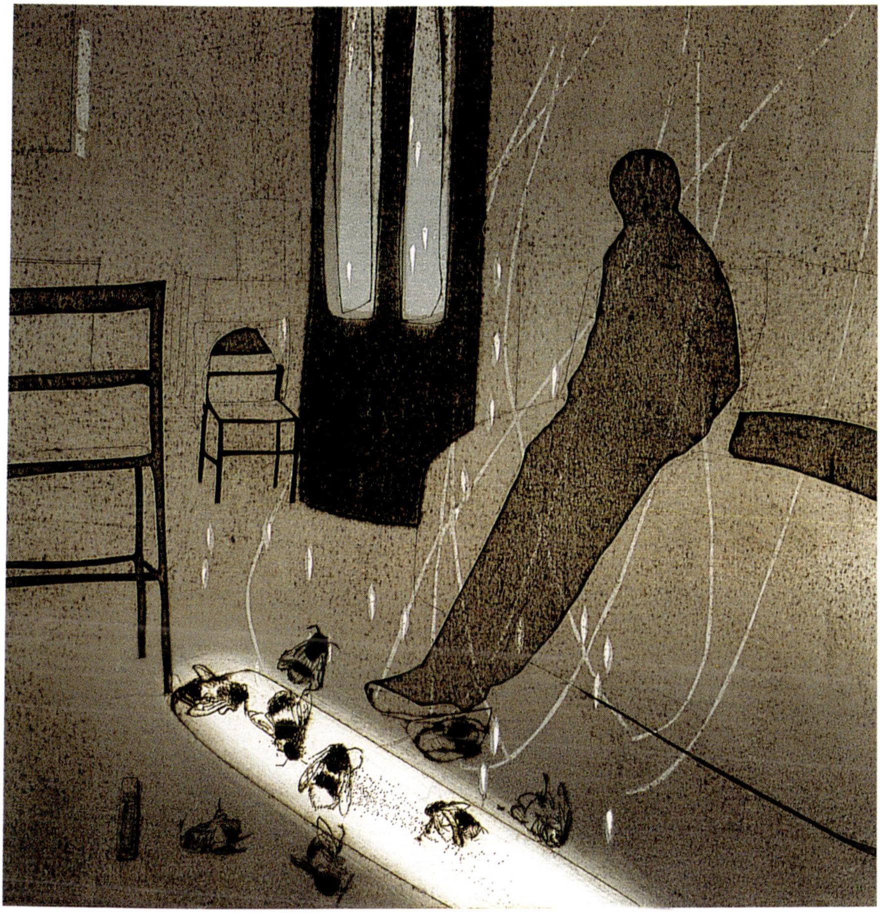

Katie Jones – *Bumble Bee*. Drypoint on card, 40 × 39 cm (15¾ × 15⅓ in.). This drypoint has been done using a thin scribe on a plastic coated mountcard. The large tonal areas such as the figure were made by cutting out the shapes with a fine razor blade and then peeling off the plastic coating from the card. The intaglio lines were inked up in sepia ink and then the plate is rolled with light grey and duck egg blue inks mixed 40/60 with extender.

The drypoint tool is held in basically the same way as a pencil. It is advisable to draw using strokes made towards your body as the tool is more prone to sticking or slipping when you draw the lines away from yourself. This will happen less with finer, more delicate lines. Holding the pen as vertically as possible, with the top angled in towards you, creates a line with furrows on either side of the tip. This line will survive printing better than one created by angling the tool slightly to the side, although the latter will produce a softer, more 'furry' line. If you want to achieve a very fluid, curved line you will need to keep the drawing stroke coming straight towards your body and move the plate as necessary. The best way to achieve this is to place a firm book or a piece of wood smaller than the plate underneath the plate and to move the plate with

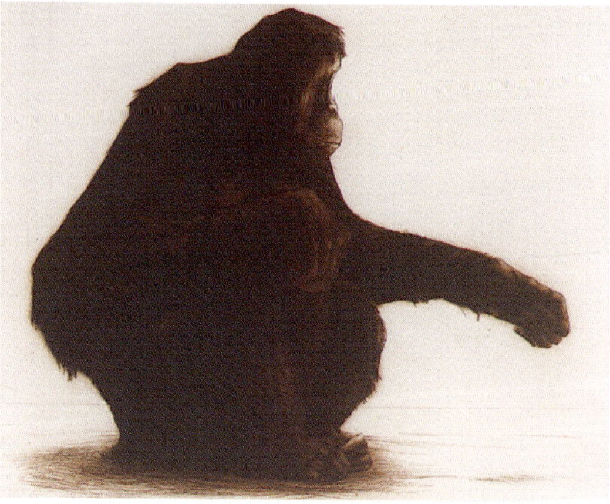

Helen Fay – *Orang Utan III*. Drypoint, 30.5 x 37 cm (12 x 14½ in.)

your free hand. You can create large tonal areas by using combinations of hatching and cross-hatching. By building up layers of cross-hatching in different directions you can create areas of pure black.

You can also use a tool called a roulette to create drawn lines or tonal areas. A roulette has a wheel covered with a pattern of raised teeth at the end of a bent shaft. They are available in a number of different sizes, in which the teeth vary in both height and spacing. You can draw with the edge of the wheel to create a line of evenly spaced dots or you can hold the tool so that the entire face of the wheel is in contact with the plate to create a column of evenly spaced dots. You will be able to exert more pressure on the roulette and create deeper impressions when using the edge than when using the whole face. Irregular roulettes have a wheel that tapers towards a rounded point with teeth arranged in a seemingly random manner rather than in a strict pattern. These make more unpredictable marks and are also quite useful for filling in areas of improperly-bitten aquatint.

Drypoint on metal

The look of a drypoint is in part the result of the choice of metal. Aluminium is a very soft metal and allows for a strong, dark, fluid line. Zinc and copper are harder and, although they make it more difficult to achieve the weight of line possible with aluminium, lighter, more delicate lines will actually hold up better. Copper is a harder metal than zinc and can be steel-faced to make it stronger still (see p.26). Steel is very hard and while it will stand up to editioning far better than any other metal, the mark making is considerably more difficult and frankly less rewarding. You can achieve a look very similar to soft metal by using Perspex® and it is available in various densities. If you use a harder version of the material it will survive larger editions.

Aluminium that is 1mm thick is available in 1 x 2 metre (3 x 6½ ft) sheets. It comes polished with a protective plastic coating on one side. It can be easily cut to size, using a Stanley knife, by deeply scoring the plate on one side only and then gently bending the plate along the scored line, then straightening it repeatedly until it breaks. The metal is very thin but still needs to have the edges filed before printing to protect both paper and blankets. You can draw directly onto the plate with pencil or you can transfer drawings onto the plate using transfer paper or carbon paper. Transfer paper has the advantage of not being easily rubbed off on your hand while working. The metal is inexpensive

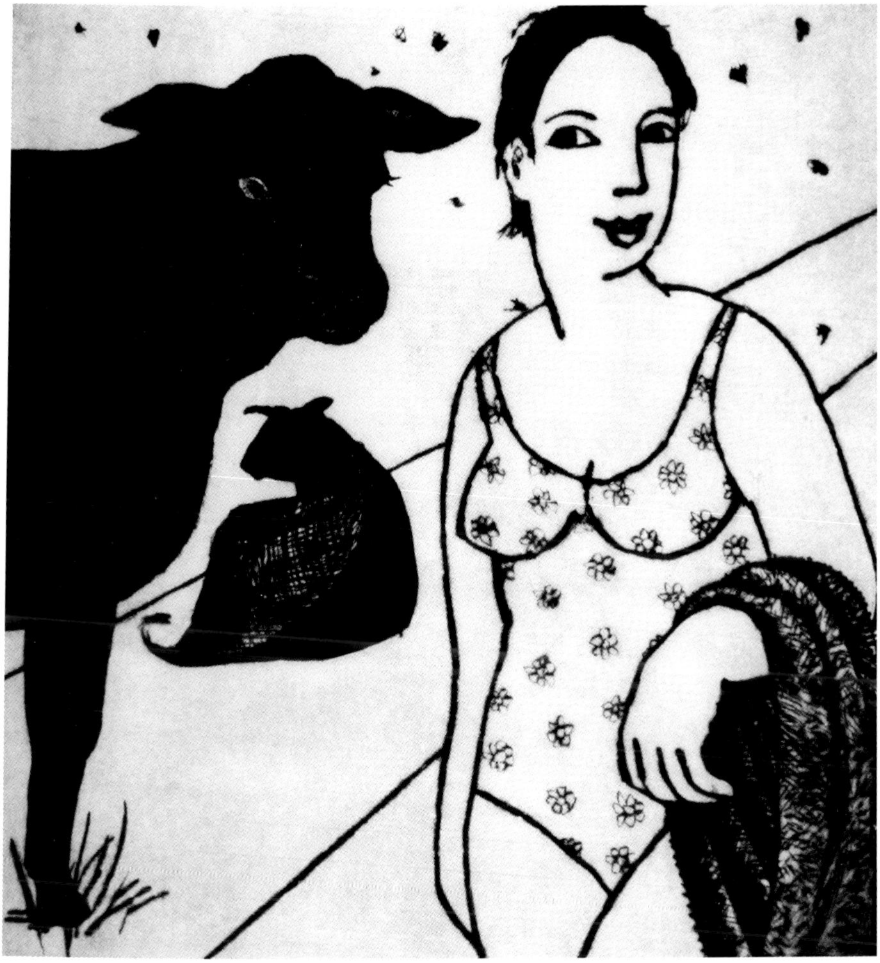

Anita Klein, *Going to swim at Bundanon*. Drypoint on aluminium, 32.5 x 29.5 cm (12⅘ x 12⅗ in.)

enough to allow you to not feel too precious about it, but I would strongly recommend doing at least one test plate before you embark on anything too time consuming and detailed. The advantage of doing a test plate is that it is very difficult to assess the difference between the varying weights of line and how they will print. To create very strong lines you do have to press surprisingly firmly. Once you actually begin working on a plate that you plan to edition it is advisable to avoid repetitive proofing; this will wear down the burr and shorten your potential edition size. You can add a little black ink to some Vaseline and gently rub it into the lines using a piece of soft paper towel to give an indication of how the lines will print. Remember to clean the mixture off with white spirit prior to inking the plate up for your first print. Sandpaper, steel wool and wire brushes are all useful for creating areas of tone but these marks will not stand up to editioning as well as drawn lines will.

When inking up, it is important to remember that aluminium is so soft that it is not advisable to wipe with scrim as it can scratch the plate. The inking and printing technique that I will outline here is that used by Anita Klein. The ink should be mixed approximately 50/50 with a compound called Easywipe as this makes for much easier wiping without affecting the look of the print. Use a loosely balled up piece of tissue paper to remove the excess ink. Prepare a stack of newsprint (newspapers or old phone books are perfect for this) torn to a size large enough to easily accommodate your hand when the fingers are splayed out. Lay a piece of newsprint onto the plate and, with your hand completely flat against the surface of the plate, wipe the plate with the paper. It is crucial at this point that you avoid the temptation to use your fingertips to wipe the plate, as you will remove too much ink. Once the newsprint in saturated with ink, flip it over and use the other side. Carry on wiping until the lines and tones are strongly defined and the white areas appear even and relatively clean. At this point you can use your fingertips on the newsprint to pick out the areas of finer detail and even use cotton buds if necessary. The first print you pull from even a very successful plate is unlikely to be perfect as the burr holds a great deal of ink so even for test plates you should always pull at least two prints.

If you are using a 1mm aluminium plate, the pressure on the press should be increased by approximately a quarter turn from the standard etching pressure on a Rochat press, but you will need to test for the optimum pressure on your press.

The techniques for plate making and printing are virtually identical to those for copper or zinc. As they are less delicate metals, they can initially be wiped with scrim although they still benefit from being wiped with newsprint at the end. The harder metals do not allow for the same intensity of single line possible with aluminium, but any type of dense mark-making (such as cross-hatching to create large areas of tone) will be much more successful and will hold up to editioning much better.

Steel-facing copper plates

A copper plate can have a thin layer of pure iron electroplated onto it to make it stonger still. This technique is called steel-facing and only does not alter the look of the subsequently printed image (except in the case of some colours which will print more true). It needs to be carried out by an experienced practitioner.

Drypoint on Perspex® using a soldering iron

You will need:

- Filed Perspex® plate or polycarbonate sheet
- Soldering iron or pyrographic tool
- Gas fume mask.

The method

Using a soldering iron to melt lines in Perspex® is an interesting twist on traditional drypoint, which I first saw used by Trevor Price. It has wonderful possibilities, but still retains the essential characteristics of an aluminium drypoint. Working on a transparent plate allows you to have your preparatory drawing underneath it as a guide, so you can dispense with transferring the drawing onto the plate.

The first thing to point out is that melting Perspex® will create fumes that necessitate the use of a proper gas mask. The heated soldering iron or pyrographic tool (traditionally used for wood-burning) should be held exactly as you would hold a drypoint scribe and, as in traditional drypoint, the more pressure you exert, the darker and heavier the line will be. As you are dealing with a heated drawing tool, the speed with which you move across the plate will also have an impact on the line. Basically, the quicker your movements, the finer the line produced will be. Lines should be drawn by moving the tool in towards your body, as otherwise it is difficult to control. One of the great advantages of this technique is that the heated tip is offered little resistance by the Perspex®, allowing for absolute fluidity of movement. You can create smooth swirling and curving lines in a manner virtually impossible with a scribe on metal. It is crucial to remember to lift the tool directly upon finishing the mark-making; pausing with the tool still in contact with the plate will continue to melt the

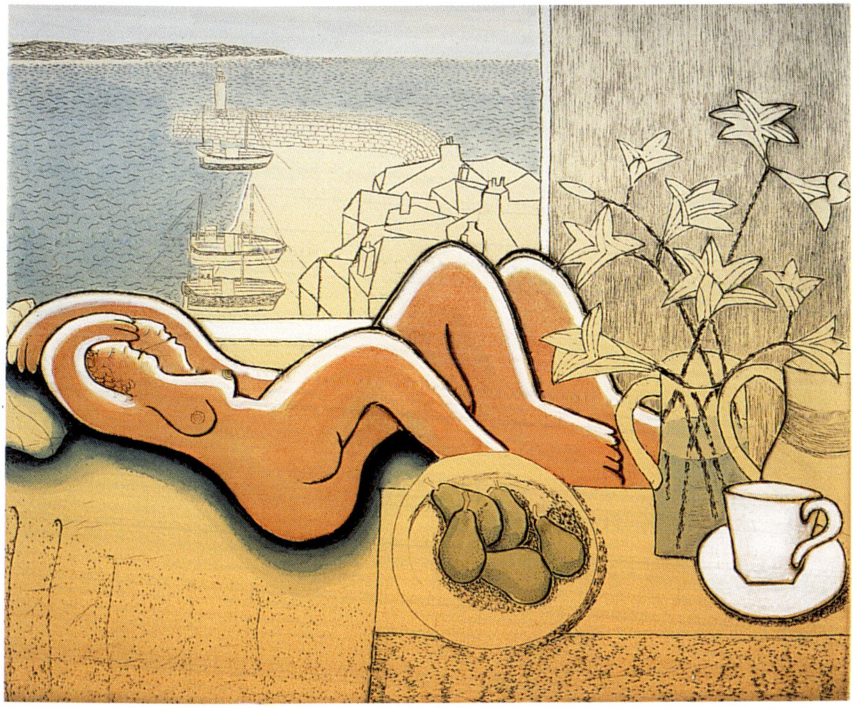

Trevor Price – *St Ives Couple I*. Drypoint on polycarbonate sheet, 30 x 36 cm (12 x 14 in.). Drypoint lines are made using soldering iron and scribe on plastic sheet, inked up in black and then the plate is rolled over the surface with a blended ochre roll that has large amounts of extender.

Perspex®. Although the lines will have that fuzziness characteristic of drypoint, upon closer inspection the burr can be seen to be very different to that of a traditional metal plate drypoint. The two furrows created by the displaced plastic, especially in the deepest lines, are very obvious and the channel running down the middle does not fill in as it does with a traditional drypoint. Very delicate lines are more difficult to achieve with a soldering iron, but you can combine conventional drypoint mark-making on the same plate to great effect. Another advantage to this technique is that Perspex® is less delicate than aluminium, so allows for wiping with scrim instead of paper and for possible edition sizes rising to 100 or 150. Do be careful when setting the pressure on the press, as these materials are considerably thicker than metal and tend to vary slightly between manufacturers.

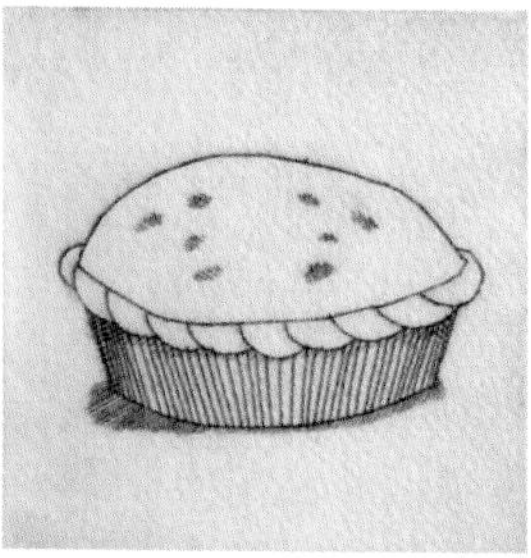

■ ENGRAVING

Engraving is a traditional technique, famously used by William Hogarth, which is so seldom employed these days as to seem completely antiquated. The line, however, has such an intrinsic character and is so unlike those obtainable with other methods that it really is worthy of consideration. The line is completely pure, unlike an etched line, which, if viewed under a magnifying glass, appears rough and irregular. This is because once the acid bites down into the exposed plate it begins to bite laterally, eating away at

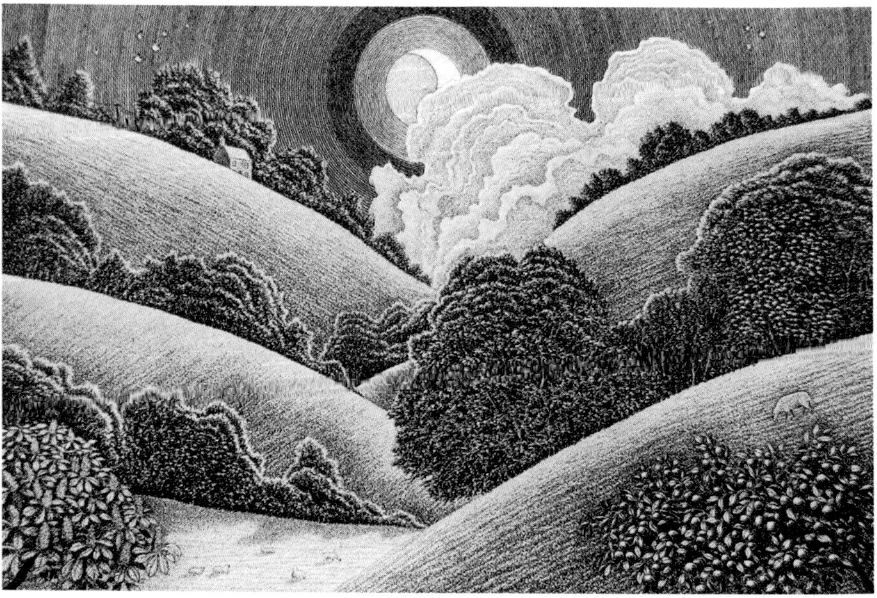

Brian Hanscomb, *Camel Valley – Cornwall.* Engraving, 8 x 12 cm (3 x 4¾ in.)

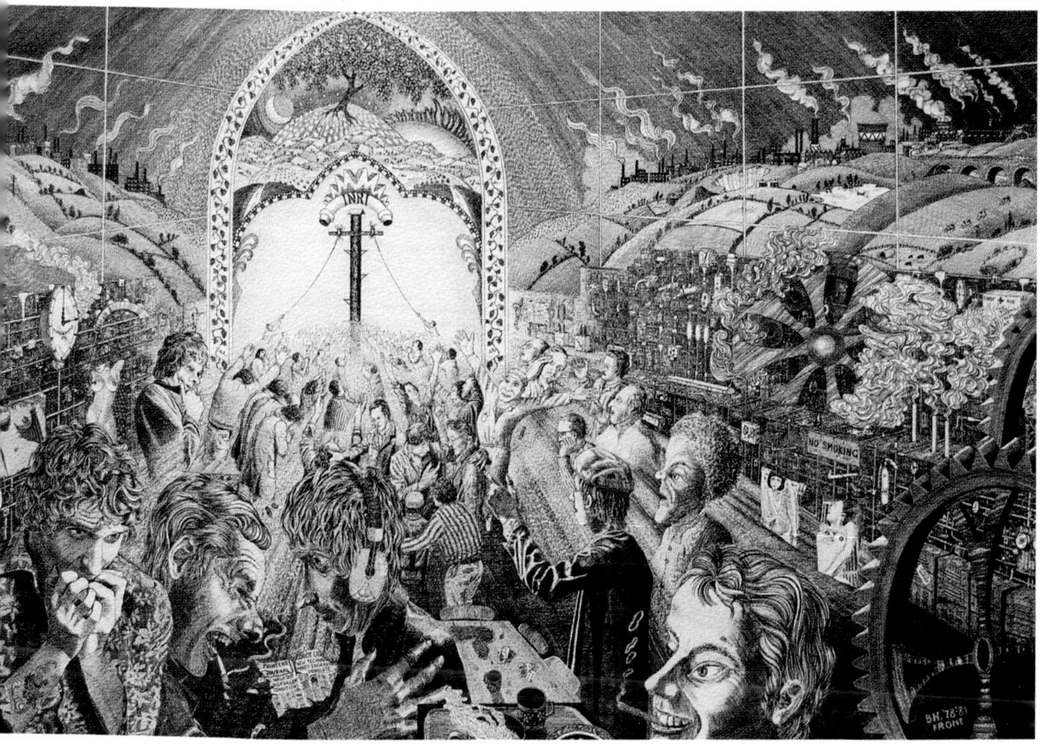

Brian Hanscomb, *Christ Appears in the Factory*. Engraving, 29 x 45 cm (11½ x 17¾ in.). This intricately detailed engraving was carried out over a three-year period and was the piece that prompted Brian to pursue full time printmaking.

the sides of the line. This happens less with ferric chloride on copper as it bites more cleanly than nitric acid, but it still cannot compare with the clear, sharp edges of an engraving. Not only does engraving not rely upon a burr (as the other direct intaglio techniques of drypoint and mezzotint do) but any burrs which do occur must be removed prior to printing. As there is no burr to wear down, the engraved line will stand up to editioning extremely well.

This is technique is usually considered best suited to copper due to the lack of plate tone but a highly polished zinc plate would also work well. In either case, you should polish the plate further with Brasso or something similar to completely remove any grain from the metal. You do not need to degrease the plate prior to engraving.

You will need:

- Filed metal plate (usually copper)
- Burin
- India Stone and Arkansas Stone (for sharpening the burin)
- Sandbag or heavy leather pad.

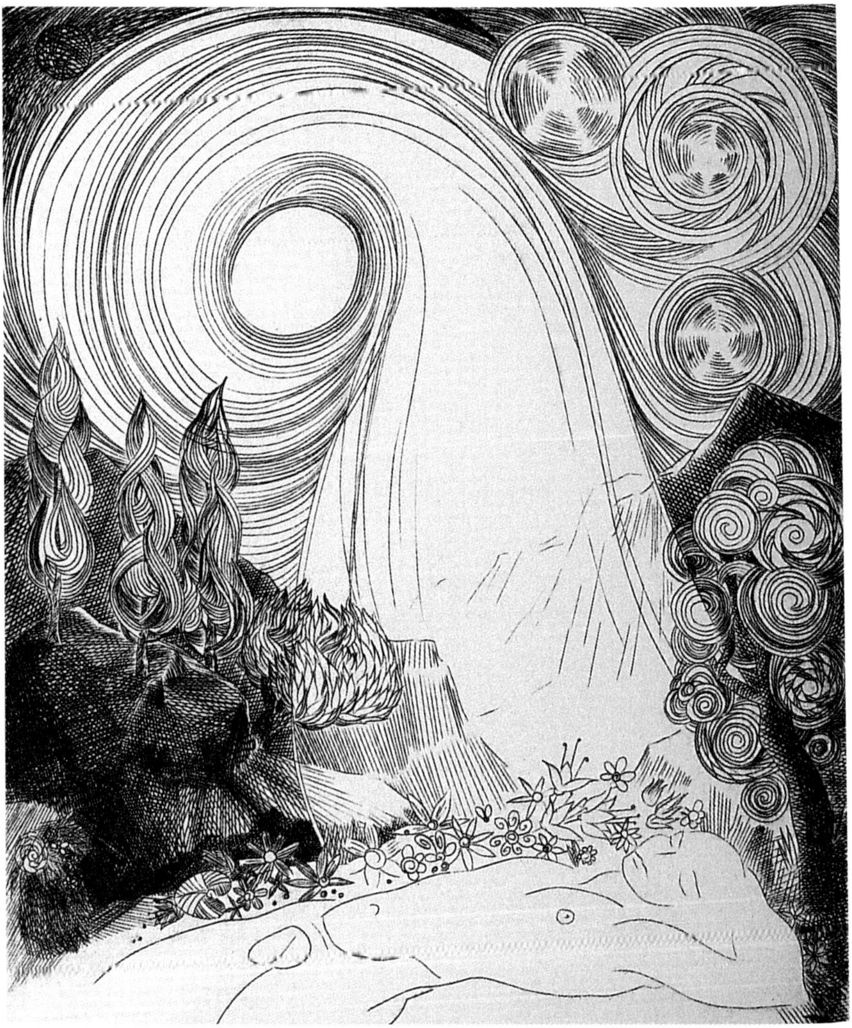

Willow Winston – *Endymion*. Engraving, 12.5 x 10.5 cm (5 x 4 in.)

Line engraving

The main tool you will need is a *burin*, a line engraving tool with a round wooden handle and a long metal shaft. The end of the shaft will be cut at an angle making a point that is either diamond-shaped or square. A diamond-point burin will create lines that are deep and narrow while a square point will make shallower but wider lines. You will also need something on which to rest the plate. This traditionally would have been a heavy leather pad resembling a small flattened medicine ball but a sandbag or even a book that is smaller than the plate will suffice.

Hold the burin so that the bottom of the wooden handle fits firmly at the base of your palm. Hold the shaft between your middle finger and thumb with your index finger on top of the shaft. You should not grip the shaft tightly with your fingers. The shaft of the burin and your index finger should run in a straight line with your forearm. Your elbow must be on the table to create a fixed point with your upper arm at a 90-degree angle to your forearm. All of this is so that the weight on the burin is transferred from your shoulder rather than your hand. The diamond or square point of the burin must be perfectly perpendicular to the plate.

To start a line, the bottom of the burin's point should be gently dug into the plate at an approximate angle of 45 degrees, but this should angle off dramatically the moment you can feel that the burin is biting. The plate should be moved under the burin rather than the burin moved over the plate to create the lines – the burin and your arm should remain fixed in position. A sharp burin will not require too much pressure to create a line. At the end of the line you should gently dip the tool right down to ease out of the biting action. This will stop the tool from slipping but also creates the distinctive engraved line that tapers off at the end. As the burin moves through the copper, the displaced metal will curl away from the point. Resist the temptation to brush these away or to try to remove them with your hand. These metal slivers are very sharp and are not only likely to scratch the plate but can also cut your fingers. Gently remove them from the side, perpendicular to the direction of the line, using a scraper; do the same with any burrs that have been created along the line. You can re-enter and continue a line that you have stopped in the middle, or you can go over the same lines again to make them stronger. From the side of the line, gently slide the burin across the

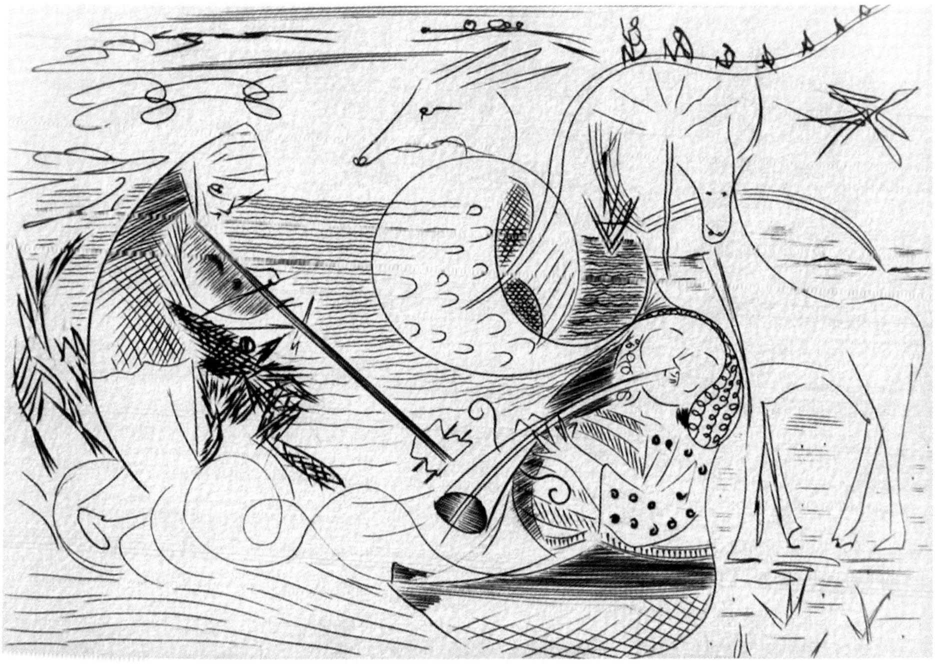

Barry Cottrell – *By the Bright Breeze*. Engraving, 14.5 x 19.5 cm (5¾ x 7¾ in.)

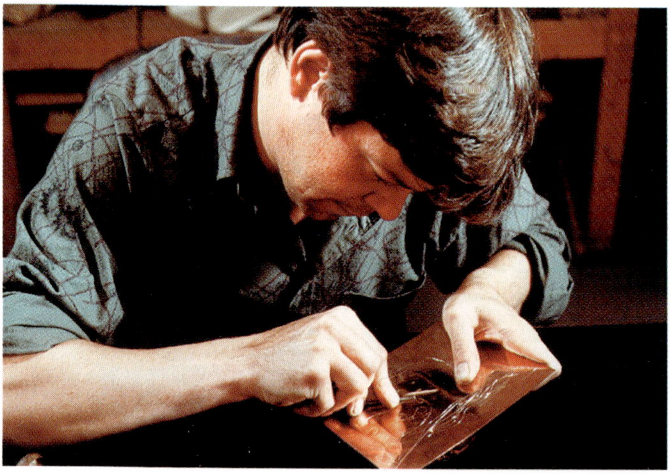

–Barry Cottrell engraving one of his plates. Note how his left hand is free to move the plate while the right hand firmly holds the burin. *Photo courtesy of Oxford Printmakers Co-operative*

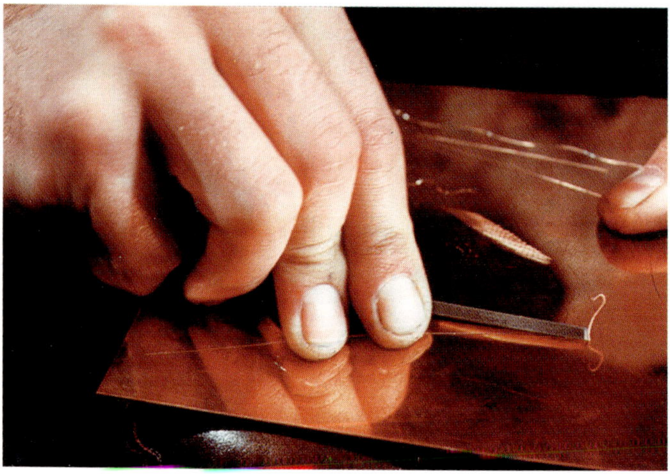

This close-up of Barry Cottrell engraving a plate clearly shows the displaced curl of metal in front of the burin. *Photo courtesy of the Oxford Printmakers Co-operative*

plate being careful not to scratch it. You will feel when the tool clicks into the engraved line. Remember, even the subtlest change in pressure will affect the weight of the line, as will alterations in the angle of the shaft of the burin.

It is a very good idea to practice on a scrap piece of copper before attempting anything too ambitious, as line engraving does require a great deal of practice. Persevere though, and with patience you will be performing the most exquisite arabesques imaginable.

Stipple engraving

A burin is also used for stipple engraving but the technique is quite different to line engraving. The tool should be held at a 90-degree angle to the plate, with the point pushed into the plate. The plate is rotated 360-degrees to make a perfectly round dot. Repeat the procedure for the next dot. Burrs should be carefully removed with a scraper. As with line engraving, the more pressure you exert the deeper the impression and the darker the printed marks will be.

Both of these techniques have great potential as supplements to etching. Combining techniques can produce some stunning effects. Remember that making corrections to a hard or soft ground is very time consuming if you have to reapply a ground and then re-etch the plate. To strengthen under-etched lines or amend drawings, engraving is preferable to drypoint as it will stand up better to editioning.

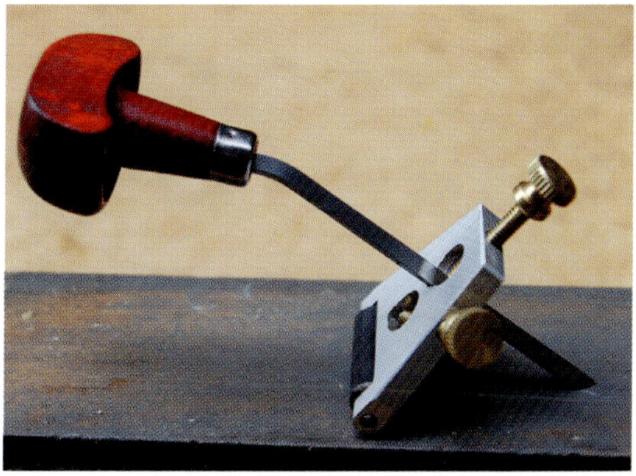

Sharpening an engraving burin using a burin sharpener that holds the end of the burin at a specific angle

Sharpening the burin

If you find beginning lines difficult, or the tool starts slipping, then you need to sharpen your burin. For this you will need delicate abrasive oilstones called *India stone* and *Arkansas stone* and some oil. Apply a touch of oil first to the India stone and, with the diamond point of the burin completely flat against the stone, gently rub your burin left and right. You will not need to do this for long to file off the tiniest amount of metal from the very end of the burin but you will then need to file the sides of the shaft as well to remove any displaced metal. When you have done all four sides of the shaft, briefly repeat with the flat diamond point. Then repeat the entire procedure with the smoother Arkansas stone.

NB: It is possible to purchase a burin sharpener. This is a tool that holds the burin at the precise angle during the sharpening process (see opposite).

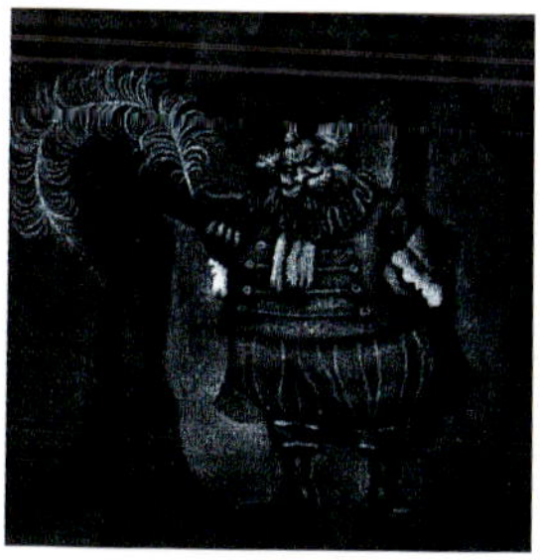

■ MEZZOTINT

The fundamental characteristic of mezzotint is a warm, soft-edged chiaroscuro with a rich and luxuriant black. Basically, the image is produced by burnishing back areas to create a range of greys on a plate that would otherwise print completely black. It is an exceedingly labour-intensive technique; just getting the plate to a point where you are ready to begin to draw into it takes considerable time and patience.

Mezzotint was first developed in the 17th century by the artist Ludwig von Siegen, and the first mezzotint print was completed in 1642. However, until the 20th century mezzotint was primarily used as a way of reproducing paintings for the mass market rather than as an art technique in its own right. It is currently experiencing a bit of a revival, especially in Japan where there are a number of very gifted practitioners.

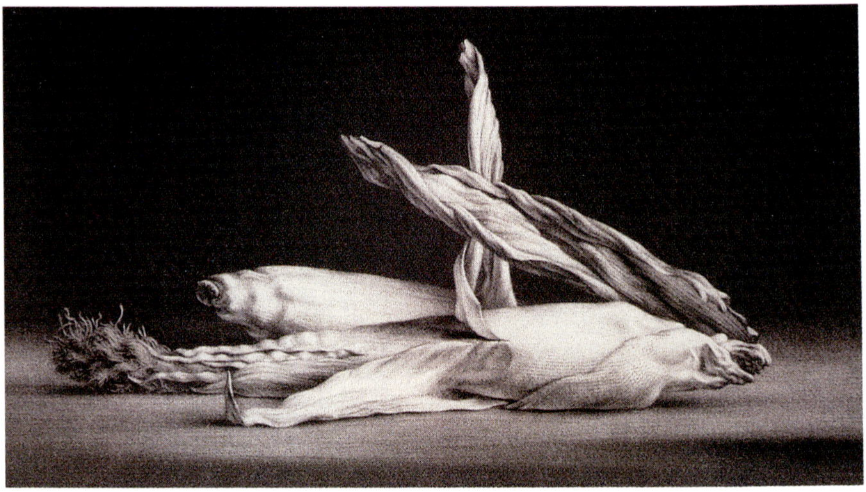

Konstantin Chmutin – *Still Life VII*. Mezzotint, 12 x 22.5 cm (4¾ x 8¾ in.)

All of the techniques and materials I will write about in this section are based on the use of 18-gauge copper plates, although some mezzotint artists favour using the thicker 16-gauge as it is less likely to bow. As the technique involves roughing up the surface of the metal, it makes sense to start with an unpolished plate. This will generally be less expensive than a highly polished plate, but check thoroughly for deep scratches or extreme flaws in the plate, as they will show up later. What is essential, however, is that you properly file and bevel the edges of the plate. They should be gently sloping, rounded edges, approximately 3mm (⅛ in.) wide to stop the blade of the rocker being damaged as it overlaps the edge.

You will need:

- Filed metal plate (usually copper)
- Rocker
- Arkansas stone (for sharpening the rocker)
- Stiff steel brush (for removing burrs from rocker after sharpening)
- Scraper/burnisher
- Rocking pattern
- Carbon paper (for transferring drawings – optional).

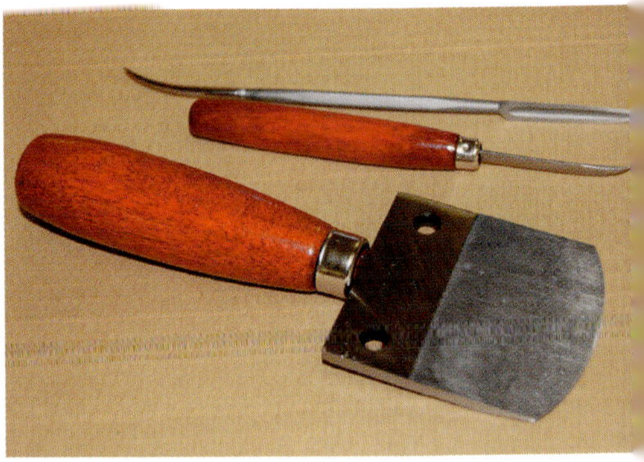

Mezzotint tools: from the top a burnisher/scraper, a wooden handled burnisher, and an 85-gauge rocker with the fluted side up showing the rows of parallel teeth. Tools supplied by Intaglio Printmakers.

Tools

Rockers

The essential requirements for creating a mezzotint are a rocker and a scraper/burnisher. The rocker has a wooden handle attached to a piece of steel with a smooth side that tapers to a bevelled edge, and a grooved side with vertical channels that end in a curved blade with evenly spaced, comb-like teeth. The advantage of having these vertical channels that form the teeth and extend the full length of the tool is that you can to sharpen the blade as often as necessary. The rocker teeth are spaced at varying intervals on each tool to create rockers of different gauges. The spacing of these teeth is measured in tpsi, which stands for 'teeth per square inch'. The standard gauges that are most commonly used are 45, 50, 65, 85, 100, 120 and 150 tpsi.

The coarse-grade rockers (those with between 25 to 50 tpsi) have larger teeth separated by bigger spaces. Because of this they displace more metal, creating much deeper impressions and throwing up larger burrs. This will produce a surface that holds more ink and will result in a denser, richer black when printed. As the burr is less sensitive to wear, it will tolerate more scraping and burnishing. This allows for a gradual reduction of the burr, widening the possibilities for tonal variation. The toughness of the burr also means that it is less easily damaged by wiping and printing and will withstand quite large editions, especially if steel-faced (see p.26). Also, the roughness of the surface

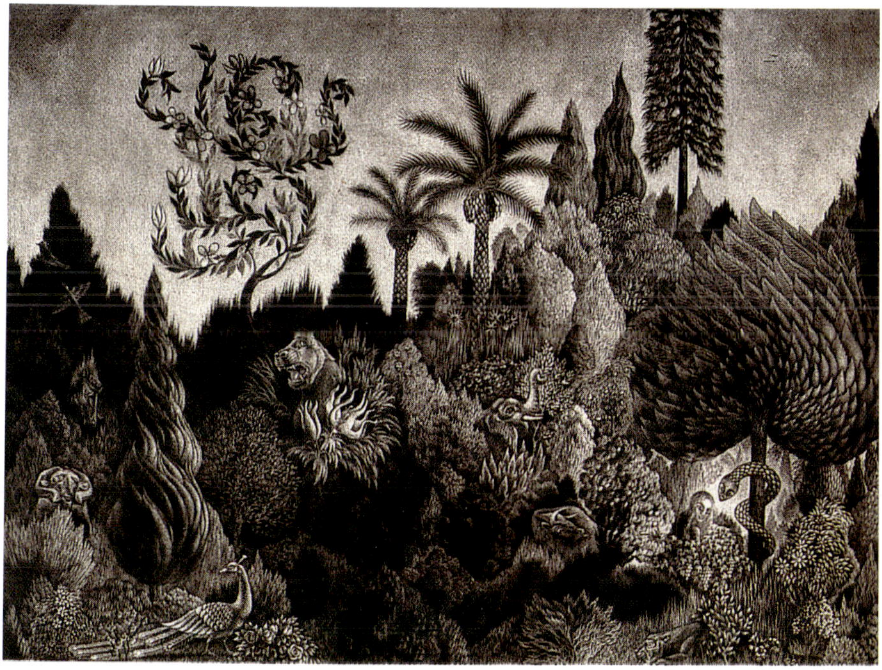

Willow Winston – *The Temptation*. Mezzotint, 27.5 × 35 cm (10¾ × 13¾ in.). This plate was rocked in an incredible 40 different directions.

means that there is less likelihood of the scrapers and burnishers slipping during plate work. On the downside, because the surface is quite tough and resilient it takes much longer to burnish, and achieving areas of white will require quite a bit of effort. It is also very difficult to create finely detailed images.

Medium-gauge rockers are those with between 50 to 100 tpsi. The most commonly used rockers are the 65 and 85 gauges, which will create blacks almost as rich as the coarse grade rockers and will also withstand large editions. As the burr created is smaller, there is not the possibility for the same range of tonal variation. What is possible, however, is a much greater potential for fine detail. It is also easier to work the plate and the paler greys or white are not quite as taxing to create. The finer the gauge of rocker, the less effort is required when rocking.

The fine-gauge rockers with 120 or 150 tpsi will produce a less intense black but make it possible to create pieces with extraordinarily intricate detail. These plates are extremely delicate and will not stand up much proofing and printing, limiting the potential edition size. Although plate work is easier, you are also more likely to have accidents involving the burnisher slipping, and these can be quite obvious in the finished piece.

The other variable where rockers are concerned is the width of the blade. They come in widths ranging from 1.5-30 cm (½-12 in.) although the most commonly used are: 4, 6.5, 10 and 15.25 cm (1½, 2½, 4 and 6 in.). You should avoid using one that is wider than the plate as you are likely to unevenly wear down or even break the teeth of the rocker. A tiny rocker on a huge plate is also not advisable, as it will take you forever to rock the plate.

Small rockers of up to 4 cm (1½ in.) are useful for correcting mistakes or for creating small areas of spot mezzotinting on larger plates.

Medium sized rockers of between 5-10cm (2-4 in.) are appropriate for most applications and plate sizes.

Large rockers of between 11.5-15.25 cm (4½-6 in.) are very tricky to use and should only be used if the plate you are rocking is extremely large.

Experienced mezzotint artists will possess a range of rockers in various gauges and sizes, and will select them depending on the image and the desired effects. If you are trying mezzotinting for the first time then you should opt for a 6.5 or 7.5 cm (2½ or 3 in.) 65- or 85-gauge rocker.

Sharpening the rocker

It is essential to the look of a mezzotint that a sharp rocker be used at all times. Although rockers are made of steel, which is much harder than the metal of the plates they are biting, they will wear down. The teeth should be examined periodically to make sure that there are no more than a few irregular or broken teeth. The tools are designed to allow for a great deal of sharpening, however, and a rocker should last a lifetime. By using a rectangular oilstone such as an Arkansas stone, you can sharpen or repair your own rocker. There are two bevelled edges, one short and adjacent to the teeth, and the other long. It is the short bevel that you should sharpen. Being careful to preserve the angle, slide

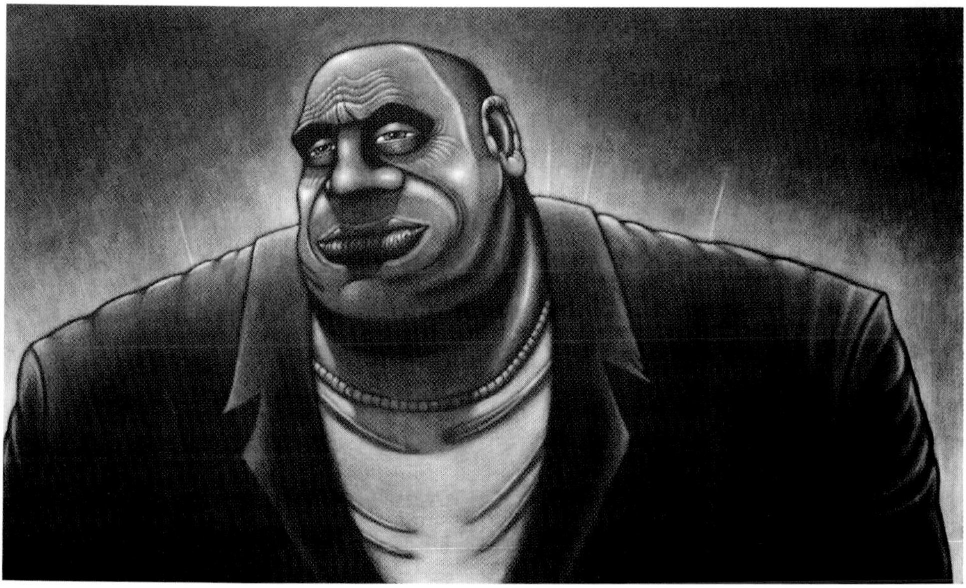

Martin Langford, *Bloke*. Mezzotint, 29 x 48 cm (11½ x 19 in.)

the stone back and forth on the short bevel of the blade until the tops of the teeth grate against the stone. You must always sharpen the entire length of the blade and remove any burrs from the blade using a stiff steel brush.

Scrapers/burnishers

The two basic drawing tools used to create images on a mezzotint are the scraper and the burnisher. Scrapers come in many varieties but the most commonly used have a triangular shaft with three hollow or solid sides. These sides taper to a point and the angles where they meet are extremely sharp. As the name suggests, the tool is used to scrape or shave the burrs off the plate. For the tool to work well it must be kept sharp. Slide the flat surface of the scraper back and forth along the length of the shaft on an oiled Arkansas stone. Always sharpen all three sides of the scraper. Scrapers come either on their own with wooden handles or at the other end of burnishers or etching needles.

Burnishers come flat or with ball ends but the most common have a curved and rounded shaft tapering to a sharp point. Mezzotint artists will generally have a number of these depending on their intended application. Martin Langford uses the burnisher on a German made scraper/burnisher for large tonal areas but a wooden-handled Lions burnisher for fine detailed work.

Other tools

Any material that can be used for sanding or polishing can be used to create tones on a mezzotint. Steel wool, sandpaper or carborundum paper can create interesting effects. Arkansas stones, traditionally used to sharpen intaglio tools, or very hard charcoal can be used for drawing – they allow for much looser and more gestural mark making than is possible with a burnisher or scraper.

Rocking the plate

As with all of the tools in this section, the name indicates how the tool will be used. In this case the rocker is worked across the surface of the plate by rocking the full width of the blade from side to side. Holding the tool at an angle allows it to advance naturally across the plate. Do not try to force the forward motion of the rocker – a constant and consistent motion to the left and right will accomplish this for you. The teeth of the rocker cut into the plate and push the displaced metal to one side to create burrs that will hold ink. When you have taken the rocker from one side of the plate to the other, it will have created a column of parallel dotted lines comprised of these burrs. All of the subsequent columns should move in the same direction and begin from the same edge of the plate. They should be positioned to slightly overlap the previous column. When the entire plate is covered with columns in one direction you will have completed a single 'pass'. The number of passes needed to create a suitable ground for a mezzotint is very much a case of personal preference. Some artists will just do two passes, which will print black but will show a strong crosshatched pattern when burnished. Martin Langford rocks in 22-26 different directions on every plate that he makes. See 'Creating a Rocking Pattern' (p.39) for tips about this.

Holding the rocker

The manner in which the rocker is held is of paramount importance. The handle should be held in the palm of a closed fist with the blade at the bottom of your hand, perpendicular to the direction of your forearm. When the rocker is in contact with the plate it should be held at an angle. The fluted or the smooth side of the blade can be facing you, providing that the fluted side is tilted towards your plate. If the fluted side is facing you then the top of the handle should be tilted in towards you at something between 5-degree and a 30-degree angle. With the smooth side towards you, the handle should be angled away from your body.

Attaching weights to the rocker helps to regulate the pressure and makes rocking the plate by hand easier. If you do this, however, be careful to use weights that do not damage the fluted side of the rocker. A rocking pole is a helpful device for controlling the space between the lines. It is comprised of two adjustable legs attached to a wooden channel or rail that can be clamped to your work surface. The rocker is attached to a pole with a large ball bearing or similar round weight at the opposite end. The round ball should fit into the channel and will allow the rocker to move forward in a straight line at an even pace. Adjusting the height of the legs will enable you to modify the angle of the rocker, which controls its speed across the plate (see photo on p.40).

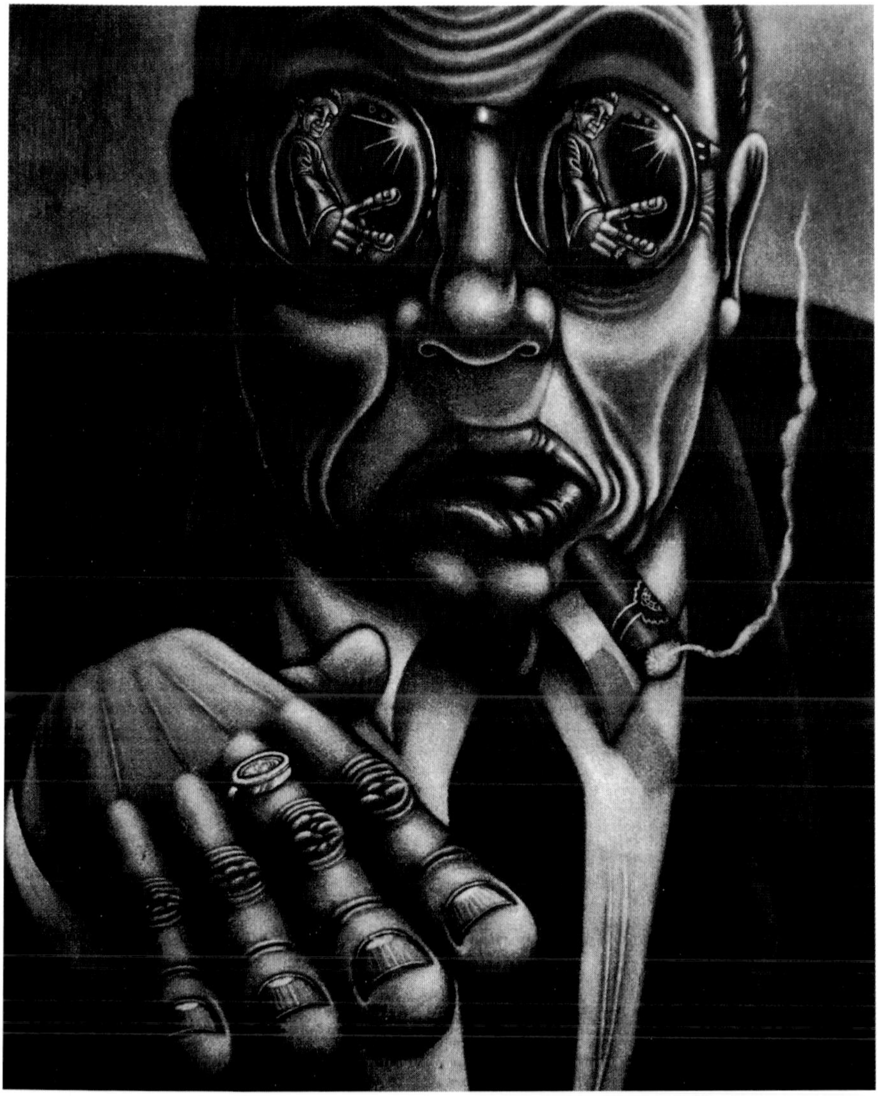

Martin Langford, *Scissors, Paper, Stone*. Mezzotint, 35 x 28.5 cm (13¾ x 11⅕ in.)

Creating a rocking pattern

If you intend to rock the plate in a number of directions, it is vital that you have a plan; the most straightforward and easy plan to follow is a 'clock pattern'. On a piece of paper larger than your plate draw a square, the height of which is longer than the longest edge of your plate. Draw a clock pattern over the square, with all lines bisecting the centre of the square; mark the 'hours' from one to twelve with arrows at the end of each line. On the back of the plate, mark the top using a piece of masking tape or an arrow drawn with a permanent marker. Place the plate face up over this rocking pattern, so that

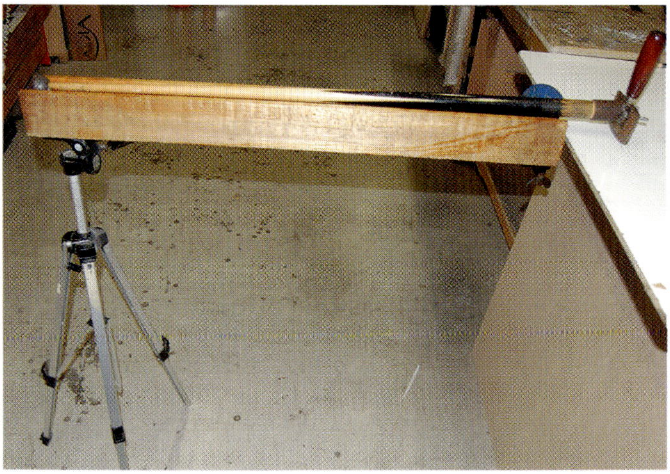

Mezzotint rocking pole. This is Martin Langford's rocking pole, which shows the adjustable legs made from a photographic tripod attached to the wooden channel. He has used an old snooker cue for the pole and attached a metal ball bearing to the end. Mezzotint rockers have holes in them to allow a) them to be screwed to the end of a rocking pole and b) weights to be attached.

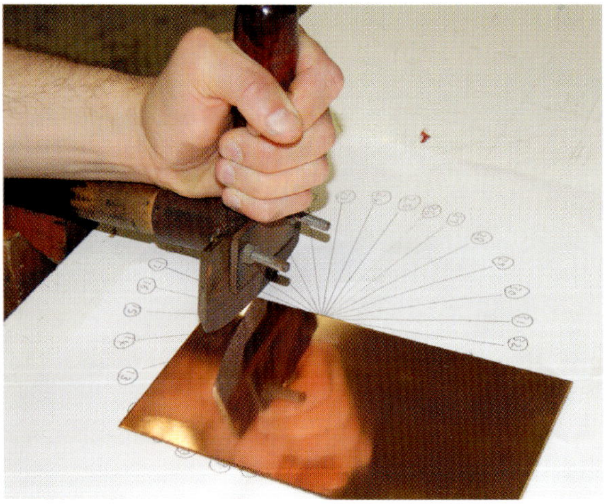

Rocking using a mezzotint rocking pole. This shows the screws attaching the rocker to the pole and you can see a small weight attached to the front. Martin is beginning the first pass and you can see the rocking pattern beneath the plate. This one has been numbered with twelve extra pass lines.

the left edge of the plate sits flush with the line numbered '1'. Starting at the bottom left corner of the plate, commence the first row of your first pass towards the arrow of the number you are working on. Continue until you have completed the first pass, make a note that you have completed number '1', and then turn the plate so that the top left corner of the plate now points towards '2'. Repeat the process.

It is essential that you keep a note of each completed pass, as you will have difficulty remembering where you are up to and it is impossible to tell how many passes you have made by examining the plate. Once you have completed all twelve passes, you can either repeat the entire process by reusing the same sequence of numbers or you can add twelve extra passes by inserting an extra line equidistantly between every two existing lines on the rocking pattern.

Martin Langford uses the clock pattern plan, but prefers a more random approach to the numbering of the lines and the rocking of the passes.

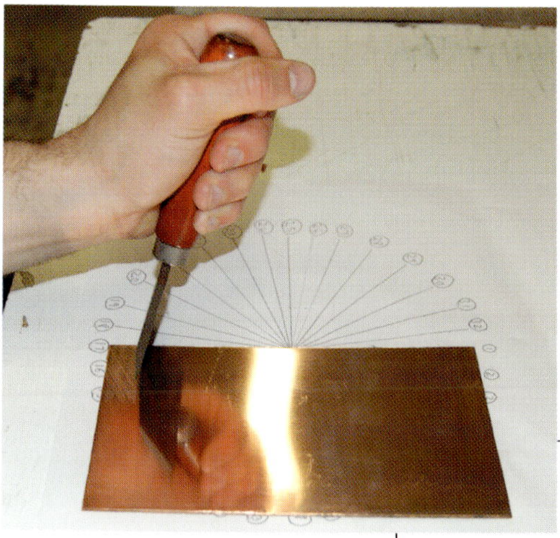

Mezzotint hand rocking. This clearly shows the correct angle for holding the rocker when rocking by hand.

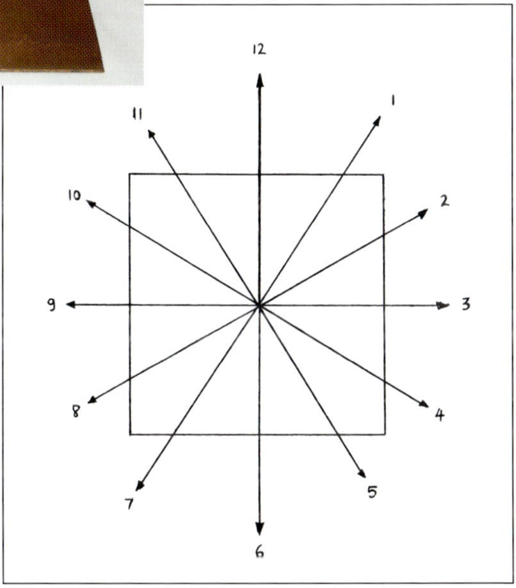

RIGHT Mezzotint rocking pattern numbered with the twelve basic pass lines.

The manner in which you choose to number the passes is completely a matter of personal preference; as long as you are systematic and keep a careful note of each pass as you complete it, the process should work perfectly.

Transferring a drawing

You can transfer a drawing onto the prepared plate by placing a piece of carbon paper or lithographers' rouge face down onto the plate and then tracing over a pre-existing drawing done on tissue. The surface of the plate is very rough and uneven so it will not be easy to do and great care must be taken to avoid tearing through the paper. You must find the right pressure to transfer the drawing adequately as pressing too hard will burnish the drawn lines onto the plate. Coloured pencils or softer lead graphite are less likely to damage the burrs than biros or hard pencils and can also be used to draw directly onto the plate.

Working the plate

The drawing process for a mezzotint is carried out in reverse compared to all other intaglio techniques; this is because you are working into the plate to create the lighter tones and the highlights. The areas that you want to remain a solid black or to read as lines will be left alone.

There are essentially two ways to approach a mezzotint image. The first is to begin cautiously altering the burrs, starting with the darkest tones and then to gradually work through progressively lighter tones until you eventually expose the very lightest tones you hope to achieve. This method allows for proofing and reworking and, as it is more difficult in mezzotint to add tone than it is to lighten tones, this way you are less likely to make mistakes. It also allows for greater freedom if you decide to alter the image.

The second method is to go straight to the scraping and burnishing of the whitest areas and then gradually work through the other tones. The advantage of this method is that once you have established the darkest and the lightest tones you have a comparison for all of the shades in between. A further benefit of this technique is that, as you have worked through the various layers of the plate, you will know how robust and resilient your ground is. This will give you an idea how much proofing and printing your plate will withstand.

When using a scraper, the blade should be held with the cutting edge parallel to the plate's surface. The idea is to pare the tops off the burrs in order to reduce the amount of ink they will hold. Burnishers are held like pencils, so that the smooth face of the curved tool is in contact with the plate but the tip does not scratch it. It is useful to use a little oil on the plate – this reduces friction and will help protect the tool from being scratched or otherwise damaged. The burnisher gradually flattens the burr to allow for a broad range of tones. A burnisher allows much more subtle work on the plate and greater freedom of movement. Moving the burnisher in varying directions will create smooth gradations of tone.

A piece of tissue paper is useful to determine how the burnishing is progressing. Trap a piece of tissue paper larger than your image size under the edge of the plate. Fold it in towards you and hold it over the plate so that shields but does not cover the image. The diffused light that falls onto the metal will allow you to see the burnished areas clearly. You can also cover the plate completely with the tissue paper to see how best to proceed, but it will be more difficult to make out the details.

Printing a mezzotint

The surface of a mezzotint is delicate and the printing process will wear down the burr. This is only partially a result of passing the plate through the press, as the paper and blankets are soft and the pressure should not be set so firm as to damage the burr. This is primarily due to the abrasive nature of the inks when wiping. It is advisable to keep your proofing to a minimum and have the plate steel-faced prior to editioning (see p.26).

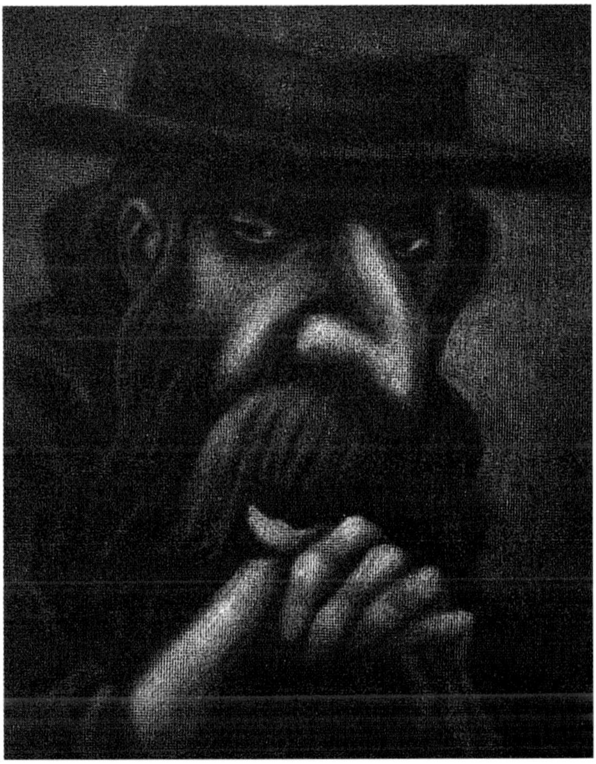

Mychael Barratt – *Shylock*. Mezzotint, 10 x 8 cm (4 x 3 in.). This mezzotint was done on a machine-rocked plate. Close examination will reveal a grain pattern in the burnished areas.

To ink up the plate you can use a tool called a brayer, which is a small, soft roller. Roll up the ink from a slab and then spread in an even layer over the entire surface of the plate. You must apply just enough pressure to gently push ink into the depths of the mezzotint without damaging the burr. You can also use squeegees made of either card or soft rubber. Avoid hard plastic varieties, as they too will damage the burr. Wipe gently with scrim and tissue.

Throughout the course of each edition it is crucial that you pay attention to the state of the mezzotint. If the colour of the copper is beginning to show when the plate is cleaned then you will need to repeat the steel facing. If the facing is intact but the prints are beginning to be affected by the wearing down of the burr then you can nurse the edition along by stiffening the ink. Martin Langford begins all of his editions with Graphic Chemical 'Bone Black' but then begins to add small amounts of Charbonnel 55981 as necessary.

4 INDIRECT INTAGLIO

All of the techniques that rely upon chemical processes are grouped here. As in the section on 'Direct Intaglio', there are techniques that favour the draughtsman (such as hard- and soft-ground etching) but there is also plenty of scope for the painter. Aquatint, especially when used with spit bite or sugar lift, allows for distinctly painterly approaches. Nothing else looks quite like an etching; however, an etching can be made to look like any number of other media. Hard ground often resembles pen and ink, soft ground can be used in a manner reminiscent of charcoal or pastel, and aquatint can look for all the world like an accomplished watercolour painting. The effects are remarkably diverse. Etchings are the product of a mysterious alchemy, according to artist Chris Orr: 'Etching is a peculiarly intimate process. Half hidden in veils of wax grounds, stinking solvents and fuming acids, it lends itself easily to a romantic and mystical dimension.'

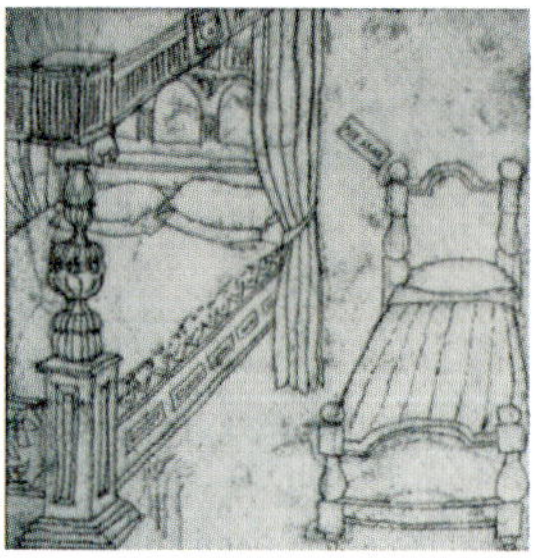

■ HARD GROUND ETCHING

Hard ground is one of the most straightforward and easily identifiable etching techniques. It features solid lines of various weights and densities that most closely resemble pen and ink drawings. It can be used on its own to create images combining lines with tones made using cross hatching, or it can be used to lay down a drawing as a starting point for a more complicated piece incorporating various other techniques.

Hard ground is the name given to the acid-resistant waxy substance that is heated and then spread evenly over the surface of a metal plate. Once the plate has cooled, the ground will harden and then the most common procedure is to use an etching needle or scribe to draw though the ground, thus selectively exposing the plate. When the plate is placed in acid only the exposed lines are bitten. If more drawing is done before subsequent immersions those lines drawn first will bite deeper. The bitten lines will hold the ink and print as positive marks with those bitten deepest printing darkest. The range of tools that can be used for mark making and exposing the plate is limitless and can include pencils, pens, sandpaper, steel wool, wire brushes, roulette wheels and white spirit applied with rags or brushes.

You will need:

- Filed, backed and degreased metal plate (copper, zinc or steel)
- Hard ground ball (either store bought or homemade – see page 49)

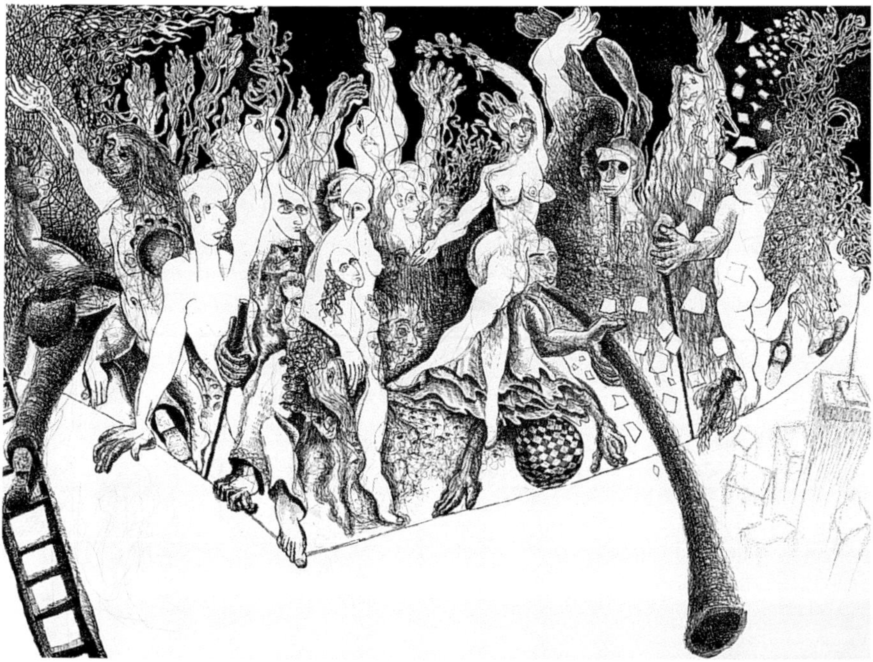

Paul Hawdon – *Reaching for Dreams*. Hard ground, aquatint and drypoint, 60 × 82 cm (23½ × 32¼ in.)

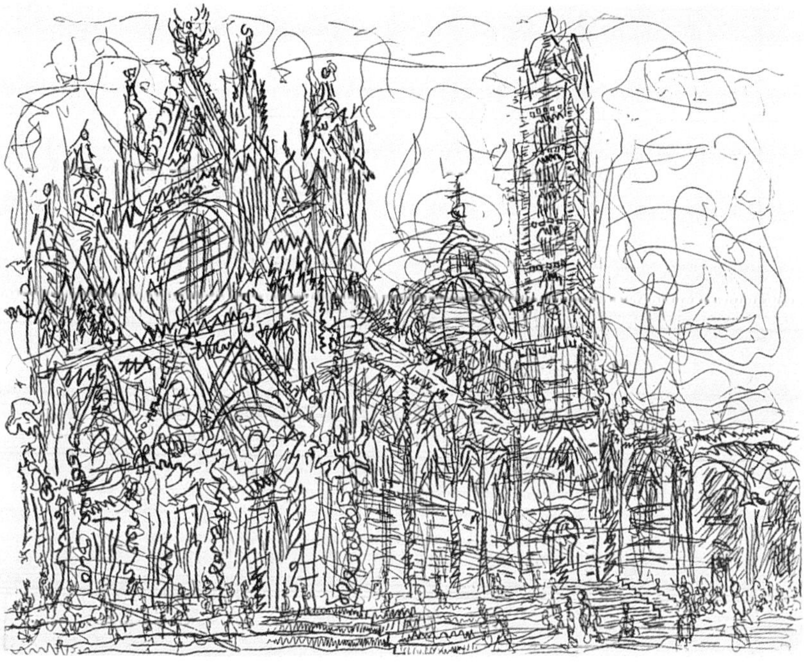

Paul Hawdon – *Il Duomo – Siena*. Hard ground, 21 × 26 cm (8¼ × 10¼ in.)

- Hot plate or liquid hard ground (no hot plate required)
- Roller or dabber
- Drawing tool
- Nitric acid or ferric chloride (don't forget to use a tray and fume cupboard)
- Fume mask, goggles and gloves
- Long feather for brushing over plate during etching to remove air bubbles.

The method

Place the filed, backed and degreased plate on a pre-warmed hot plate. Once the plate is hot enough for the hard ground ball to melt on contact you are ready to begin. Spread the ground over the surface of the plate, using either a leather pad or a roller. If you are using the leather pad, apply a liberal amount of the ground to the plate and work it evenly over the surface of the plate using a gentle, rolling motion of the hand. It is quite an art to achieve a perfectly even coating of ground using the pad, and for this reason most printmakers prefer to use a roller. The traditional technique for applying the hard ground with a roller is melting the ground onto the hotplate and loading the roller from there. However, as you ideally want a clean, grease-free surface and most printmaking studios use their hotplates for everything from inking up plates to preparing soft and hard grounds, and clean them only erratically, I've never wholly trusted them. So I melt the hard ground directly onto the etching plate and roll it up using a rubber or PVC roller. You can use traditional leather rollers as well, although as it is very difficult to clean them properly and traces of other grounds are not helpful it is advisable to have designated hard and soft ground rollers. It is essential that the hotplate be set to the right temperature. If the roller is not turning properly or slides across the surface of the plate then your hotplate is too hot; if the roller sticks or the hard ground is tacky then your hotplate is too cold.

Liquid hard ground is useful for those without access to a hotplate. Pour the ground onto the degreased plate, tipping it to cover the entire surface. Then, tip the plate to pour the excess liquid off one of the corners back into the original container. Allow the ground to dry completely before beginning work on the plate. This should take about 24 hours.

Smoking the plate

Store-bought hard ground is very dark and opaque so this traditional technique, which darkens the ground so you can more clearly see the lines you have drawn, has almost vanished. However, as smoking the plates has the added benefit of making the hard ground harder and more impervious to foul biting, I feel it is worthy of inclusion. You will need a bunch of waxing tapers twisted together and a hanging plate clamp. The hanging plate clamp is comprised of two sticks joined with a hinge at the top with small feet facing in at the bottom. The sticks should be made from pieces of 2.5 x 5 cm (1 x 2 in.) wood approximately 60 cm (24 in.) long. Attach a metal chain to the hinge end so that you can suspend the apparatus

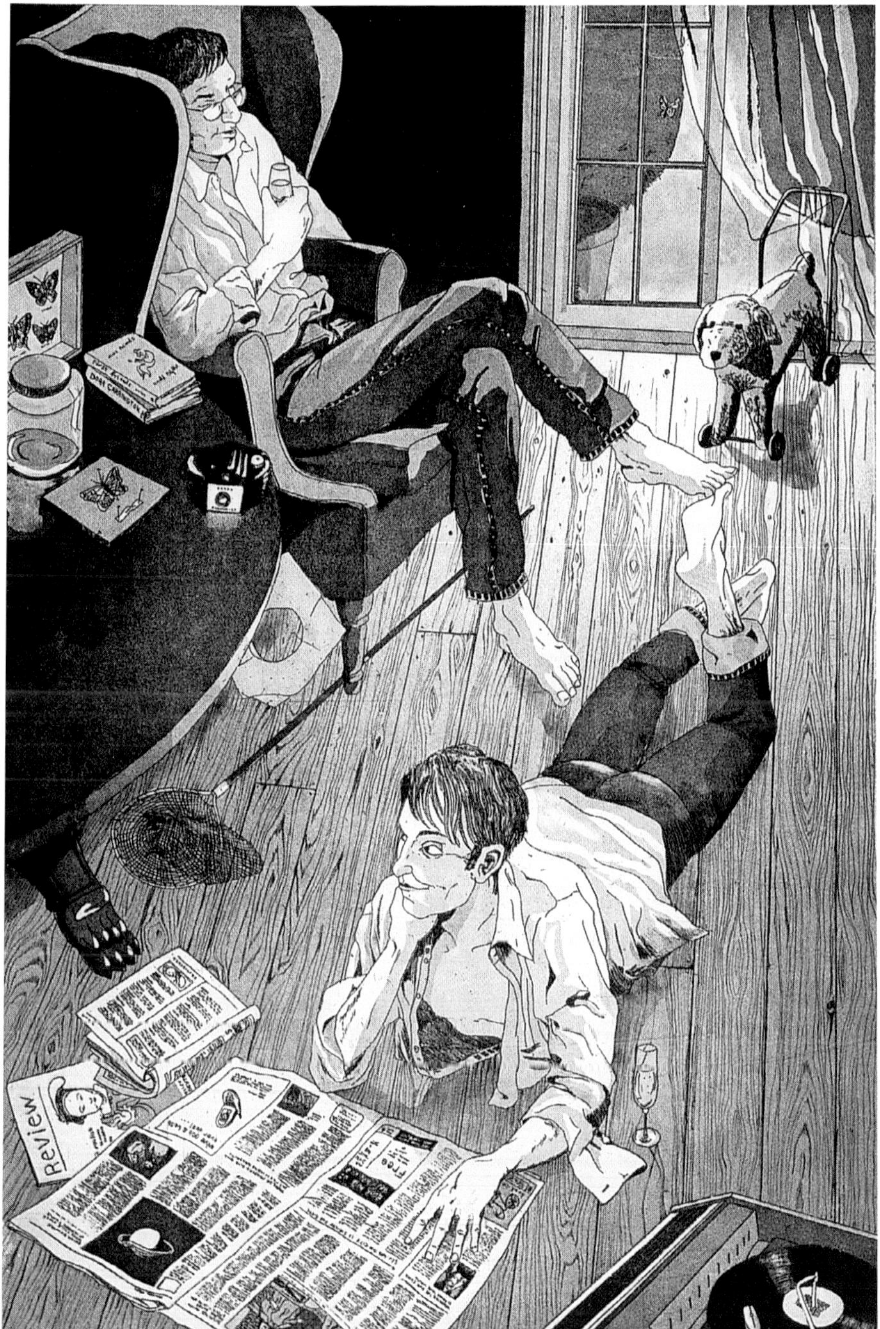

Martin Ridgewell – *I remember everything*. Hard ground and aquatint, 53 x 35 cm (21 x 13¾ in.)

from a hook. You should then hang the plate, hard-ground-side down, between the two arms of the clamp and light the tapers. Move the tip of the flame over the surface of the plate so that the wax absorbs the smoke and turns uniformly black and shiny.

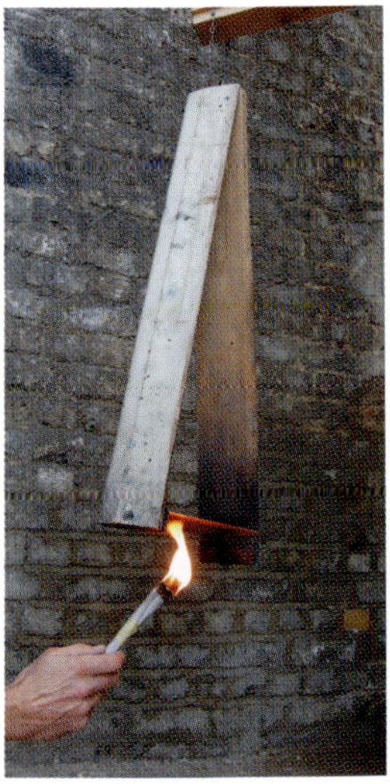

Smoking a hard ground plate. You can see how the plate rests on the feet, which face in at the bottom of the hanging plate rack

Guide drawing onto the plate

Guide drawings can be done lightly and directly onto the ground or they can be transferred from other sources. You can offset the image by placing a soft pencil drawing face down onto the plate and running them through the press together. Reduce the pressure from that you would use for normal etching to avoid damaging the ground. Offsetting the image has the added advantage of reversing the image onto the plate so that your eventual etching will be the same way around as your original drawing. You can also use carbon paper or lithographers rouge paper to transfer drawings onto the plate. Try not to press too firmly as this will also damage the ground.

Drawing into hard ground

As previously stated, the range of tools you can employ for drawing through the ground is limitless and you will quickly find the ones that suit you best. Drypoint tools are not ideal – they will catch on the plate making it difficult to draw unimpeded. They have the added disadvantage of marking the plate where you have drawn, which is very irritating if you decide to alter the drawing prior to etching. Etching needles are preferable as they are not as sharp as drypoint tools. Sharp pencils, ink pens and roulette wheels are also useful. For looser, more unpredictable marks you can use solvents, such as white spirit, oil of spike lavender or lighter fluid, on rags, stiff paintbrushes or toothbrushes to wipe the ground off of the plate. You will get very gestural marks if you use rags and brushes on the plate while the ground is still wet. If the marks are very wide then the exposed areas will open-bite. This will result in marks that are roughly and unevenly etched in the middle and much darker at the edges.

Another way to achieve painterly marks is to paint onto a dried hard ground using oil of spike lavender. Leave the marks for a short while to allow them to react with the ground and then wipe them off with a cloth and briefly run the plate under water. This will result in very specific removal of the ground exposing the plate for etching either in lines or areas of open-bite, depending on the size of the brush strokes.

Prior to etching the plate, degrease it again to remove any grease from the exposed lines. Etching times are critical for hard ground and if you want a range of line weights then the lines that you want to print darkest should be

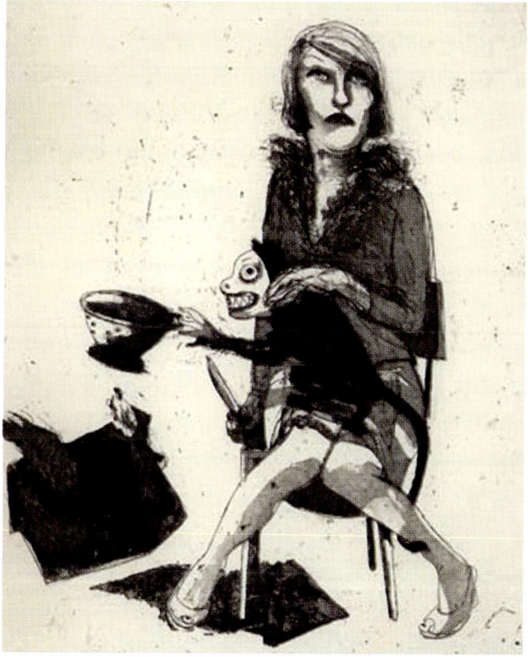

Marcelle Hanselaar – *Liar, Liar, House on Fire*. 26 x 21 cm (10¼ x 8¼ in.). Hard ground and aquatint

drawn and etched first. Plates etched in nitric acid should be frequently brushed with a long feather to remove air bubbles that form during etching and will impede the clean biting of the plate. If you are using copper and ferric chloride then you will need to place the plate face-down in the mordant or agitate the tray often during etching and rinse the sediment out of the lines occasionally. When you have finished etching, clean the plate thoroughly with white spirit or paraffin prior to printing.

Mixing your own ground

The store-bought hard and soft ground balls are of a very good quality but are each limited to a single consistency. If you would like to try using different consistencies, especially in the case of soft ground, then you might like to try mixing your own. This also has the advantage of being less expensive over time. You will need beeswax, bitumen, fine colophony resin, a saucepan (one that you never plan to use again for domestic application), a stir stick or wooden spoon and non-porous containers such as waxed paper cups or plastic egg cartons to be used as moulds.

Dark hard ground

- 40% beeswax
- 40% bitumen
- 20% colophony resin

All of these amounts should be measured precisely by weight and not by volume. Melt the beeswax in a pan and then gradually add the bitumen while constantly stirring. Once you have added all of the bitumen, begin to gradually add the colophony resin still stirring consistently. Once you have a smooth mixture, reduce the heat as much as possible and simmer for three hours, still stirring occasionally. Remove from the heat and allow the mixture to cool slightly, still stirring occasionally, until it begins to thicken. Then pour it into moulds and leave to set and harden. These balls are a perfect hard ground or can be used as a base mixture for soft ground (see p.54).

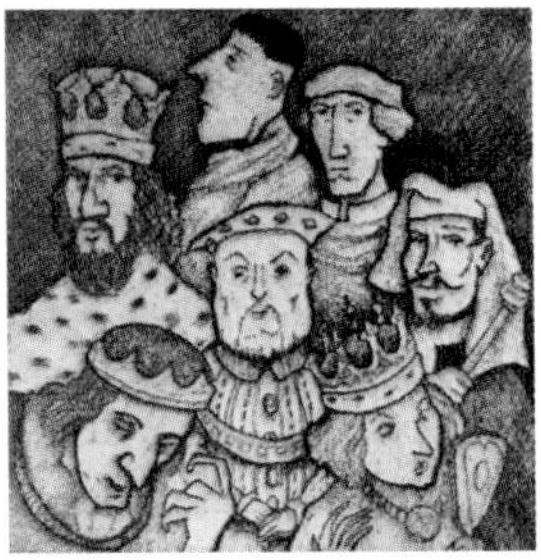

■ SOFT GROUND ETCHING

Soft ground etching is very similar to hard ground etching except that the acid-resistant ground never dries but stays soft and tacky to the touch. You do not work directly on the ground but instead draw through a piece of paper laid over the surface of the plate. The ground will stick to the paper where you apply pressure, exposing the plate along the lines you have drawn. The drawn lines, depending on the paper and drawing tools used, will have a soft-edged appearance resembling anything from a pencil to pastel or charcoal. In addition, anything pressed into the surface of the ground and removed will leave impressions that will print surprisingly accurately. Lace, crumpled tissue paper or leaves can all be used effectively.

You will need:

- Filed, backed and degreased metal plate (copper, zinc or steel)
- Soft ground ball (either store bought or homemade – see p.54)
- Hot plate
- Roller
- Paper (to draw through; experiment to find your favourite)
- Drawing tool (to draw with; again, experiment to find your favourite)
- Nitric acid or ferric chloride (plus tray and fume cupboard)
- Fume mask, gloves and goggles.

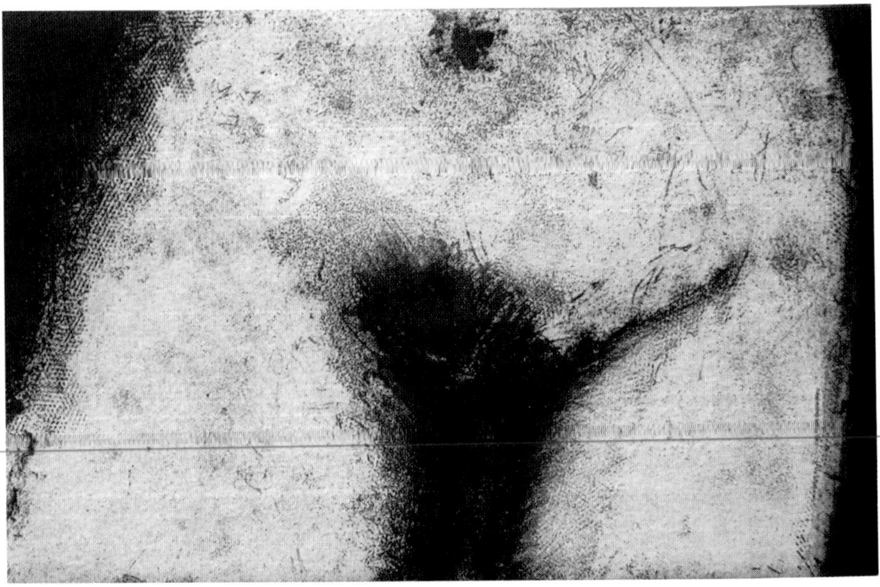

Iain Perring – *Bella Figura*. Soft ground, roulette, 15 × 23 cm (6 × 9 in.). This image has been created by drawing through paper and by impressing textures into the soft ground.

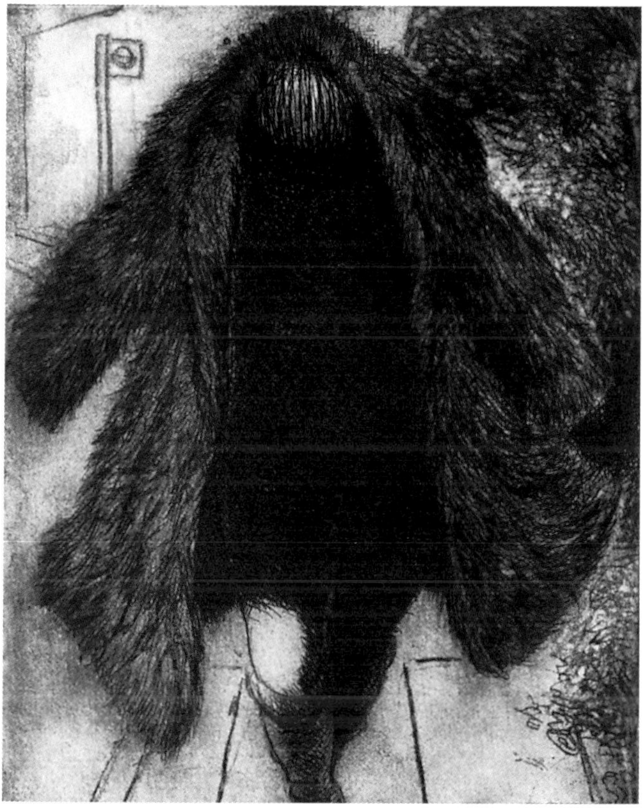

John T Freeman, *South Lambeth Road*. Soft and hard ground etching and aquatint, 17.5 x 12.5 cm (7 x 5 in.)

The method

Place the clean, filed and degreased plate onto the pre-warmed hotplate. It is crucial that the plate be protectively backed before you apply the ground, as soft ground is delicate and you will not be able to handle the plate afterwards. If you trust that your hotplate is clean and grease-free, melt some soft ground directly onto it but, as stated on p.46, I prefer to apply the ground directly to the warmed etching plate. Roll the ground over the plate until you have achieved an even layer of ground over the entire surface. A thin coating of ground will be sensitive to delicately drawn marks but is extremely easy to over-etch and very prone to foul biting. If you want lines that will etch deeply and print very dark then you should apply a slightly thicker layer of soft ground. It is useful to make test plates, trying out different densities of ground and varying times in the acid. Once the plate has cooled it is ready to use, however the sensitive nature of the ground means that great care should be taken when handling the plate as any fingerprints or accidental knocks will etch and print.

If you wish to draw on the plate then you will first need to carefully fix your plate to the work surface using small loops of masking tape or Blu Tack (Fun Tack), remembering to handle the plate only by its filed edges. Avoid strong

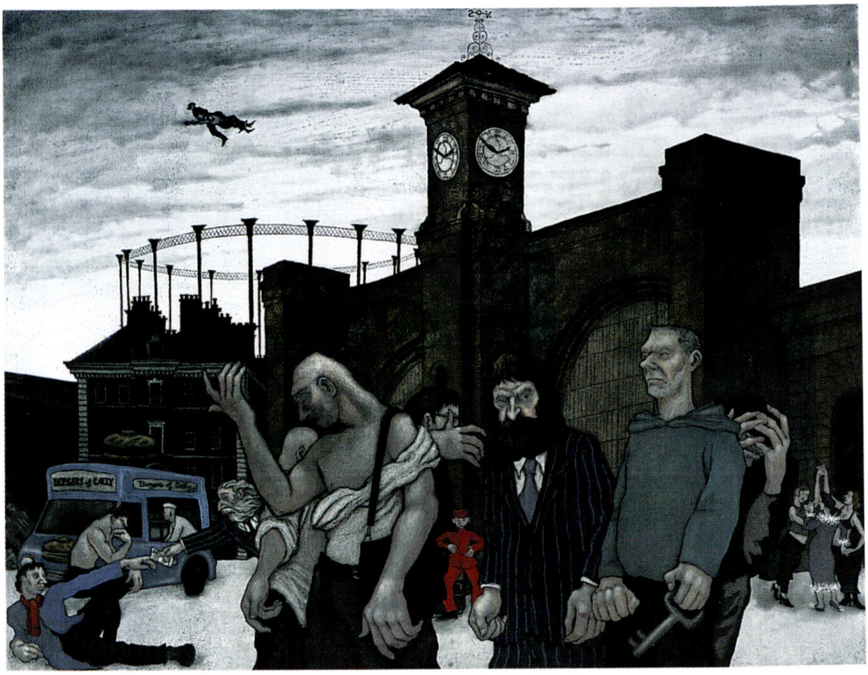

Mychael Barratt – *Life Imitating Art VII*. Soft ground, aquatint and spit bite, 50 x 66 cm (19¾ x 26 in.). The entire drawing is done as a soft ground etching in a single biting. The variation in the weight of line is all from the weight applied to the pencils.

adhesives such as parcel tape, as these will cause problems later when you need to lift the plate. The piece of paper that you intend to draw through must be larger than the plate; tape this paper firmly into place across the top and in the two bottom corners, to allow you to check the drawing on the plate without misregistering when you replace the paper. You can also make a window mount slightly larger than the plate with the paper attached to it. This makes registering easier if you plan to redraw on the plate between bitings in the acid.

The choice of both paper and drawing tool is crucial to the look of the etched lines. A hard, sharp pencil or pen drawn through tissue paper will create very fine, strong lines, whereas a soft litho crayon or a cotton bud drawn on newsprint will give the etched line the appearance of a crayon or charcoal drawing. One of the great advantages of tissue paper is that you can place the drawing face down on the plate and still be able to see the drawing well enough to follow the outlines. This makes it possible to create an etching that will print the same way round as your original drawing. It is a good idea to place an extra piece of tissue paper between the drawing and the plate as any traces of soft graphite from the drawing on the tissue can stop the acid from biting properly. You can also use a tissue paper drawing with a different type of paper between to vary the line. Norman Ackroyd uses graphite sticks drawn through soft Japanese tissue paper to create broad painterly strokes. To do this properly he mixes up his own soft ground, which is very supple. He makes up the hard ground as in the recipe on p.49, but rather than adding the usual 50% tallow to make a medium soft ground he adds 60% or 70% tallow. For this surface to etch properly it is imperative that the plate is etched face-down in ferric chloride which is colder than room temperature.

Once your plate and paper are in place it is a good idea to create a raised platform to rest your hand on. I use strips of 1cm (½ in.) thick foamboard taped into place surrounding the plate to create a frame and then I rest a rigid piece of plywood or 6 mm (⅕ in.) MDF over the frame. You can also protect the plate by using a curved piece of wood (e.g., from a barrel). Soft ground is very susceptible to foul biting so once you have finished the drawing it is advisable to stop out the entire plate around the drawn lines if possible, particularly if you want a very white background. Alternatively, you can etch the plate for a couple of minutes and then check it as the foul biting will show up clearly but will not yet have etched very deeply. Stop out the areas of foul biting and return to the acid (for more information on stopping out see p.59). Another useful technique involves using a counterproof for registration when you want to proof and rework a soft ground. A print is pulled from an early state etching and this is then passed through the press at an increased pressure with a piece of dry, fine Japanese paper. You can reapply a soft ground to the plate, place the counterproof print face up onto the plate and draw through it to perfectly register with the existing drawing.

As the ground stays tacky it is possible to imprint flat objects such as leaves, feathers, fabric, clothing, textured paper, sandpaper and crumpled tissue. It is important that you do not use normal etching pressure as you will remove too much of the ground. Take the pressure off by approximately a quarter turn or remove the heaviest blanket and place the plate on the bed of the press. Lay the object you want to imprint on the surface of the plate and cover the entire plate with tissue paper to protect the blankets. After slowly winding it through the

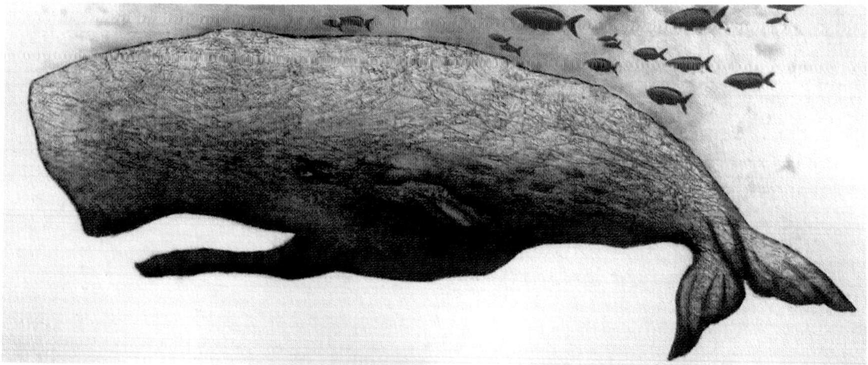

Mychael Barratt – *Jonah and the Whale* (detail). Soft ground offset etching. This texture was created by laying a crumpled piece of tissue paper over a soft ground and running it through the press at a low pressure.

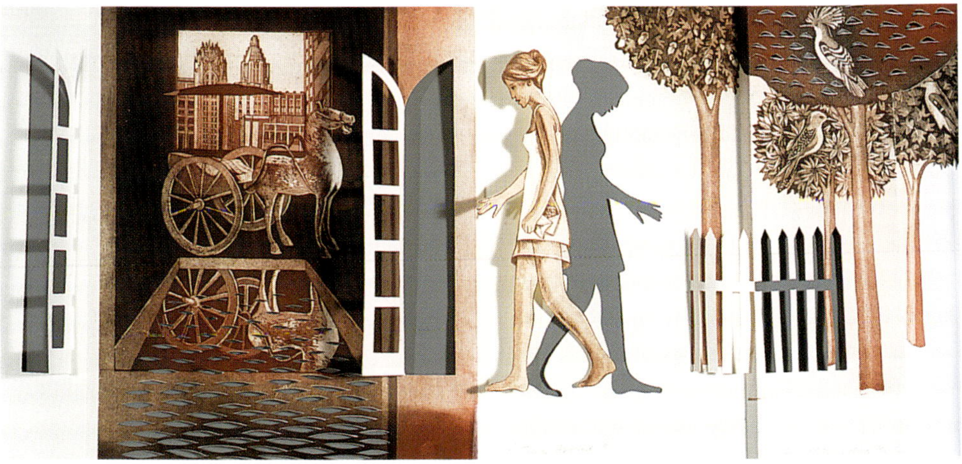

Mila Judge Furstova – *Turn Around*. Hard ground, aquatint and paper sculpture, 56 × 100 cm (22 × 40 in.)

press, carefully remove the objects from the plate. In the case of objects with a clear border such as leaves and feathers it is advisable to stop out the entire area around the object.

The traditional wisdom regarding etching copper plates in ferric chloride is to etch them face down but this is extremely tricky with soft grounds. If you want to do it then you will need to stop out small areas in the four corners of the front of the plate to which you attach 'stilts' such as small balls of Blu Tack (Fun Tack) or slices of cork. Holding the plate by the edges, lower it gently into the acid until the stilts come to rest on the bottom of the tray. This is not possible if you have a soft ground texture or drawing covering the whole plate, as there will be no suitable areas to stop out. I must say that I seldom etch my soft grounds face down and providing you agitate the tray during etching and rinse the plate regularly in cold water to flush out the sediment from the lines it works almost as well. When you have finished etching, clean the plate thoroughly with white spirit or paraffin prior to printing.

Soft ground

- 50% hard ground mixture (see p.49)
- 50% tallow

A medium soft ground is made up of a combination of the hard ground mixture and tallow. You can start to add the tallow to the above mixture after the three hours simmering but it is quite helpful if you have already mixed up the hard ground, as it is much easier to measure the weight of set hard ground. Re-melt the appropriate amount of hard ground until it is completely fluid, then gradually add the tallow while continuing to stir constantly for five minutes. Simmer for a further 15 minutes and then allow the mixture to cool slightly before pouring into moulds as for the hard ground (see p.49). This mixture with the 50% tallow will make a medium soft ground, which has the consistency of the store-bought balls.

You can vary this mixture considerably depending on your intended application. Less tallow will make the soft ground stiffer, which is useful if you are going to be using it in high temperatures such as outside on a summer's day. More tallow will make the soft ground softer, which is appropriate if you are using it in a cold setting such as an unheated studio in the winter. Norman Ackroyd uses a mixture with much more tallow when he wants a more sensitive surface. For this technique to etch properly it is imperative that the plate is etched face down in cold ferric chloride. In addition to varying the amounts of tallow, you can also make a softer soft ground by thoroughly mixing in 10% Vaseline to the liquid soft ground mixture. Cool slightly and then pour into moulds as above.

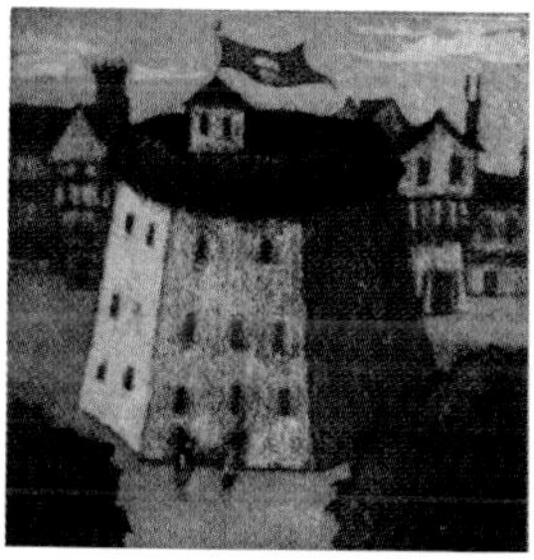

■ AQUATINT

Aquatint is the intaglio technique used for creating areas of tone and shading. A layer of rosin covers the plate and each particle of rosin creates a barrier around which the acid bites, creating the impression of a consistent tone. By selectively stopping out areas of the plate during the etching process you can create a dramatic variety of tones. It is an extremely versatile technique and can create anything from bold areas of solid black resembling a carborundum collagraph to the most delicate watercolour-type wash.

You will need:

- Filed, backed and degreased metal plate (copper or zinc)
- Aquatint rosin
- Aquatint box or hand shaker
- Gas burner
- Wire rack (for suspending plate over gas burner)
- Fume mask, goggles and gloves
- Methylated spirits to clean off the aquatint prior to printing.

The method

The most popular technique for aquatint is applying a fine dusting of powdered rosin in an aquatint box. This rosin is dangerous if inhaled, so it is advisable to wear a gas mask when using an aquatint box. Your plate must be clean and degreased, and must bear no trace of hard or soft ground in any etched lines. Place the plate onto a piece of hardboard that is approximately 5 cm (2in.) larger than the plate in every direction. This prevents patchy aquatint close to the edges of the plate. Rotating the handle on the front of the aquatint

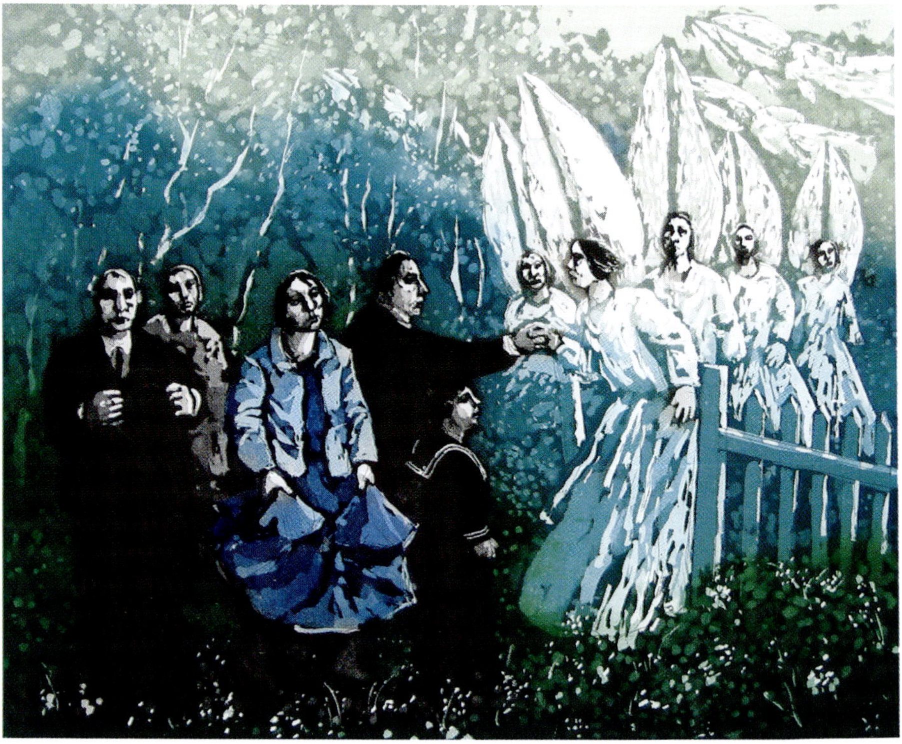

Karolina Larusdottir, *The Good Gathering*. Hard ground and aquatint, 40 x 50 cm (16 x 20 in.). Aquatint is applied to a plate with a hard ground drawing and all of the tonal work is carried out using stop-out varnish between the various bitings. It has been inked up on one plate *a la poupée*. Karolina was assisted in the plate work by Linda Richardson, who also did the colour proofing and printing.

box creates a cloud of dust inside. For a coarse, grainy aquatint, place the plate in the box immediately after stirring up the dust. For a finer aquatint you should wait 30 seconds after agitating the box before placing the plate inside as the heavier particles of rosin will have settled to the bottom of the box by then. If you want a very fine aquatint then wait for at least a minute after agitating the box before placing the plate inside.

When you remove the plate from the box, an even layer of aquatint rosin will then have settled onto your plate. Ideally, 50% of the plate should be covered with dust particles. Too much rosin will actually form a ground, which stops the plate from etching at all. Too little rosin will have the aquatint etching too quickly and then burning off before you can achieve a full range of tones. It is difficult to impart how to know when there is sufficient rosin on the plate beyond just saying that it is a matter of trial and error and experience. However, I have found that if, under reasonable studio lighting, the plate looks opaquely covered with dust when you look down on it from above then it probably has too much rosin. It should look to be opaquely covered only when

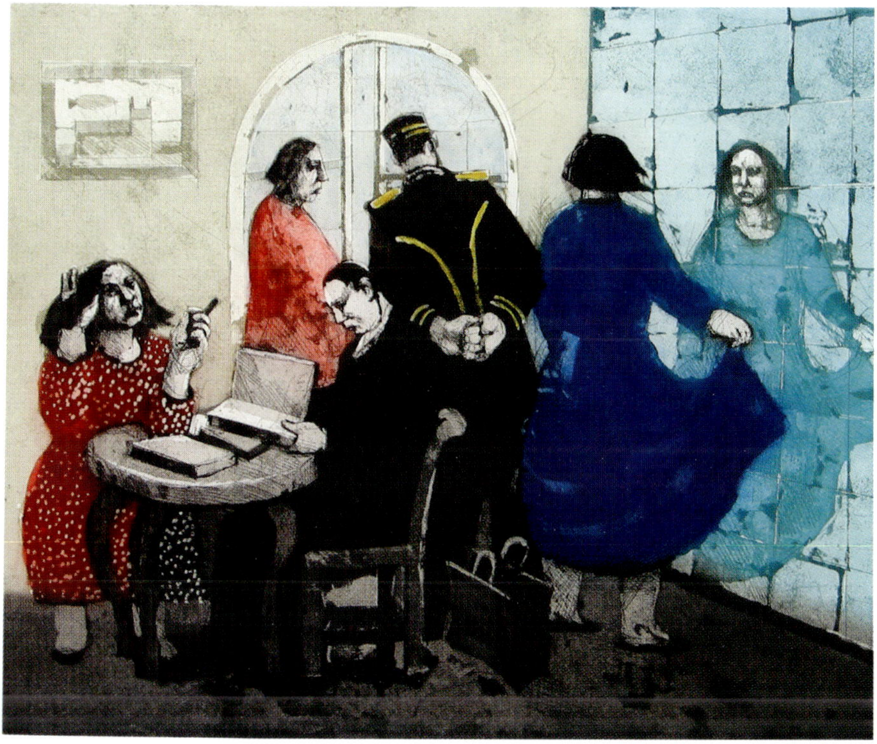

Karolina Larusdottir, *Mirror, Mirror*. Hard ground and aquatint, 40 × 50 cm (16 × 20 in.). Inked up on one plate *a la poupée*. Plate work and printing by Linda Richardson

viewed across the surface of the plate at eye level. If it does not appear opaque from that angle then you probably have too little rosin on. You can check the plate and if it needs more coverage replace it inside the box any number of times at this stage before the aquatint is fused. If you realise that there is too much rosin on the plate you must wipe the plate clean with a dry paper towel, degrease it and begin again.

When you are satisfied that you have a good coverage of rosin, carefully remove the plate from the hardboard place it onto a wire rack and heat it from below with a gas burner. Watch the plate across its surface at eye level if possible and once the aquatint rosin begins to turn transparent start slowly moving the flame across the bottom of the plate. It is important that you keep the flame in motion as overheating the rosin stops it from etching properly. Only when the rosin is uniformly transparent will it be fused onto the surface of the plate. At this point you can remove your gas mask. The added benefit of wearing the mask during the heating of the plate is that it is easy to blow the dust off the plate just by breathing.

If the plate were immediately immersed in the acid it would etch a solid, consistent tone over the entire surface. The tone is entirely time-dependent, so the longer the plate is in the acid the darker the tone will be. Through repetition of selective stopping out and re-biting a range of tones is achieved. Areas that you wish to remain white should be stopped out (see p.59) before the plate goes into the acid for the first time. If the plate is then placed in the acid for a short time (perhaps 30 seconds or one minute), the entire plate not previously stopped out would print a very light grey. The plate should be thoroughly rinsed in water, front and back, and then dried with a hair dryer or fan. Any areas then stopped out would remain light grey even after successive bitings. This progressive process of stopping out and re-biting should continue until the plate is finished. Once areas of the plate are etched to black, any successive immersions will start to burn the aquatint off the plate. This can be used to good effect but the process is very difficult to predict or control.

Stopping out

Anything that protects the plate from the acid will work as a stop out. Stop out varnish applied with a brush can produce very hard-edged areas of tone or painterly brushstrokes depending upon your technique. You can also apply the stop out with rags, paper towels or cotton balls to achieve different effects. Oil-based drawing mediums such as oil pastels and litho crayons also work well. Oil pastels and soft litho crayons will give very loose, gestural marks while hard litho crayons can create highlights that resemble burnishing. The weight of application, as well as the density of the medium, alters the level of stopping out enormously. Care should be taken not to touch the plate during this process, as grease from your fingers will impede the biting.

Hand shaken aquatint

If you do not have an aquatint box, or if you wish to create a less predictable surface, you can use a shaken aquatint. For this method you need a clean, dry jam jar partially full of aquatint rosin. Stretch a piece of porous fabric (such as nylon stockings or layers of scrim or muslin) over the top of the jar and secure it with an elastic band. Hold the jar on its side and gently shake it over the plate until it is covered with an even layer of rosin. The rosin should then be fused as described for the aquatint box method. Try experimenting, as the type of fabric used will have an effect on the type of coverage you achieve and the look of the aquatint. I have also heard of printmakers successfully using cake dusters (icing sugar shakers) for this task.

Car spray aquatint

Another method for those without an aquatint box is car-spray aquatint. This method gives the visual appearance of that achieved with a coarse aquatint box. Lean the plate against a vertical surface and hold the spray can completely upright about 30-50 cm (12-20 in.) away. Move your hand in a straight line across the plate; start spraying before you reach the edge of the plate and finish after you leave the plate to ensure even coverage. Do this in consecutive, slightly

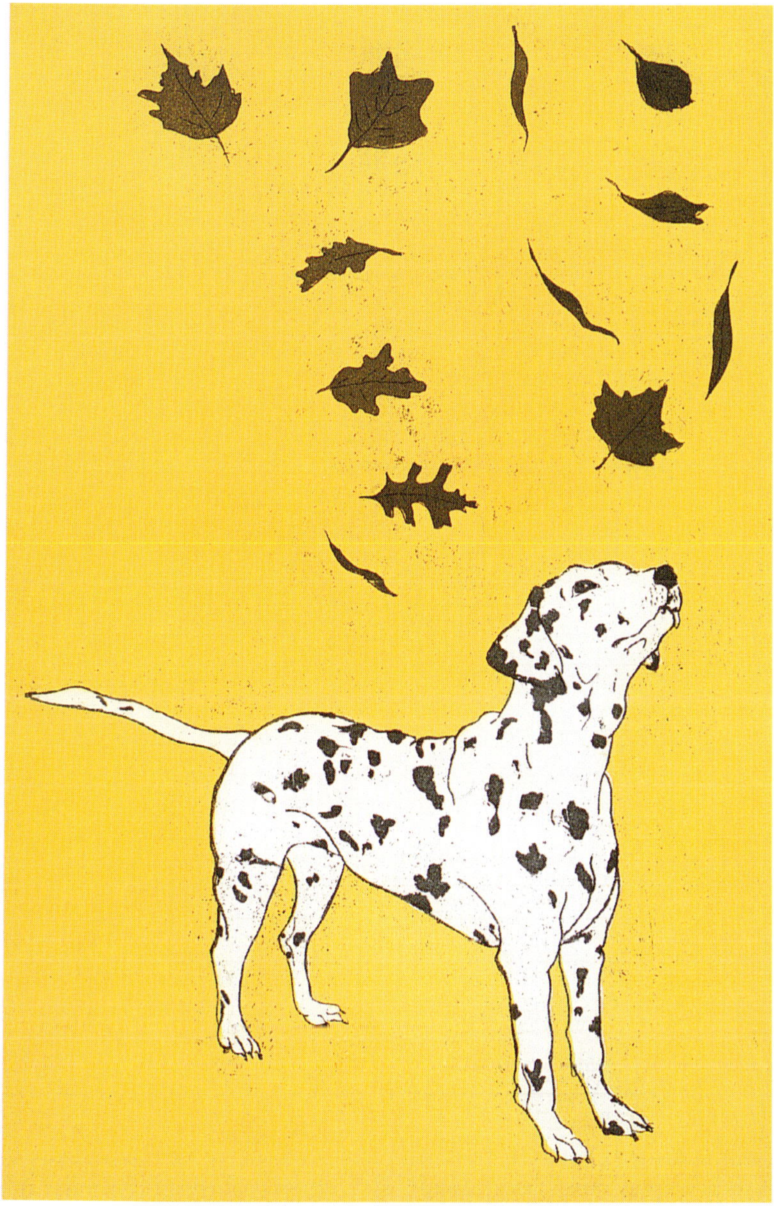

Sonia Rollo – *How the Dalmatian got her spots, oh best beloved.* Hard ground and aquatint, 37 x 25 cm (14½ x 10 in.). This is a two-plate etching, one black carrying all of the drawing and one yellow for the background.

overlapping rows until the plate is covered to the same extent as with the powdered rosin – ideally 50%. Once you have finished etching the plate, clean any stopping-out grounds with white spirit and then clean the aquatint rosin with methylated spirits prior to printing.

Notes on metals and tools

A quick point to note here is that all of the techniques cited above are for copper or zinc, as aquatint rosin is not needed if you plan to etch on steel. An open bite on steel will etch as if aquatinted, which makes it the perfect metal of choice for those wishing to achieve a fine aquatint without an aquatint box. As it starts off with a strong plate tone, it is very difficult to achieve areas of white.

A plate that has been aquatinted can be worked into using any number of tools, the most common of which are scrapers and burnishers. A scraper generally has a vicious-looking triangular shaft with three sharp edges and a sharpened point. As its name implies, it is used to scrape off areas of etched aquatint tone but can also remove lines or any other intaglio impressions. Burnishers come in a variety of shapes but the most common have a curved shaft that tapers to a point. These are used to polish areas of aquatint so that they will hold less ink, in order to lighten areas of tone or to create highlights.

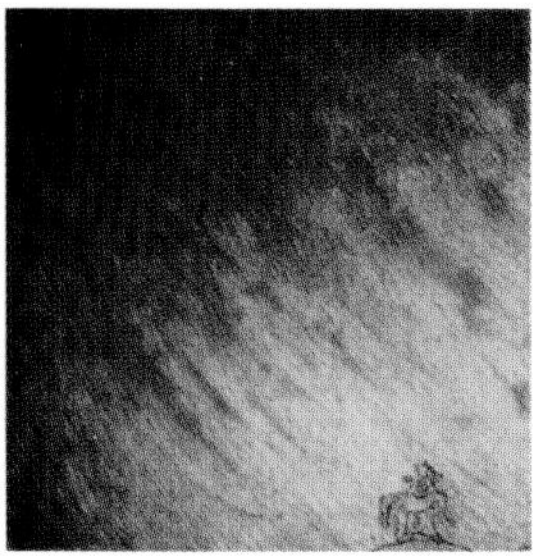

■ SPIT-BITE

You will need:

- Metal plate with aquatint applied (only for copper or zinc; no aquatint required for steel)
- Nitric acid or ferric chloride (tray and fume cupboard)
- Paint brush
- Surface tension breaker (water with washing-up liquid).

Spit-bite is a technique that allows you to paint acid directly onto the plate. It derived its name from the practice of printmakers spitting onto the plate as they worked so that the acid would stay where it was painted. This is no longer deemed to be a desirable practice, primarily because you should always wear a gas mask when working with nitric acid and this is not conducive to spitting! When used well, spit-bite can create the same full range of subtle and dramatic effects available to the watercolour painter.

The method

You will need a plate covered with aquatint rosin. Any of the aquatint techniques listed above will work, but the best results will be achieved using a fine aquatint box application. Start by stopping out any areas that you do not want to etch, as it is difficult to completely control the acid. If you plan to work on copper then you can paint directly onto the aquatint with ferric chloride. I usually have one undiluted pot and one mixed with water (with an approximate ratio of 1:1). When using nitric acid, I usually mix up two or three different strength acids of perhaps 12:1, 7:1 and 4:1, remembering always to add the acid to the water, rather than the other way around. If you are working

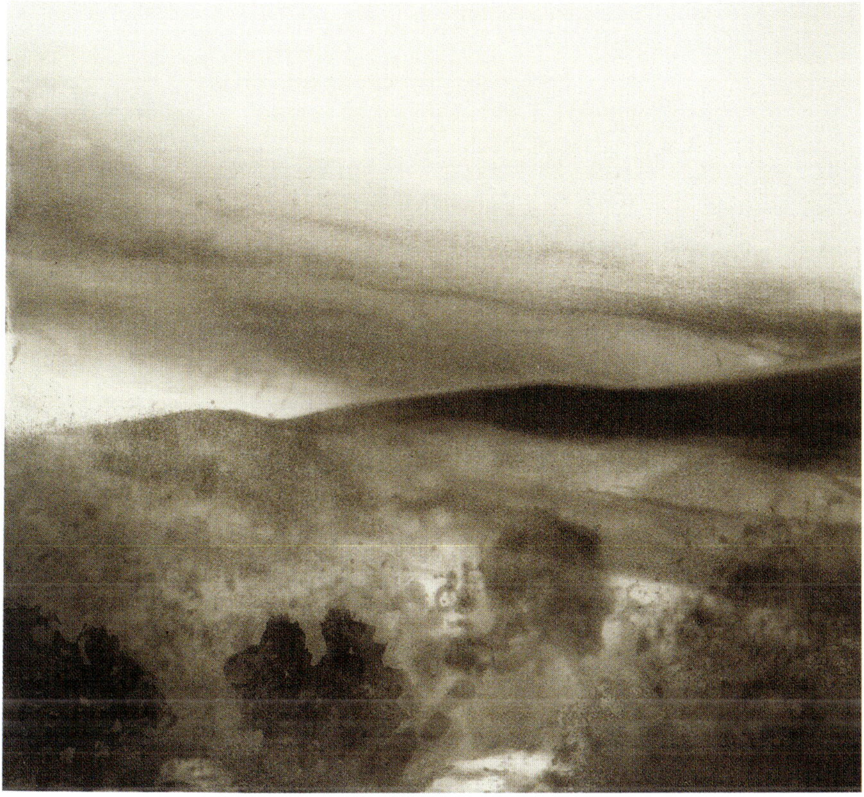

Norman Ackroyd – *Wenlock Edge*. Spit bite aquatint. 16 x 21.5 cm (6⅓ x 8½ in.). This spit bite has been done in stages so that the aquatint is layered.

on zinc, mix slightly weaker solutions. I start painting with the weaker acid and build up to the stronger acid as the image develops. The acid will bubble and turn slightly blue as it etches and the plate will darken, allowing you to see the image more clearly. When the acid stops bubbling it is no longer biting so at this point you should add more. Be careful not to over-etch it, as you will burn off the aquatint.

Painting directly onto a dry plate will give hard edges to your tones, but if you want to paint large areas that bleed into each other (e.g., skies or water) you will need to paint onto a wet plate in the same manner as a watercolour artist would paint onto wet paper. Dip the plate into a tray containing water and a few drops of washing-up liquid. Remove it and allow the excess water to drain off until the plate is covered with an even layer of water and then lay it on a flat, level surface. Acid painted onto this surface will quickly dissipate and spread. Experiment with tipping the plate to move the acid; this gives some interesting results. In addition to brushes, acid can be applied using paper towels or rags, cotton balls or it can even be flicked off the bristles of a toothbrush.

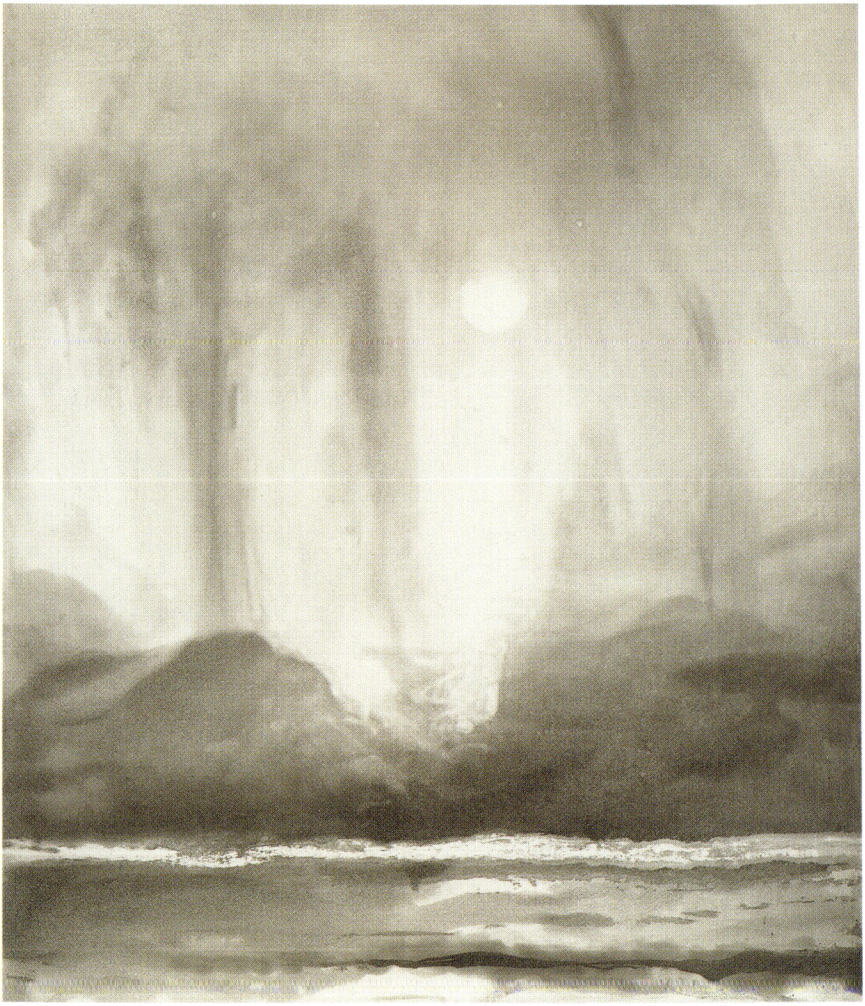

Norman Ackroyd – *Puffin Island – Kerry*. 28 x 25 cm (11 x 10 in.). Spit bite aquatint. This started *in situ* as a spit bite but was then articulated with reference to watercolour studies back in the studio. The dramatic weather conditions meant that the initial spit biting had to be done from land rather than from a boat.

The above techniques apply to nitric acid, as ferric chloride will adhere to the plate and stay where it is painted in a very different manner. Furthermore, the use of surface tension breaker is not necessary when you are using ferric chloride. If you merely keep the plate wet and keep applying fresh water as needed you can paint with the ferric chloride as if with watercolour. For this to work at its best it is crucial to work on a warm plate. Warm the plate using either a hotplate or hairdryer, and use warm water to wet the plate. The importance of having a very well degreased plate cannot be overemphasised.

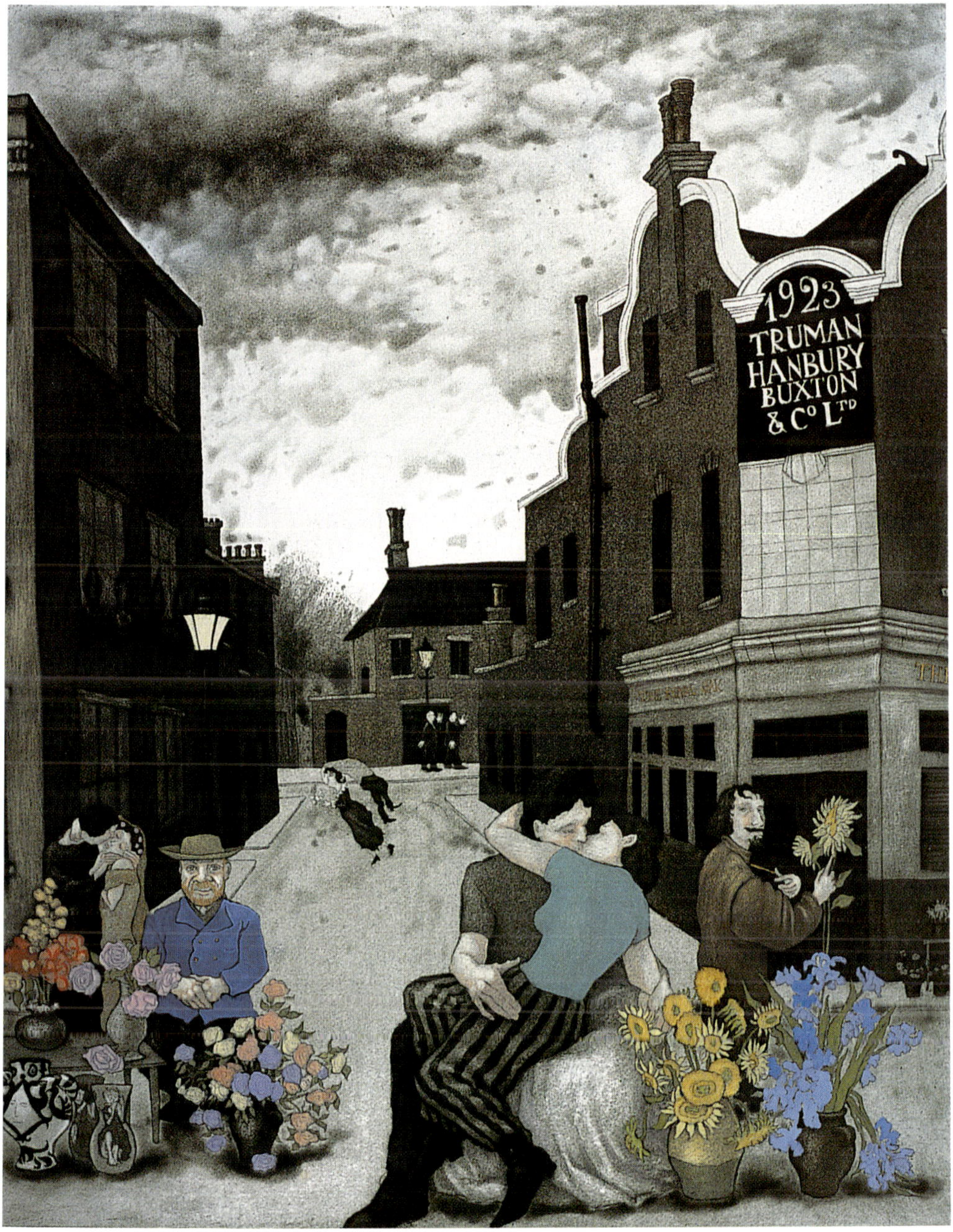

Mychael Barratt – *Life Imitating Art III*. Soft ground, aquatint and spit bite, 50 × 40 cm (20 × 15¾ in.). The tonal work on the ground and sky was done with a nitric spit bite with no surface tension breaker.

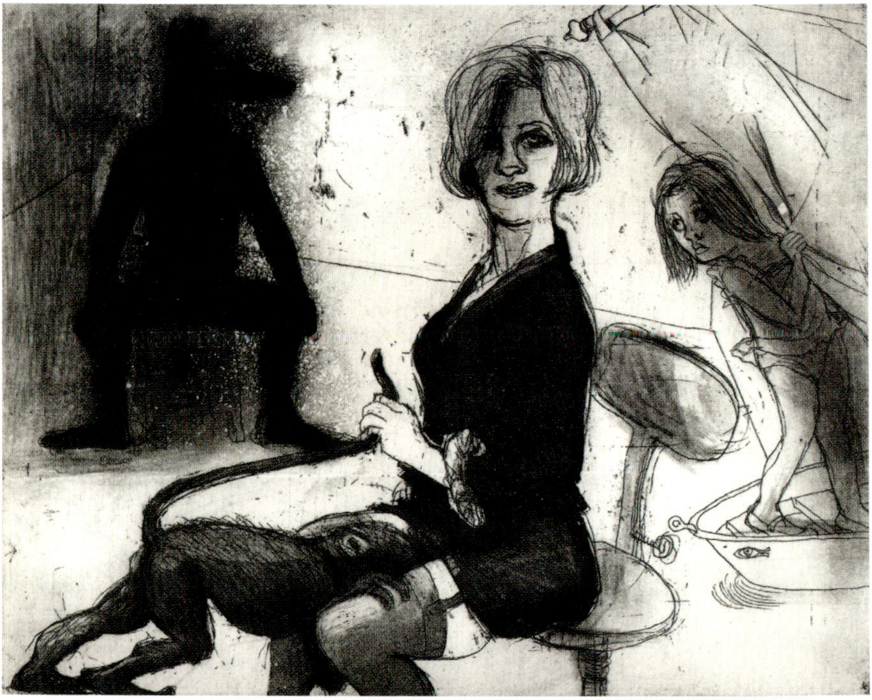

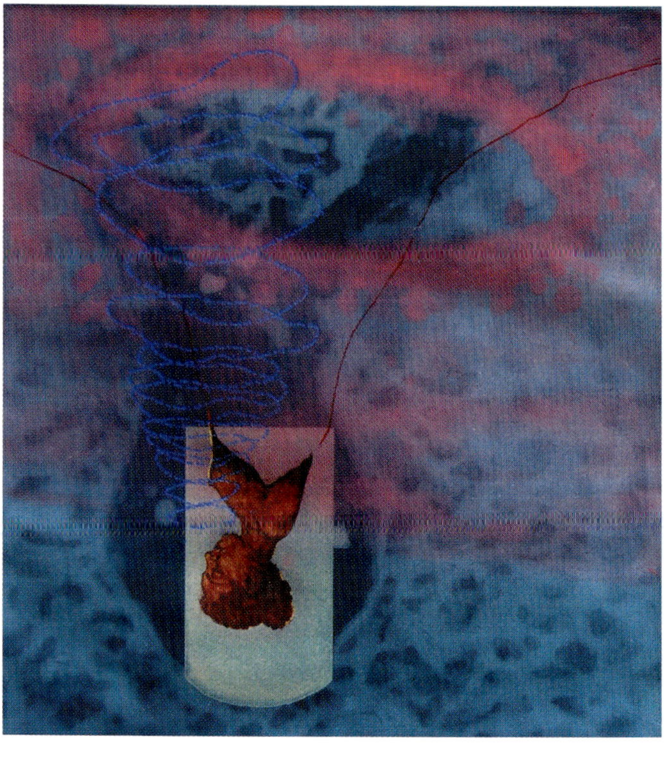

ABOVE Marcelle Hanselaar – *Petite Mort 4*. Hard ground, aquatint and spit bite, 20 x 25 cm (8 x 10 in.). Hand shaken aquatint has been used to great effect around the background silhouette.

LEFT Freya Payne – *Mute*. Hard ground, aquatint and spit bite, 23.5 x 22 cm ($9\frac{1}{4}$ x $8\frac{3}{4}$ in.). This print has been through the press five times but was allowed to dry between printings. A spit bite has been inked up in white and then rolled over with blue. A pink spit bite plate has been added afterwards. The head is brown ink on a cut out yellow *chine collé*.

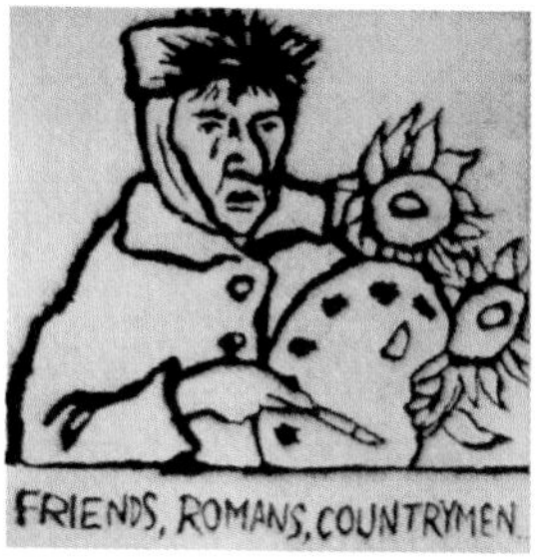

■ SUGAR LIFT

Sugar lift is a technique that allows you to use brushes or a pen nibs as drawing tools. By directly applying the sugar lift solution to the plate you can perfectly replicate hard-edged painterly brushstrokes or pen and ink lines that are far more sensitive and varied than lines achievable with hard ground. Printmaking materials suppliers sell a sugar lift solution, or you can use 'Camp' coffee directly out of the bottle. To mix your own home-made saturated sugar solution take an empty jam jar and make marks on the outside of the bottle that are 2.5 cm and 5 cm (1 in. and 2 in.) from the bottom. Fill the jar to the 2.5 cm (1 in.) mark with household granulated sugar and then top up to the 5 cm (2 in.) mark with water. Once the sugar has dissolved, mix in approximately half of a 60 ml (2 oz) tube of black designers' gouache or India ink.

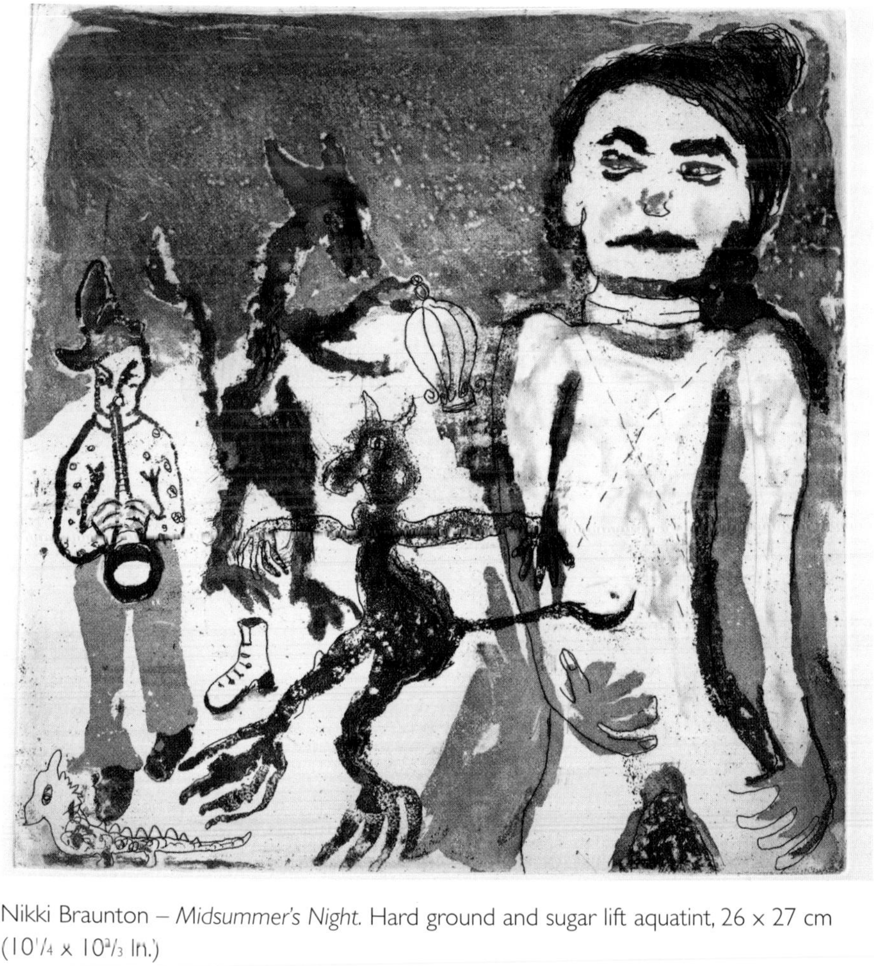

Nikki Braunton – *Midsummer's Night.* Hard ground and sugar lift aquatint, 26 x 27 cm ($10\frac{1}{4}$ x $10\frac{2}{3}$ in.)

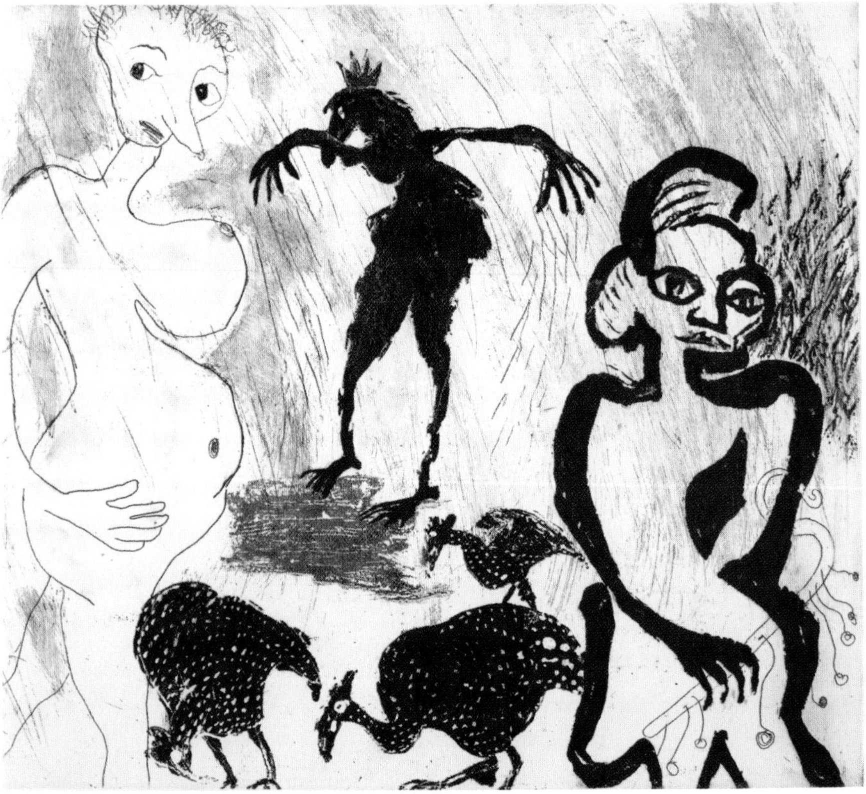

Nikki Braunton – *The Kraal of Modjadi.* Hard ground and sugar lift aquatint, 25 x 27 cm (10¼ x 10⅔ in.)

You will need:

- Filed, backed and degreased plate (copper, zinc or steel)
- Sugar lift solution
- Acid-resistant ground (dark straw hat varnish and methylated spirits)
- Paint brush or pen (to apply the sugar lift solution)
- Lithographic crayon (optional)
- All ingredients listed for 'Aquatint' (see p.55).

The method

You paint or draw with the sugar lift solution directly onto the plate. However, it is absolutely essential that the plate be degreased, as the marks will not adhere to the plate otherwise. To avoid dragging your hand through the marks, try using a frame as described in the Soft Ground Etching section (p.52-3). When the drawing is complete, allow it to dry. It will not dry hard but will remain tacky to the touch. In a clean, airtight jam jar make up an acid-resistant ground that is a 1:1 mixture of dark straw hat varnish and methylated spirits. Pour this mixture onto the plate and gently move the plate until it is covered with a thin layer of the ground. Drain the excess back into the jar and replace the lid. Allow the ground to completely dry before immersing the plate in a tray of tepid water for 20 minutes. The sugar lift solution will then magically lift off revealing areas of the plate which will print dark when aquatinted, faithfully reproducing the original marks. If the sugar lift has not completely lifted, add some hot water and gently rub the drawn areas with cotton wool. When the entire area previously covered by sugar lift is exposed, dry the plate completely making sure not to touch the areas of open plate. If you do, then you will need to degrease the plate again before you apply an aquatint and etch the plate as described above. This technique will also work on plates that are already holding an aquatint, although you will not be able to use a pen nib as more care must be taken to avoid damaging the surface of the aquatint. Similar effects can be achieved by painting oil of spike lavender onto a hard ground. This is described in the 'Hard Ground' section covering 'Drawing into hard ground' on p.48.

Another variation that works well is using a litho crayon instead of the liquid sugar lift. You can draw directly onto the aquatinted plate with the litho crayon and then cover it with the straw-hat varnish and methylated spirit mixture as above. Remove the litho crayon with white spirit or paraffin that is allowed to sit on the plate for about five minutes. Gently scrub the lines with a cotton ball to remove all traces of the litho crayon and degrease the plate before placing it in acid. This gives a mark reminiscent of a soft ground etching.

Reworking plates

One of the most wonderful elements of intaglio printmaking is its completely fluid nature. Although most printmakers work in a very linear manner, gradually building up lines and tones as they progress, the metal plates are extremely thick and resillient, and allow for quite extensive alteration. These alterations can be made subtly with a burnisher, a little more thoroughly with a scraper or radically with a power sander. It is possible to completely remove an etched line or area from your plate and, providing it is not pitted or bordered by a harsh edge, even huge dips in the level of the plate will not be apparent in the finished print. Less comprehensive reworking will leave behind traces of previous states, which can be used to great effect.

I have used a number of proofs of different states of an etching *Because I do not think* by Freya Payne to illustrate this point. The first proof (1) is a hard-ground drawing on which some ideas for the next stage of plate-working have been painted in using an ink wash. If you tape down your early proofs using gummed tape then you can work on them in this manner soon after pulling the print.

In the next state (2), some of the ideas that were painted onto the previous proof have been etched onto the plate and the original hard ground drawing has been strengthened with further hard ground etching, a fine roulette wheel and a fine box aquatint. Freya has then once again used an ink wash to add some lettering onto the scroll at the bottom and to darken some of the tonal areas in the background (3).

By the next state (4) a further aquatint has been applied and the background has become so dark that some of the elements from previous states are just barely visible while others have become completely obscured.

Freya then decided that the print was too dark and had taken a direction that she was no longer happy with, so she decided to radically rework the plate (5). Using a combination of power sander and scraper she completely obliterated the background of the image leaving only mere traces and hints of the previous states. She then began to work back into the plate using a combination of hard ground etching and drypoint. The proof taken at that point was again reworked with a pencil and some pale grey paint.

For the final state of the print (6) she added some hard ground drawing and an aquatint with some spit-biting. A little bit of burnishing completed the plate work. The finished piece varies significantly from her original concept but the stages of plate development have all added to the print.

Nothing that happens to a metal plate cannot be reversed or altered at a later stage. Engraving lines are incised into the plate, so will obviously require more effort to remove, but even a very coarse aquatint can be successfully scraped back. In some cases you may even end up with a piece where the surface is far more interesting than it would have been otherwise; it is like discovering a playwright's original manuscript with the revisions intact.

OPPOSITE **1** Freya Payne – *Because I do not think;* 1st state. Hard ground and ink
2 Freya Payne – *Because I do not think;* 2nd state. Hard ground, aquatint, drypoint and mixed media
3 Freya Payne – *Because I do not think;* 3rd state. Hard ground, aquatint, drypoint and mixed media
4 Freya Payne – *Because I do not think;* 4th state. Hard ground, aquatint, sugar lift and drypoint
5 Freya Payne – *Because I do not think;* 5th state, Hard ground, aquatint, sugar lift, drypoint and mixed media
6 Freya Payne – *Because I do not think;* 6th state. Hard ground, aquatint, sugar lift, spit bite and drypoint

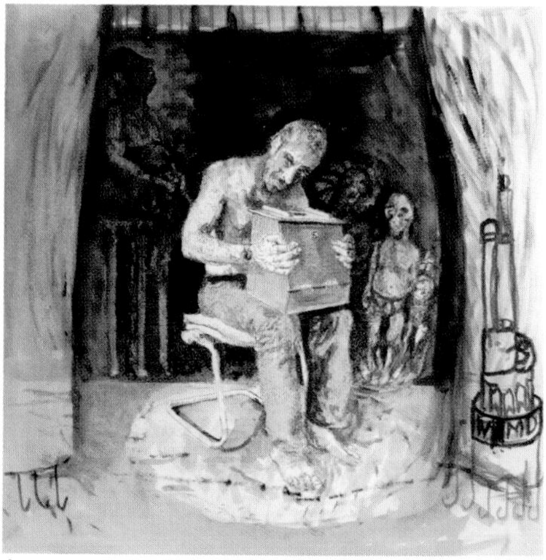
1

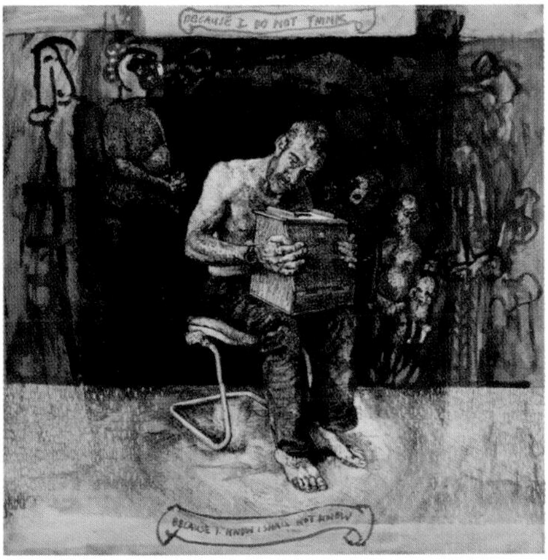
2

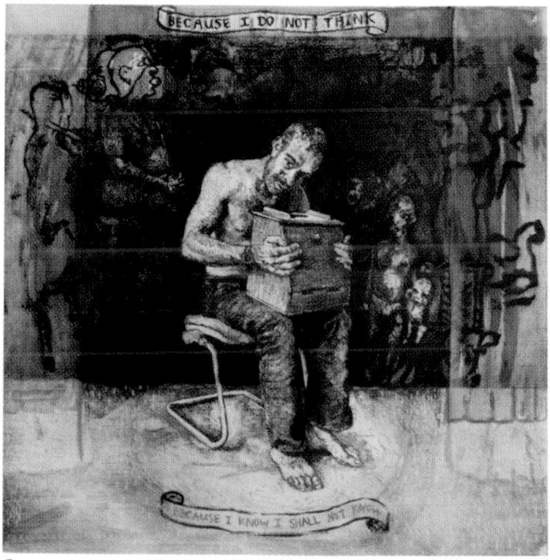

3

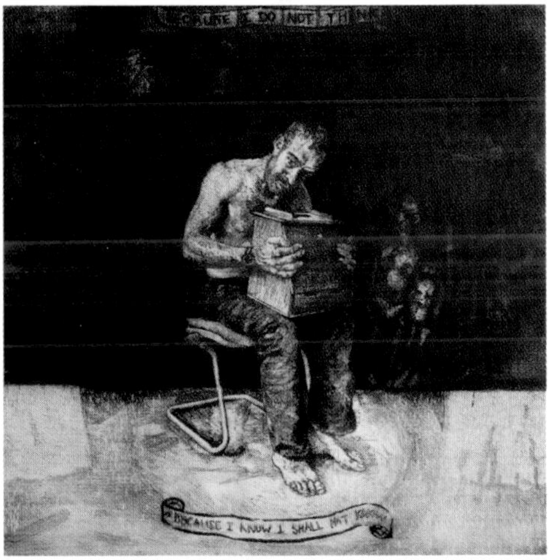
4

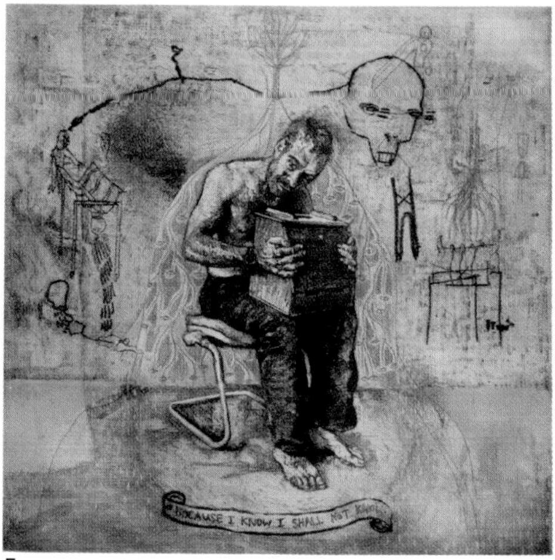
5

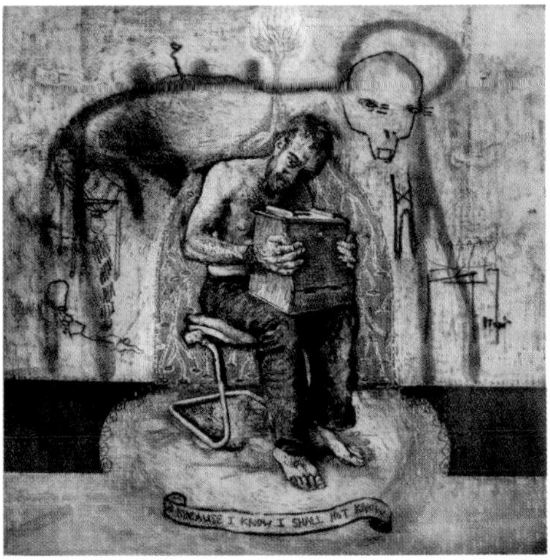
6

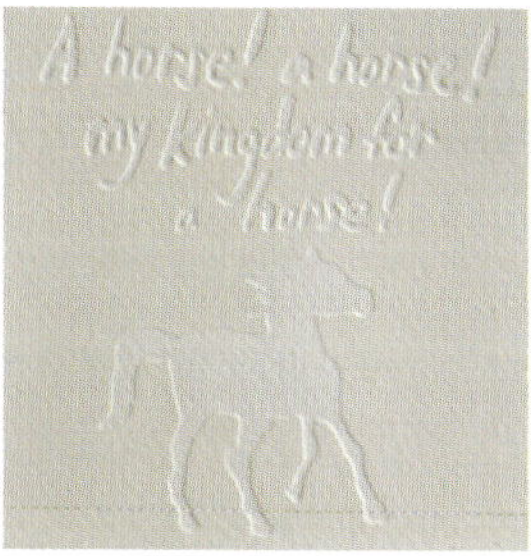

■ DEEP-BITE ETCHING AND EMBOSSING

One of the greatest features of etching is afforded by the three dimensional nature of the plate, which is never more apparent than in deep open-bite etching. Open bite is the result of extremely lengthy immersion in strong acid. This technique was shown to me by Brenda Hartill, whose work I have featured on these pages.

You will need:

- Filed, backed and degreased plate (copper, steel or preferably zinc)
- Brush, pen, and any other tools for applying grounds
- Roller (optional if printing a relief print)
- Sugar lift (optional)
- Stop out varnish or liquid hard ground
- Oil of spike lavender (optional)
- Strong nitric acid (70% acid mixed 1:4 with water)
- Brasso.

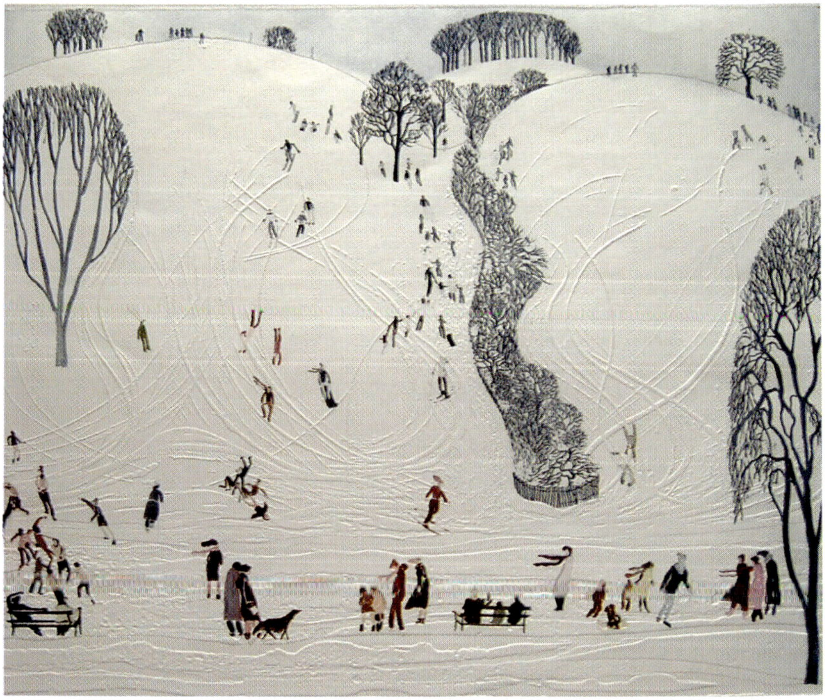

Brenda Hartill – *The Day it Snowed.* Aquatint and blind embossing, 40 x 50 cm (15¾ x 19⅔ in.). When printing a two-plate etching where one of the plates features blind embossing, it is essential that the embossed plate be printed second.

RIGHT Brenda Hartill – *El Tajo de Ronda III*. Hard ground, aquatint and deep bite etching, 56 x 46 cm (22 x 18 in.). This plate has been inked up *a la poupée* in warm browns but then separate balls of scrim impregnated with yellow, red and blue have been subtly wiped over the surface. The ink is caught on the surface of the deeply etched plate.

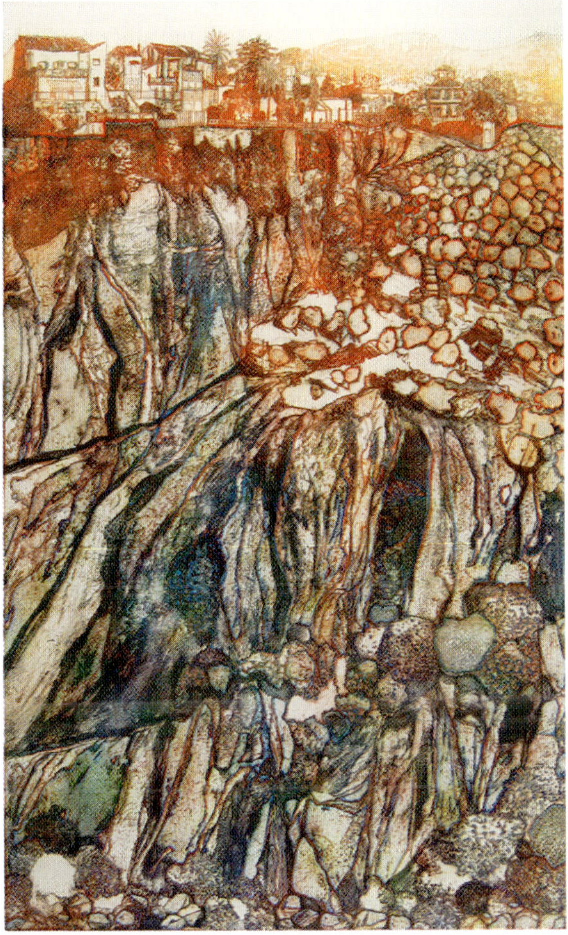

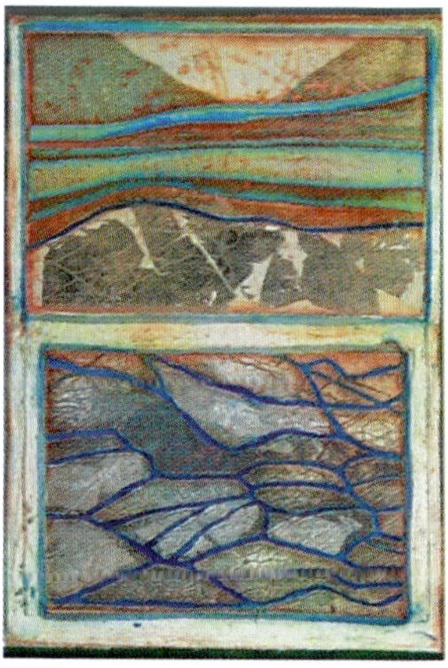

LEFT Brenda Hartill – *Silver Life Elements VII*. Aquatint, deep bite etching, silver leak *chin collé* and carborundum, 38 x 27 cm (15 x 10⅔ in.). Deep bite etching where the intaglio has been inked up using a warm brown and then the surface has been gently wiped with scrim impregnated with yellow and blue.

The method

The best metal to use is high quality backed zinc or jet plate in either 16 or 18 gauge. Cheap roofing zinc will also work, but it will leave the acid mucky. Copper will etch in a clean, refined way while a steel open bite will print with a dark tone. For marks that you want to print positive, you can use sugarlift or oil of spike lavender. Apply the sugarlift marks and then cover the entire plate with either a thin coating of liquid hard ground or a mixture that is one part dark straw-hat varnish and one part methylated spirits. Sponge off the sugarlift with warm water to expose the plate. For finer, more detailed marks, paint oil

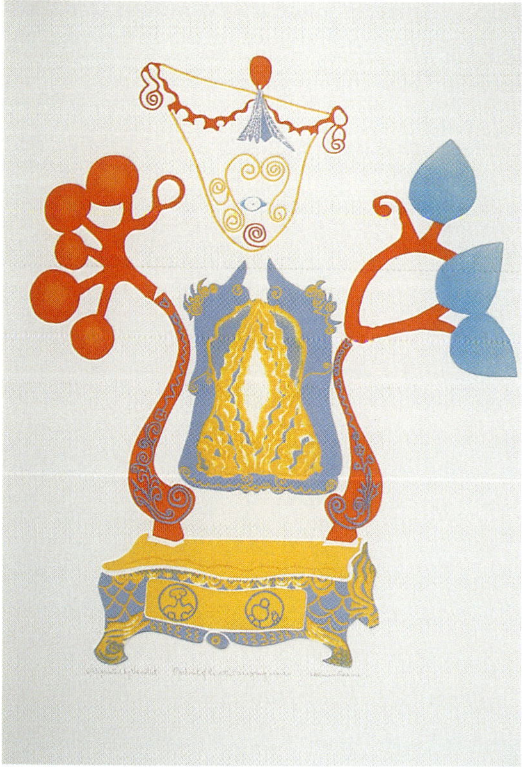

LEFT Carmen Gracia – *Portrait of the artist as a young woman*. Deep bite etching and relief etching. Carmen has assembled a number of intricately cut plates and on each of these she has deeply etched the lines and rolled over vividly contrasting colours.

BELOW Peter Ford – *The Wilderness*, 20 × 30 cm (8 × 12 in.). Deep bite etching where the intaglio has been inked up in one colour and a second colour has been rolled over the surface.

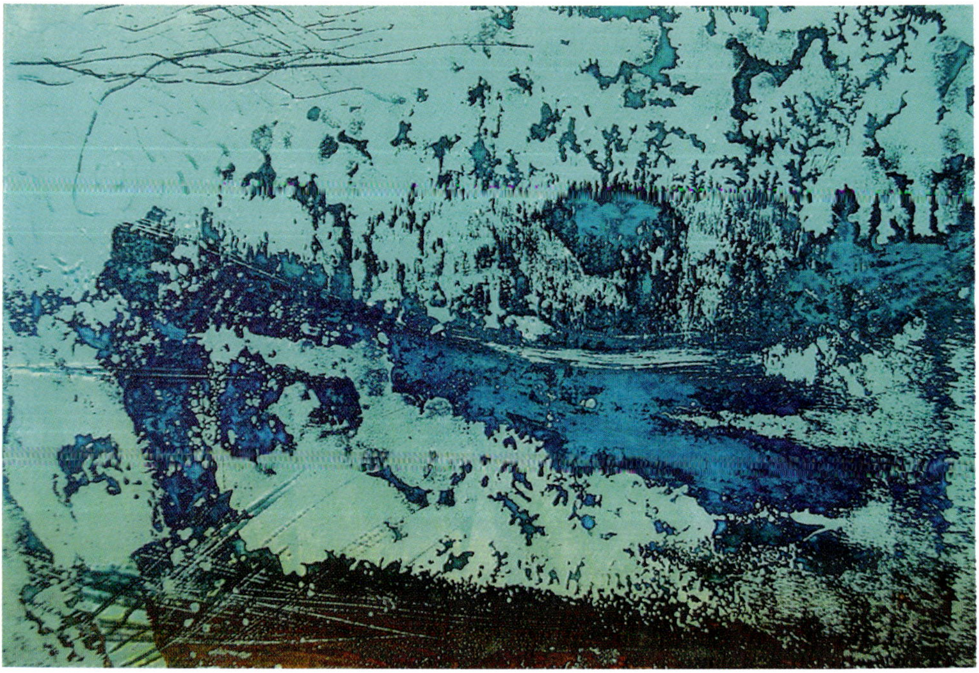

of spike lavender onto a plate covered with hard ground and then wipe away firmly with a soft cloth. Negative marks can be made using liquid hard ground or stop-out varnish. The exposed areas of plate should be thoroughly degreased. If it is important that there is no foul-biting on the areas of plate that you do not want to etch, then it is advisable to double protect them with two layers of varnish using preferably a meths-based varnish (such as straw hat) for the first layer and a spirit-based stop out for the second layer.

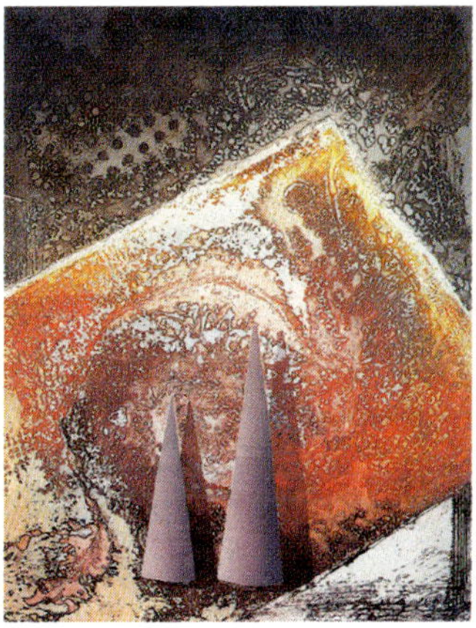

Peter Ford – *Zenith*. Deep bite etching, 48 x 38 cm (19 x 15 in.). The different levels of deep bite etching are clearly visible in this print.

Once the plate is ready, gently lower it into the acid. A mixture of one part 70% nitric acid, one part used acid and four parts water will give a strong mix that will produce speedy and dramatic results. This acid will exhaust itself very quickly. A weaker mix of one part acid to six parts water will produce slower and more controlled bites. Watch the plate and remove bubbles carefully with a goose feather. Rinse and inspect the plate frequently to check for foul-biting; if this is occurring then dry the plate and re-varnish.

The longer the plate is left in the acid, the more dramatic the results will be. To achieve interesting textures, stop out the plate progressively using a variety of techniques so that the plate ends up with several different levels. When the deep biting is complete, it is always best to polish the areas of open bite with metal polish such as Brasso as there is always a tone or false aquatint that will fade after the first few prints.

Printing an embossed plate

Once you have a finished plate there are a number of ways that you can print it. Blind embossing is printed without colour on an etching press. This brings out textures that are caught by the light and the results can be subtle or very dramatic. It is most effective when heavyweight textured paper is used.

Embossed plates can also be inked using a roller to create a relief print. It can be inked like a traditional intaglio and then rolled using inks of different viscosity so that they reach different levels of the plate. (For more information about ink viscosity see Steve Hoskins' book *Inks*, A & C Black, 2004.) You can also ink the plate traditionally and then, using separate scrim pads saturated with primary-coloured inks, you can gently tint the different levels of the plate. Brenda Hartill uses this technique to great effect, but also uses combinations of all of the other techniques above.

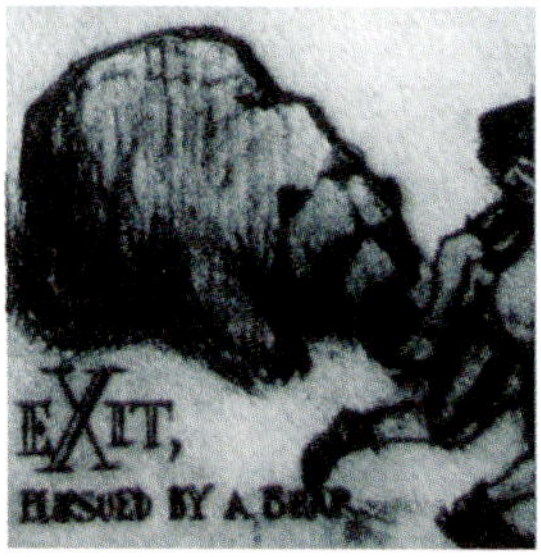

■ PHOTOCOPY TRANSFER TECHNIQUE

There are a number of reasons why one may wish to directly transfer an image onto a plate. It is essential if you wish to create multiple plate etchings where the registration is crucial. Traditionally, a first plate would be created, printed and then transferred by offsetting the image onto the additional plates. I have touched upon this technique in the section on Counterproofing (p.76). Susie Perring uses a clever photocopy transfer technique to achieve this, which also allows her to transfer a drawing that has not yet been etched onto another plate.

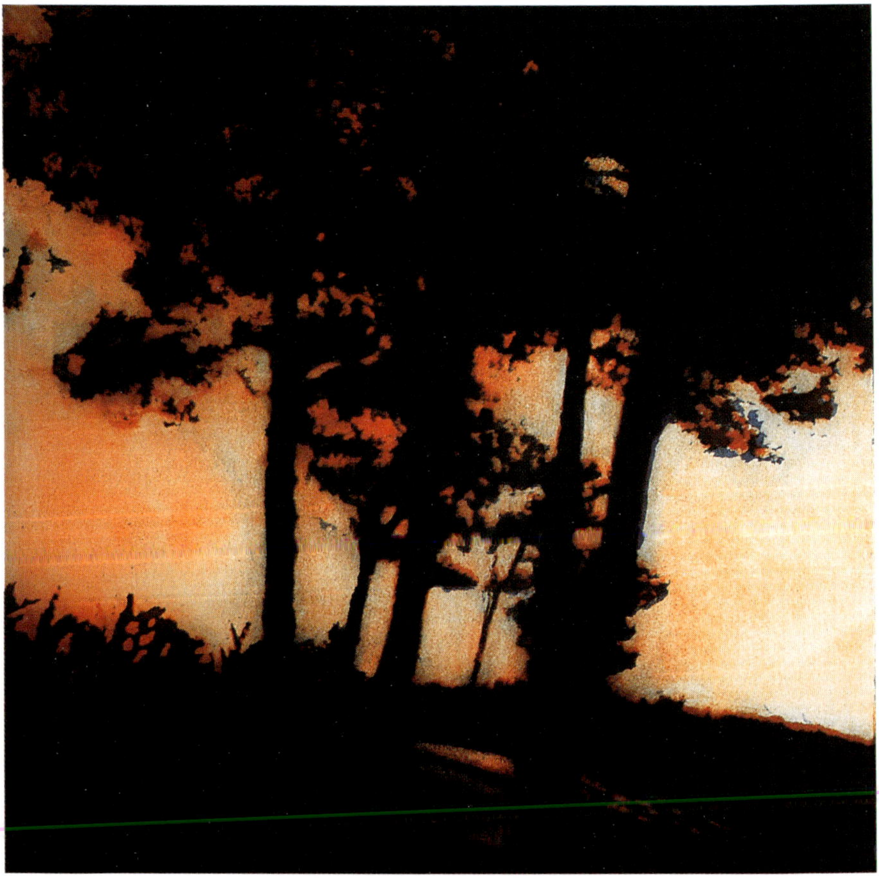

Suzie Perring – *Pacific Pines*. Aquatint using photocopy transfer technique, 49 x 49 cm (19¼ x 19¼ in.). This is a two-plate etching where identical images have been transferred. The two plates are then inked up in complementary colours, first with an orange lithographic ink and then phthalo blue intaglio ink. The blue plate is cleaned in some key areas to let the orange and the white of the paper show through.

You will need:

- Filed, backed and degreased metal plate with aquatint applied (see p.55)
- Ferrario fixative spray
- Household cream cleanser (for degreasing)
- Photocopy
- Nitric acid or ferric chloride (tray and fume cupboard)
- Fume mask, gloves and goggles.

The method

The drawing you begin with should ideally be much smaller than the plate you wish to etch. This is because the drawing will be photocopied and the technique works at its best when the image is blown up to make it more graphic. Enlarge the image, using a photocopier, to the point where the image area is slightly larger than your plate. Then apply a fine aquatint, preferably using an aquatint box, onto a degreased copper or zinc plate. Etch the plate for approximately ten minutes in room temperature nitric acid to achieve a mid-grey tonal aquatint. Wash the rosin off using methylated spirit and degrease the plate using a household cream cleanser. It is important not to use whiting and ammonia at this point, as some traces of the whiting will remain in the aquatint which would inhibit the next stage of the technique.

Place the plate onto the bed of the etching press and set the pressure for a conventional etching. Then take your photocopy and a can of Ferrario fixative spray (this brand is not transposable, as it is the only product that works perfectly for this application). Spray the photocopy front and back with the fixative, so that it is shiny but not too wet. Place the photocopy face down onto the plate and

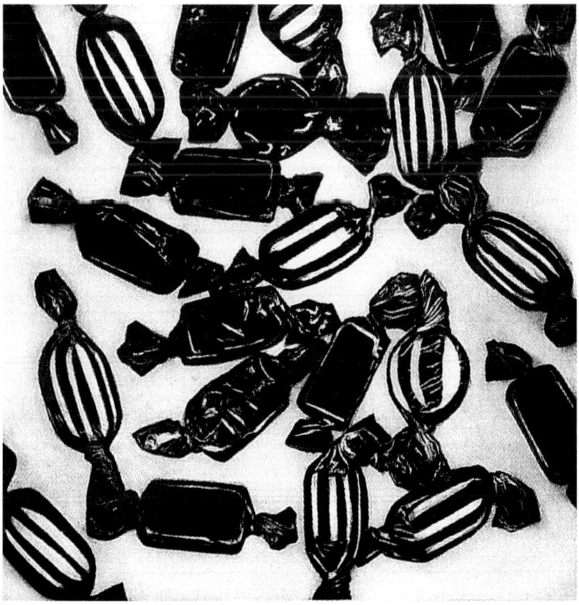

Suzie Perring – *Sweet Dreams.* Aquatint using photocopy transfer technique, 38.5 x 38.5 cm (15 1/6 x 15 1/6 in.). The original image was made from positioning sweets on the bed of the photocopier. The photocopy was then enhanced, redrawn and photocopied again before transferring it onto the plate.

protect it with a piece of paper large enough to cover the entire drawing, or the photocopy ink will bleed through and mark the blankets. When you have run the plate through the press the drawing will have been offset onto the aquatint.

Return the plate to the acid. The acid will open bite the areas of aquatint not protected by the drawing and they will be largely burned off. The protection afforded by the offset photocopied lines and tonal areas is porous and allows the drawing to continue to etch, but at a very slow rate. Remove bubbles from the open bite areas frequently using a feather or a firm hogshair paint brush. Begin to check after approximately 20 minutes to see if the uncovered areas have been burned off and to make sure that the drawing remains intact. Keep etching until the image areas have a raised pronounced edge. When you have finished etching, the plate is ready to be cleaned and printed. The lines and tonal areas will print very dark and they will have a ragged, soft-edged quality that is difficult to achieve with any other process. In addition, the areas where the aquatint has burned off will have a soft, irregular plate tone. In the case of multiple plate etchings, the drawing to be photocopied can be reworked for additional plates, making overcoming the technical hitches of registration considerably more straightforward.

Another approach to the same technique is to start with a photocopy on which the blacks and whites have been reversed. Spray the photocopy with the Ferrario fixative, then transfer it onto a clean degreased plate using the etching press as above. The areas that appear black but will eventually print white should then be painted out with varnish, preferably stop-out varnish and not straw hat. Once the varnish is dry the plate should have a box aquatint applied and should then be placed into the acid for between 50 minutes and one hour. This variation on the above technique is especially useful in cases where you want a sharp contrast and pure areas of white.

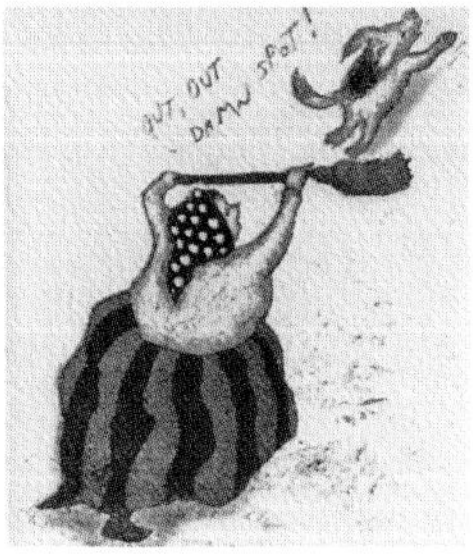

■ OFFSET ETCHING OR COUNTERPROOFING

Counterproofing is basically an image printed directly from another print rather than from a plate. Traditionally, the main use of this technique is in multiple plate etching to transfer images to secondary plates to allow for proper registration. This is usually done when the drawing on the first plate is at a very early state with perhaps just a line drawing in soft or hard ground. The plate is printed at normal etching pressure onto a piece of etching paper large enough that it can be trapped in the press after the plate has come out from under the roller.

Pull the blankets and the paper back over the roller and carefully place registration blocks against two adjacent sides of the plate. Remove the first plate and replace with a clean plate exactly the same size, being careful to not move the registration blocks. When the plate is in place remove the registration

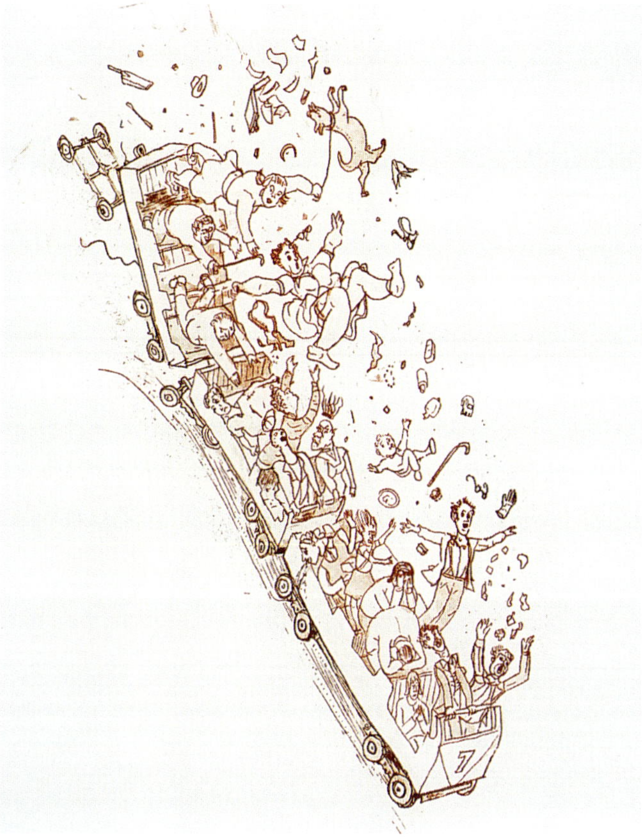

Chris Orr – *Happy Days* (detail) 25 x 10 cm (10 x 4 in.). Offset etching

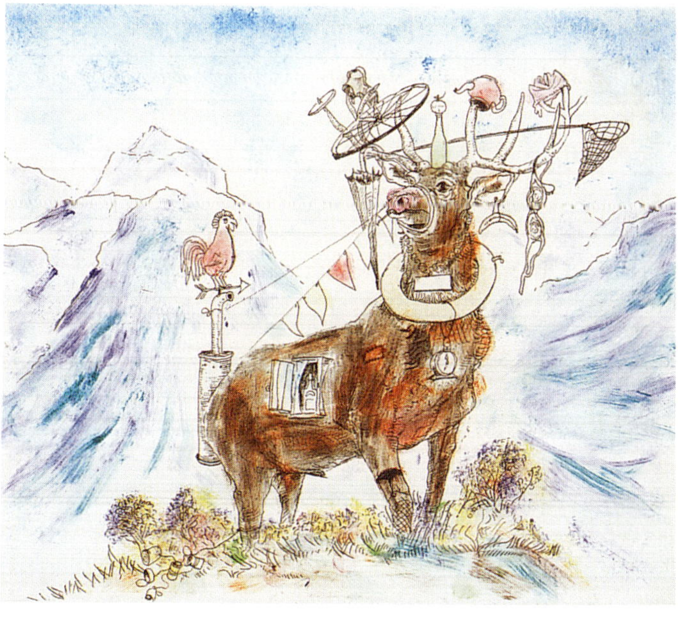

Chris Orr – *The M of the Glen*. Offset etching inked up *a la poupée*

blocks and run the plate back through the press. The etching will have transferred to the new plate allowing you to work on the two plates confident in the perfect registration of your images.

This can also be used as an effective printing technique, which I first saw used by Chris Orr. It allows for overlapping images, for elements of a print to bleed out beyond the plate mark or for images to be printed with no plate mark at all. You can also incorporate language in an image without the need for writing backwards.

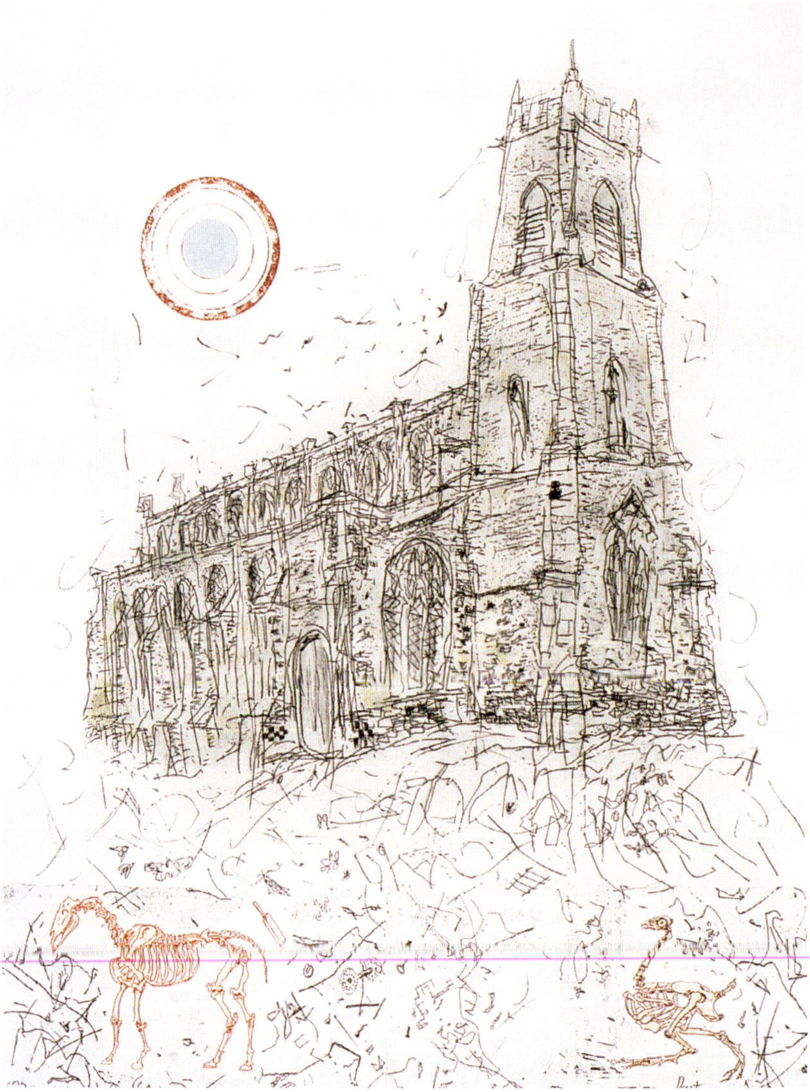

Chris Orr – *Spit.* Offset etching from two plates and frottage which is created by offset printing from a cut out, inked piece of paper

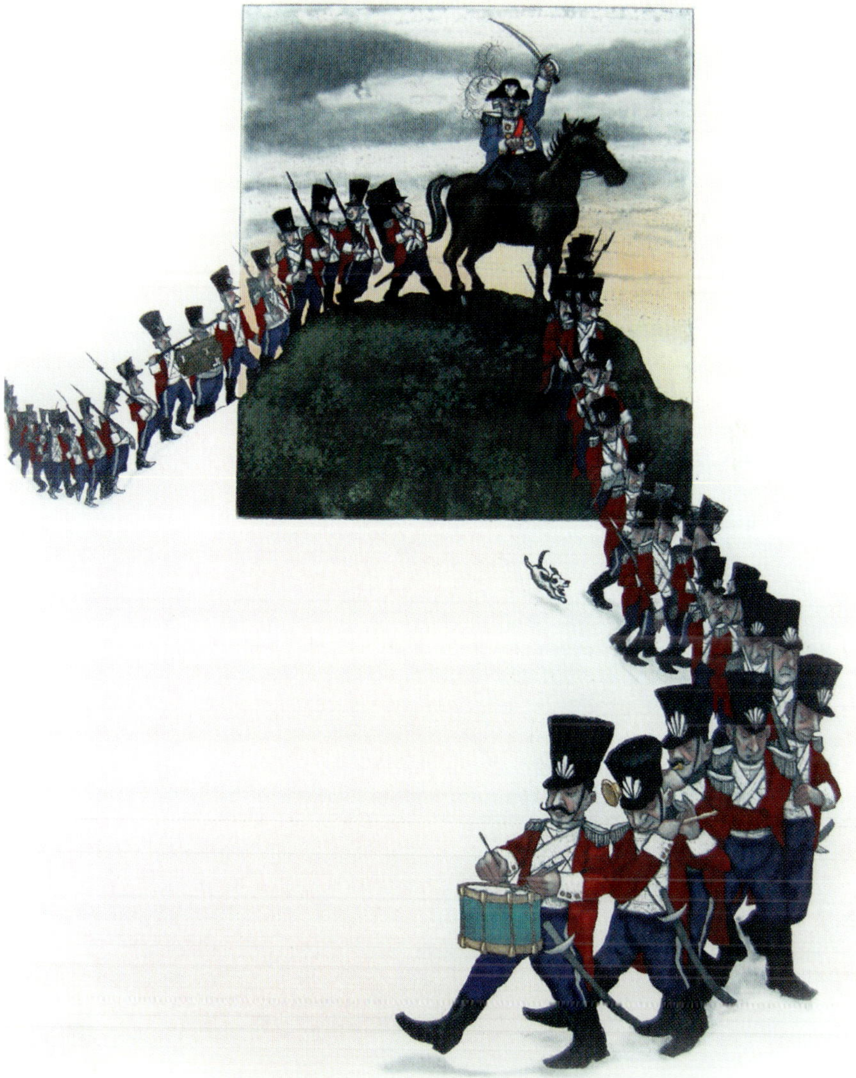

Mychael Barratt – *The Grand Old Duke of York*. Offset etching, soft ground, aquatint and spit bite, 66 × 52 cm (26 × 20½ in.). In both this plate and *Noah's Ark* (p.81), there is a combination of direct printing in the square plate and offset for the elements of the image that spill out. It is essential that the second plate is etched much darker than the direct plate as it will lose some intensity of tone when offset.

You will need:

- Filed etched plate
- Strong tissue paper
- Plant sprayer.

The method

This works best when the image to be offset is printed on a strong, acid-free tissue paper such as Kozo. Ink up the plate and place it on the press bed. It is not necessary to soak the paper, as it only needs to be slightly damp. Just before printing, spray the tissue with water using a plant sprayer. Leave for a minute, blot off the excess water and lay the tissue on the plate. Laying a piece of very slightly damp printing paper larger than the plate on top of the tissue allows you to print with normal pressure and also stops the ink from bleeding through the tissue and damaging the blankets. I hang on to old trial proofs for just this purpose and can use each piece of paper about four or five times before it starts to buckle. Print as a normal etching but leave the tissue and covering printing paper on the plate and place to one side. Lay the print or piece of paper that you wish to receive the offset image face up onto the press bed and increase the pressure by approximately half a turn. Then remove the tissue from the plate and place it printed side down on the print or piece of paper. Cover it with a large piece of tissue paper to protect the blankets and print as normal.

This technique can be used on either a dry or damp print. The main thing to remember is that there will be an inevitable degradation of the image between the first print on tissue and the final offset image. To compensate for this you will need to etch the offset plate much darker than you would normally.

Offsetting onto plaster tiles

Traditionally, intaglios are printed on paper but there are no rules stating that they must be. Trevor Price has found a way of printing on plaster tiles that create a truly 3-dimensional image.

You will need:

- Filed etched plate
- Paper – either strong tissue paper or printing paper
- Hard board
- All-purpose Polyfilla
- PVA glue
- Sandpaper
- Foam blanket (neoprene foam).

The method

The plate making for the offsetting is carried out in very much the same way as described above but it should be noted that this technique is not subtle enough

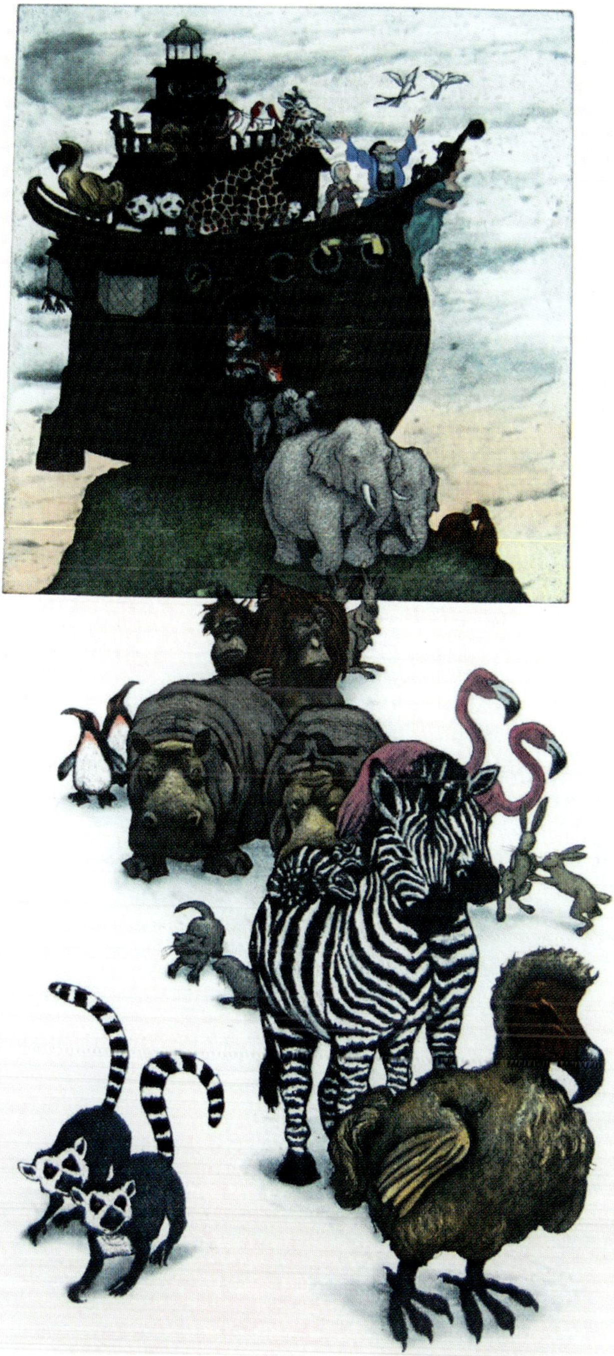

Mychael Barratt – *Noah's Ark*. Offset etching, soft ground, aquatint and spit bite, 66 x 52 cm (26 x 20½ in.)

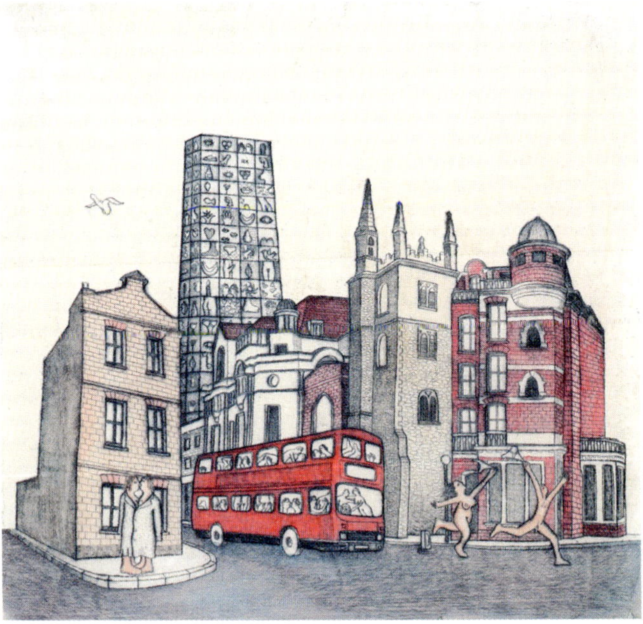

Trevor Price – *Everyone having sex everywhere*. Drypoint on plaster tile, 27 × 29 cm (10½ × 11½ in.). This has been printed onto a hard board tile as described in the text. It has then been attached to a thicker piece of board and the sides have been plastered to make a tile about 3cm (1⅕ in.) thick.

to work well with aquatint. Linear processes such as hard ground, soft ground and drypoint work best.

To prepare the plaster tiles, cut a piece of hardboard to the size of your finished image. Mix up some all-purpose, interior and exterior Polyfilla according to the manufacturer's instructions, apart from the liquid element which must be equal parts water and PVA glue. The quantities are crucial because if there is not enough PVA the printing surface will be too brittle and if there is not enough water it will be too plastic. Apply the Polyfilla with a palette knife in a thin layer to the rough side of the hardboard. Allow the plaster to set for 24 hours, then sand it down so that it is quite smooth while still retaining some of the character of the palette knife marks.

Print the plate onto normal printing paper (such as Somerset 300 gm) using undiluted ink preferably in a strong black or ultramarine. Leave the paper on the plate and place it to one side until you are ready to print the offset. Replace the etching blankets with a 2.5 cm (1 in.) neoprene foam blanket (made of the same type of rubber as camping sleeping mats). The pressure on the press will need to be adjusted to accommodate the foam blanket and the plaster tile. Lay the plaster tile face up on the bed of the press and once you have removed the still-damp print from the metal plate, place it face down onto the tile. Run the foam blanket and the plaster tile gently through the press. Patience is quite critical at this point and to avoid the print sticking, leave it on the tile for about an hour before you try to remove it. Once the offset has been allowed to dry for about 24 hours you can hand-colour it if you wish.

5 ARTISTS' PROFILES

I am convinced that it is through example that artists are most likely to be inspired to try out new techniques. The following pages feature works by a number of artists who are particularly adept at using one or more of the intaglio techniques described in the previous chapters. I have given details of how the pieces were made where appropriate.

NORMAN ACKROYD

Very few artists venture outdoors to do their plate making, due to the perceived studio-based constraints of printmaking. I will take to the Victorian railway arches behind my studio when I am spit-biting, as I feel the fume extraction is insufficient indoors, but the difficulties of transporting toxic mordants and plates with delicate surfaces mean that on no other occasion will I work outside. Norman Ackroyd is uniquely impervious to these limitations.

He is one of the great landscape artists of our age and works *in situ* whether he is painting small watercolours in a leather-bound sketchbook or etching enormous copper plates. He travels to remote corners of the British Isles to find

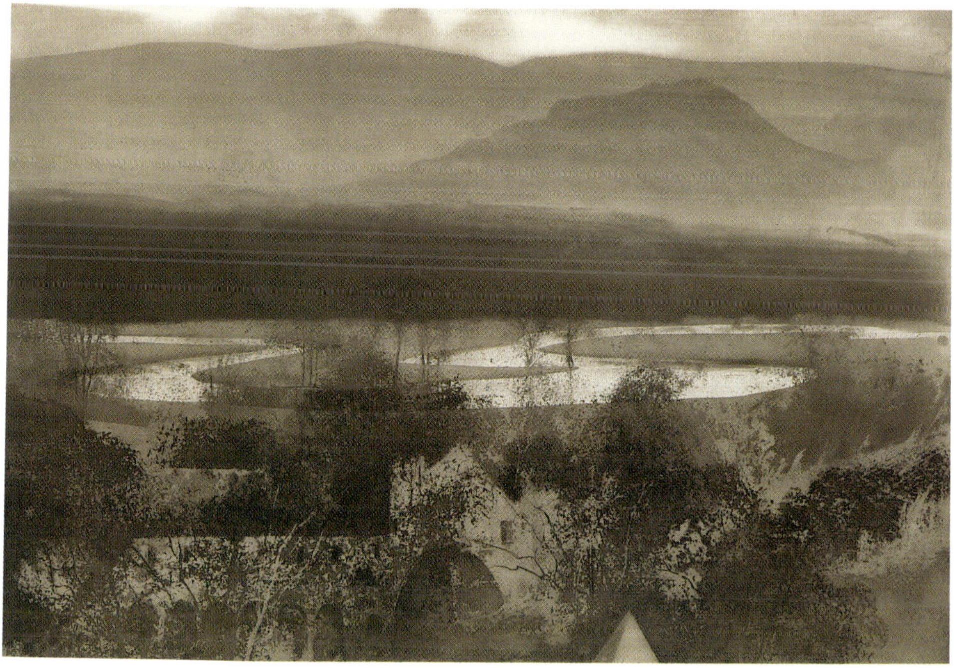

Norman Ackroyd – *Shropshire*. Aquatint, sugar lift and spit bite, 66 x 89 cm (26 x 35 in.)

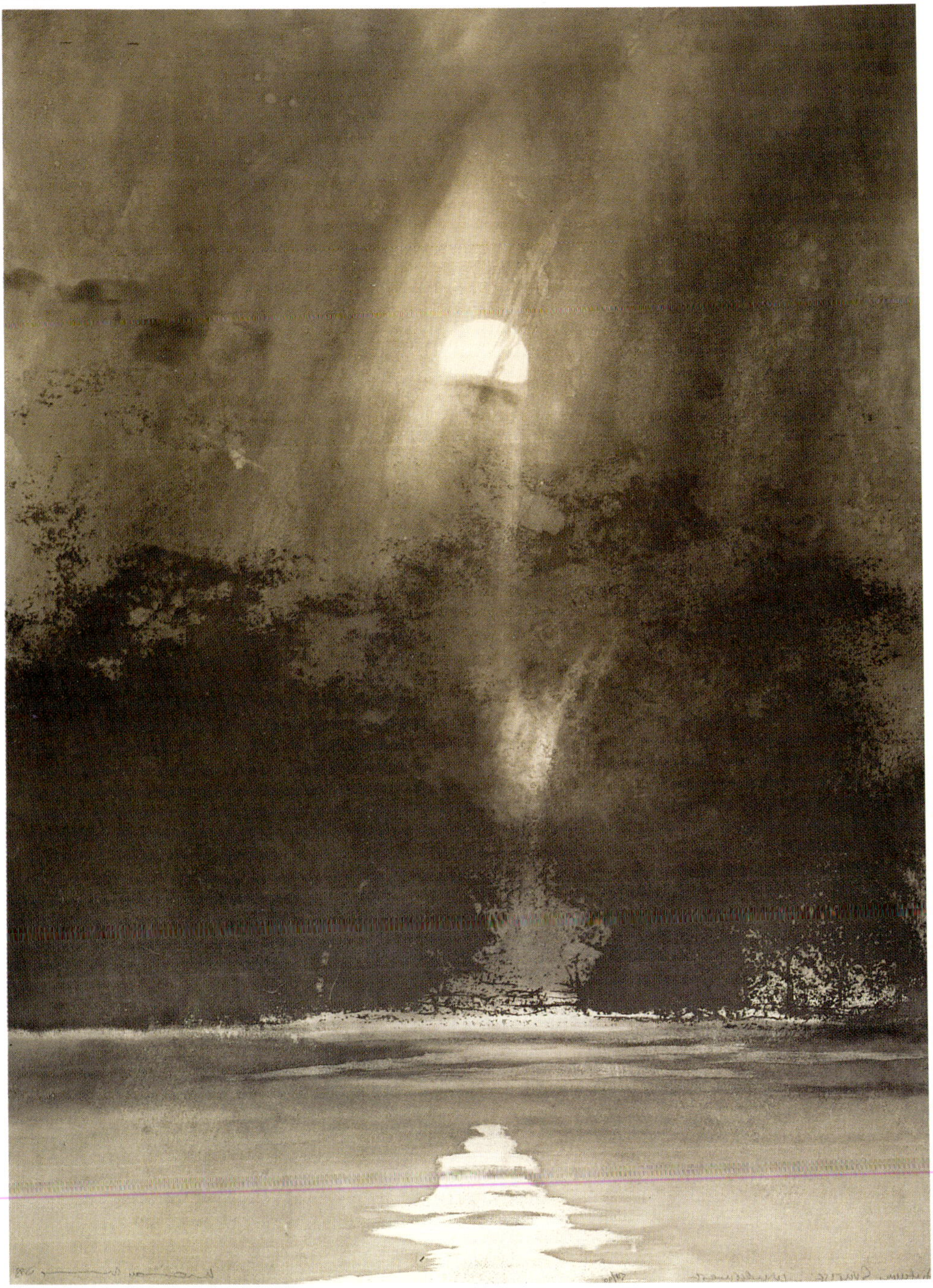

Norman Ackroyd – *Autumn Sunrise, Windermere*. 75 x 56 cm (29½ x 22 in.). Aquatint, sugar lift and spit bite

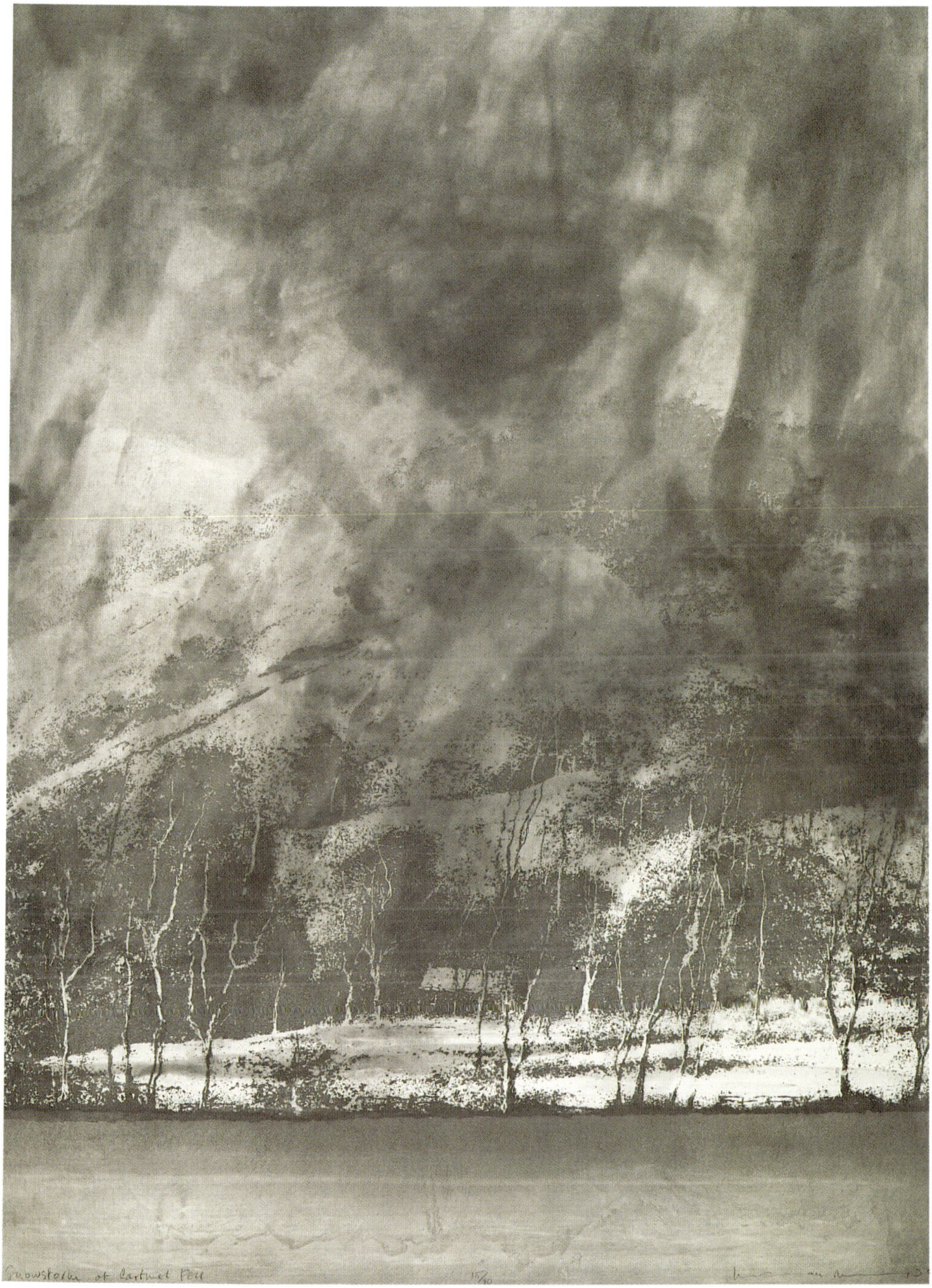

Norman Ackroyd – *Snowstorm at Cartmel Fell*. 87 x 64 cm ($34\frac{1}{4}$ x $25\frac{1}{4}$ in.). Aquatint: sugar lift and spit bite

the perfect locations for his work. He prepares a vast number of plates either degreased for sugar lift, or covered with hard ground, soft ground or aquatint. The soft ground is mixed to exacting consistencies depending on the weather conditions he is likely to encounter: it will be anything from a very fluid, soft mixture if it is likely to be cold to a much stiffer, more robust mixture in the height of summer. He arms himself with an array of brushes, pens, paper and other essential printmaking tools plus jars of nitric acid, ferric chloride and sugar lift solution; a thermos of strong coffee and an ample supply of tobacco and papers to make roll-ups.

Ackroyd's most powerful landscapes are those viewed from, and reflected in, large expanses of water. To place himself in the ideal location to capture these he will hire a small boat and either he or a hired boatman will row out off coastlines or to the middle of lakes, regardless of inhospitable weather. His starting point for each individual etching is fluid and depends somewhat on the ground. He will work on the drawing in the foreground of a hard ground plate in a detailed manner, then set it aside and apply gestural sugar lift marks with brushes and cloths to the next plate. He uses cotton buds to draw on very supple soft ground through Japanese paper, which gives a gentle charcoal appearance to the marks. He will approach a plate covered in aquatint rosin very much like a watercolour, laying in large areas of loose washes with nitric acid while spraying the plate with a plant sprayer to keep it wet. The details of the image will be worked on with progressively stronger acids while the wind blows away the clouds of fumes. When Ackroyd wants to stop the etching, he will lean over the edge of the boat and dip the plate into the water. His plates are seldom completely finished *in situ* and the watercolours that he paints at the same time, along with a few photos taken on a disposable camera, provide invaluable reference tools for further work.

When back in the studio, Ackroyd tends to work in series based on the latest trip. He will simultaneously work on nine or ten plates, with various proofs hanging from drying racks or lying on the floor. He finishes the odd plate in a single state but views this almost as a happy accident. His pieces are generally completed in between three to 30 states. In the studio he is remarkably pragmatic and efficient, and has a methodology imbued in common sense rather than habit for every element of studio practice. He rarely uses any store-bought grounds as he prefers to mix his own. The sugar lift and hard and soft ground recipes cited in the relevant sections of this book were contributed by Norman – he is remarkably generous when discussing printmaking techniques. He owns vintage presses that he treats with such care and respect that he is still using their original blankets.

Ackroyd studied painting and printmaking at the Leeds College of Art 1956-61 and at the Royal College of Art 1961-1964; he made his first etching in 1958. He has a real passion for printmaking history, techniques and traditions and has a wonderful collection of prints built up over the years either by purchasing or swapping for his own work.

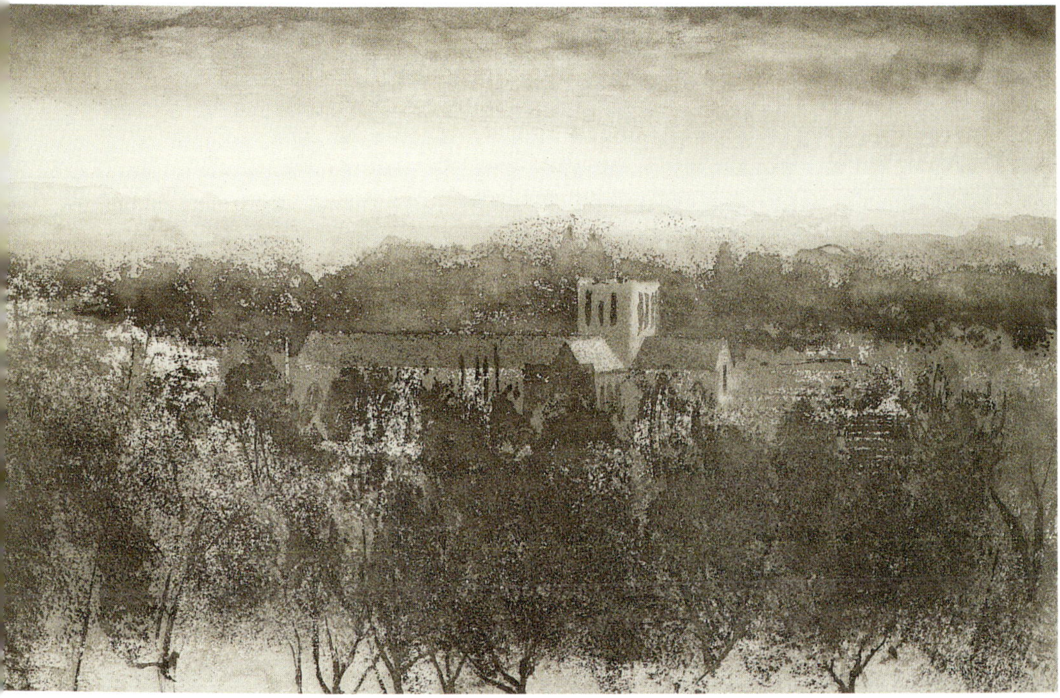

Norman Ackroyd – *Winchester from St Catherine's Hill.* Sugar lift and spit bite aquatint, 21 × 33 cm (8¼ × 13 in.)

His technical ability is incomparable and each variation of technique is customised to suit the specific requirements of the subject matter. He will cut out positive stencils of elements within a composition and stop out around them to create silhouettes. In *Shropshire* (p.83) he has used stencils for the mountains in the background and stopped out around them using spray paint to give a subtle gradation to the tone. He will also use stop out on sponges around stencils to give a dappled look to the stopped-out areas. In pieces such as *Winchester from St Catherine's Hill* (above) he has drawn the wooded areas in the foreground with sugar lift applied with a sponge or cloth. He has used this technique again in the middle ground of *Snowstorm at Cartmell Fell* (p.85), but before etching the sugar lift he drew in the highlights of the foreground trees using oil pastels. At the next stage he has painted sugar lift in for the shaded areas of the foreground trees and etched them to be darker than the trees in the middle ground. The water, some of the shadows in the middle ground and the clouds were created using spit biting.

There is a master class of etching techniques in every one of Norman's prints but ultimately they succeed by virtue of the draftsmanship of a truly remarkable artist.

■ CHRIS ORR

I have a long-standing admiration for Chris Orr, as it was when I first discovered his work that I decided to take up printmaking. He had an exhibition primarily featuring prints at the Royal Festival Hall and his enthusiasm for the medium is contagious. Few artists utilise the breadth of techniques available to the printmaker to quite the same extent as Chris Orr. The autographic drawing style and idiosyncratic humour remain constant, but each successive print is remarkably technically diverse from its predecessors. You should not be surprised upon examining one of his prints to discover lines which are created using drypoint, hard ground, soft ground and lifted lithographic pencil and aquatint tonal areas laced with roulette wheel meanderings and a spray of stipple engraved dots. All this before you even begin to investigate whether elements are printed directly from a plate, relief printed from a piece of inked-up paper, offset from another print, or perhaps even printed from a lithographic plate. It is an absolute delight for a printmaker to visit one of his shows or his studio, especially if you fancy yourself an amateur intaglio sleuth.

Chris's father worked in the printing industry and his early visits to the printing works made a huge impression on him. He remembers fondly the stacks of metal type and reams of paper that were the fringe benefits of his father's trade. From the time at art school when he made his first print with a linocut and an ancient Gestetner he was hooked.

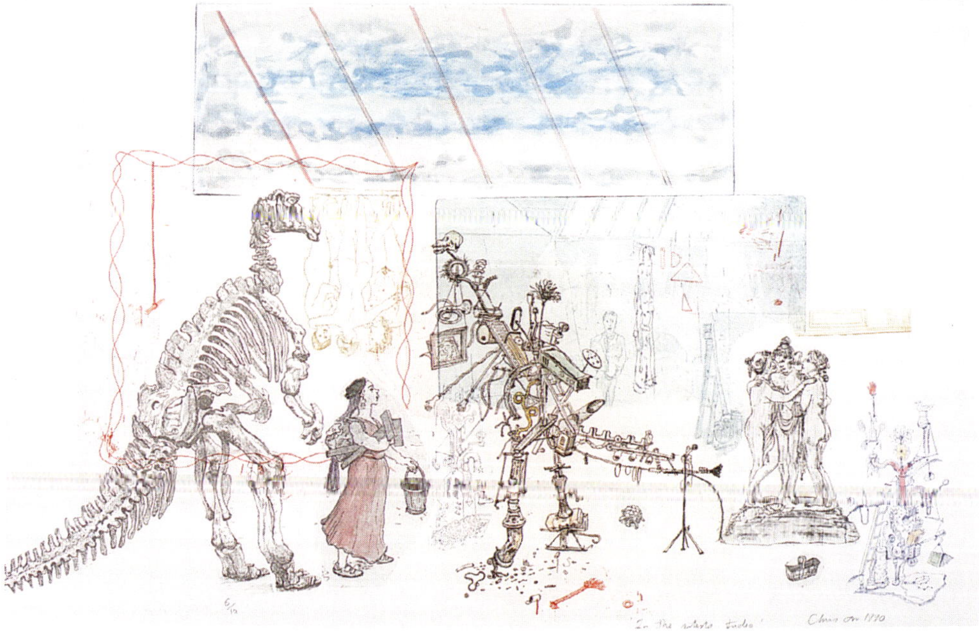

Chris Orr – *In the studio*. Offset etching, hard ground, aquatint, (paper size) 56 x 76 cm (22 x 30 in.). This print has no variants but is an editioned offset piece from ten separate plates.

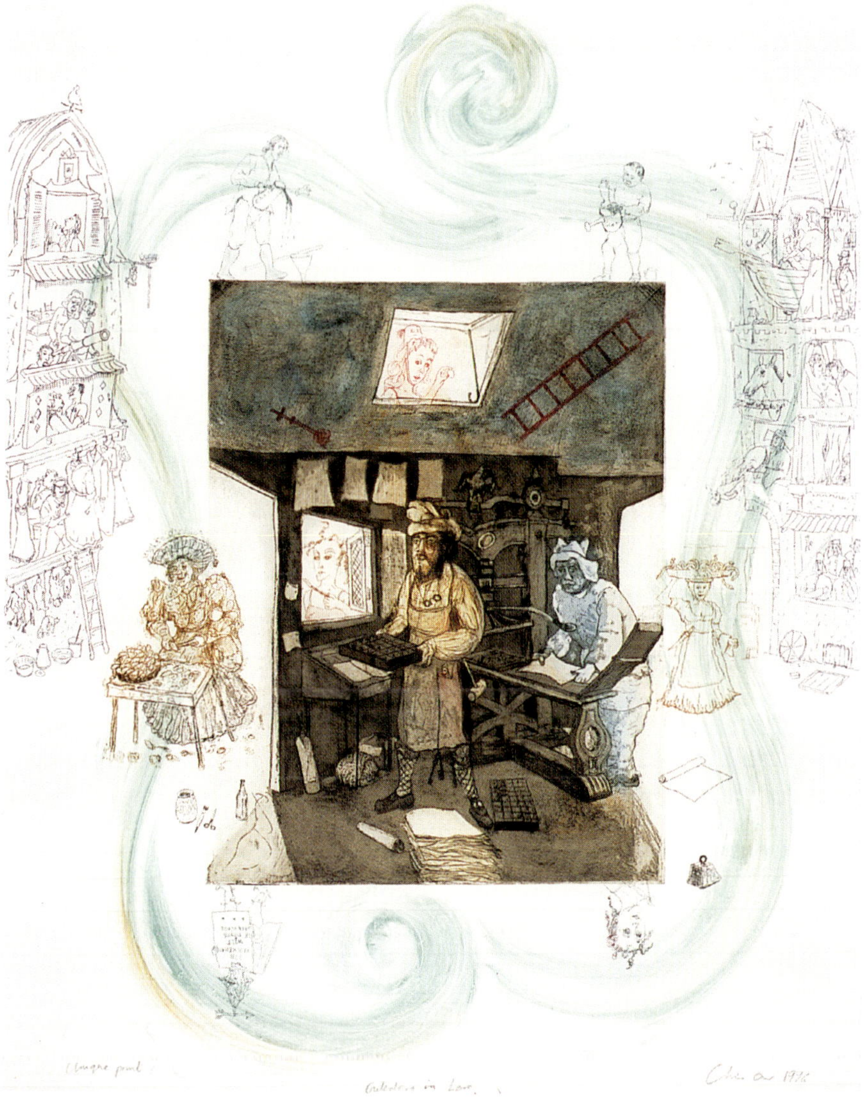

Chris Orr – *Gutenberg in love*. Hard ground, aquatint, spit bite, offset etching and monoprint, (paper size) 76 x 56 cm (30 x 22 in.). This is a unique variant of an editioned piece. The offset details around the border are quite different to the editioned piece and have been added in an improvisational, painterly manner.

Although Chris has been printmaking continuously since graduating from the RCA in 1967, he sees himself as an artist who makes prints. He is interested in the act of image making and he works in phases between painting and printmaking. His work is the product of hours of play in the studio and, especially in the case of the unique prints containing elements of counterproof, manages to retain a very improvisational, painterly quality. He enjoys creating

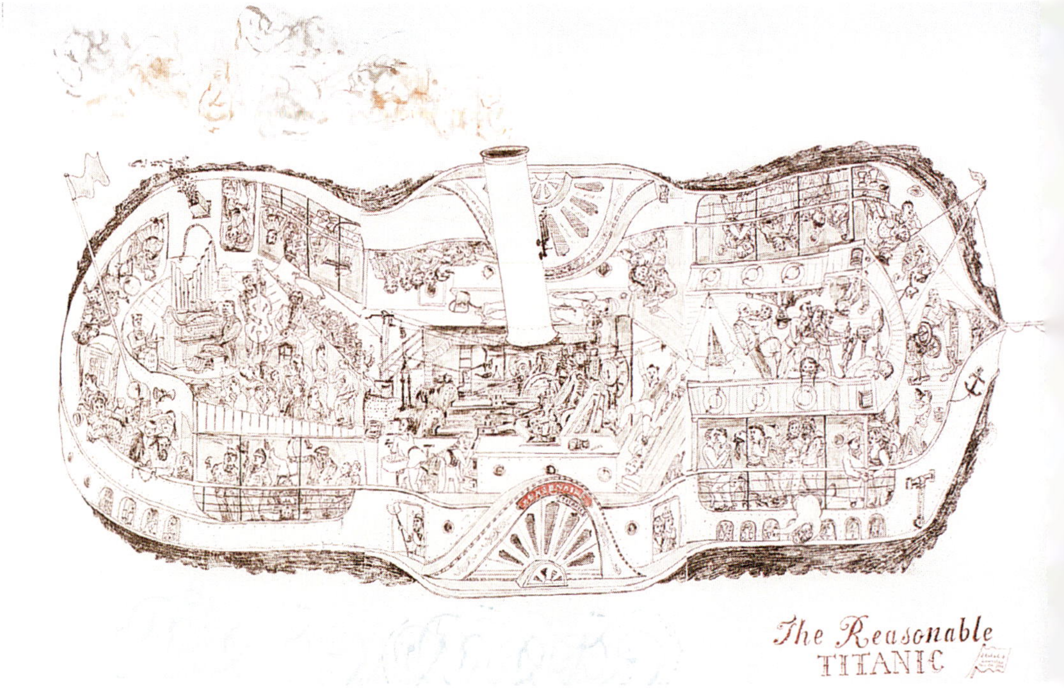

Chris Orr – *The Reasonable Titanic*, paper size 76 x 112 cm (30 x 44 in.). Offset etching from four plates. The top plate, which appears like a monoprint, is actually a spit bitten, counterproofed plate.

the unique prints but gains familiarity with and fondness for editioned pieces through the process of editioning them. He works from numerous preparatory drawings, which are not transferred onto the plate but are drawn freehand generally into hard ground. These drawings sometimes have the feel of automatic drawings where any errors are unedited. These are most successful in pieces where they are combined with sections that are detailed and carefully observed, such as *Gutenberg in Love*.

There is a boyish, quintessentially English nature to Chris Orr's work that harkens back to a more innocent time when the sun always shone over cricket grounds and the crack of ball on willow was always followed by polite applause, but there is an edge to his observations reminiscent of Gillray or Hogarth. Careful examination of the various staterooms and boiler rooms of *The Reasonable Titanic* will reveal some wonderfully barbed observations and offer insights into the workings of the artist's mind.

Although he clearly enjoys making his art and has always managed to retain a level of spontaneity, Chris revealed the effort and premeditation involved in printmaking in a lecture he gave at The Royal College of Art. 'There is nothing accidental about making a print. It requires planning, cohesive and controlled action supported by machines and materials.'

I find this quite a pleasing notion but then I enjoy the sight of a duck gently bobbing on the water all the more for the knowledge that its feet are pedalling away madly beneath the surface.

■ HELEN FAY

Helen Fay is a member of the Glasgow Print Studio, which is an independent printmaking studio. The environment for an artist and printmaker in Scotland in general, but particularly in Glasgow, is very healthy and supportive. Helen uses the studio's facilities for her own work but also editions prints for other artists such as Elizabeth Blackadder. She loves the challenge of editioning, especially in the case of colour multi-plate etchings which diverge hugely from her own monochromatic drypoints.

Helen is a draughtsperson first and foremost; virtually all of her pieces are drawn from life and depict animals to be found in Scotland's parks or the Glasgow Zoo. She will work *in situ* for hours doing scores of quick, gestural sketches that she will then take back to the studio and transfer onto plates. She prefers to work on zinc, as it is soft enough to be fluid but hard enough to withstand editions of 35 or 40. She has worked on polished jet plate but prefers to get her zinc from non-ferrous metal merchants, because she likes the unpredictability of the rough bits of metal. As you have to choose from whatever metal is available she ends up working on various thicknesses of zinc and likes the random scratches and imperfections as they stop the finished pieces from becoming too slick. This also helps them to be clearly read as works on metal so

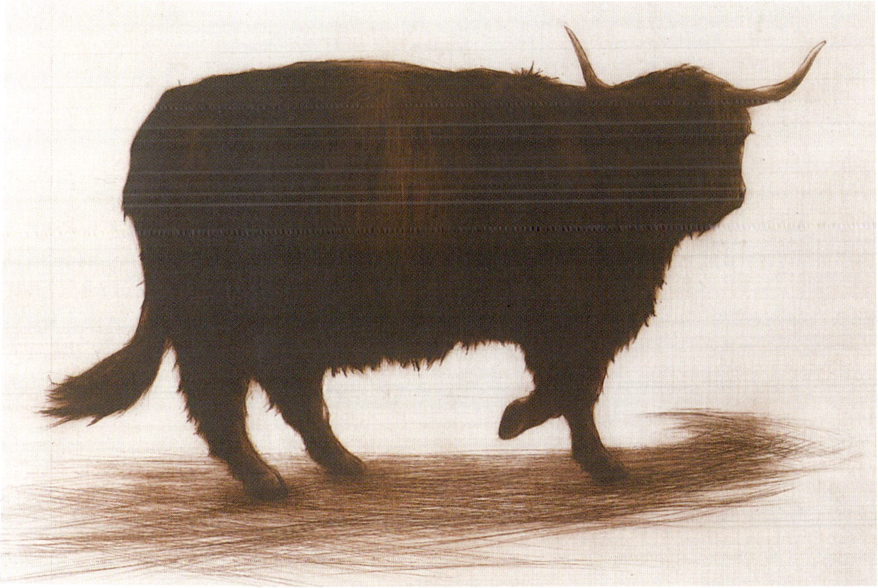

Helen Fay – *Dancing Coo*. Drypoint, 39.5 × 56 cm (15½ × 22 in.)

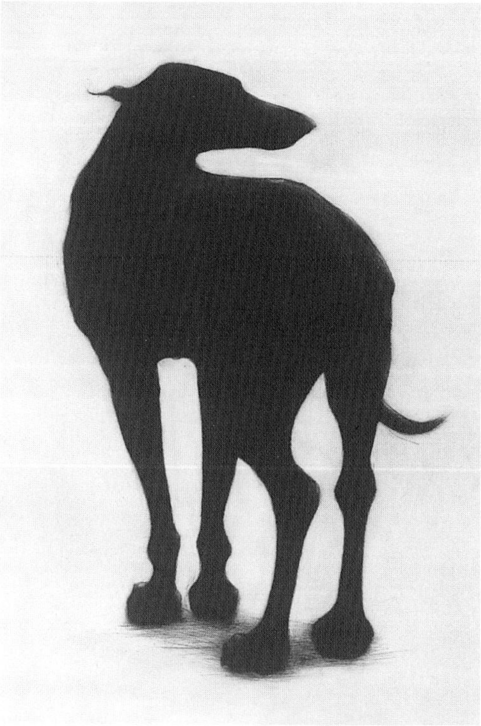

Helen Fay – *Hound Dog*. Drypoint, 60 × 42 cm ($23\frac{1}{2}$ × $16\frac{1}{2}$ in.)

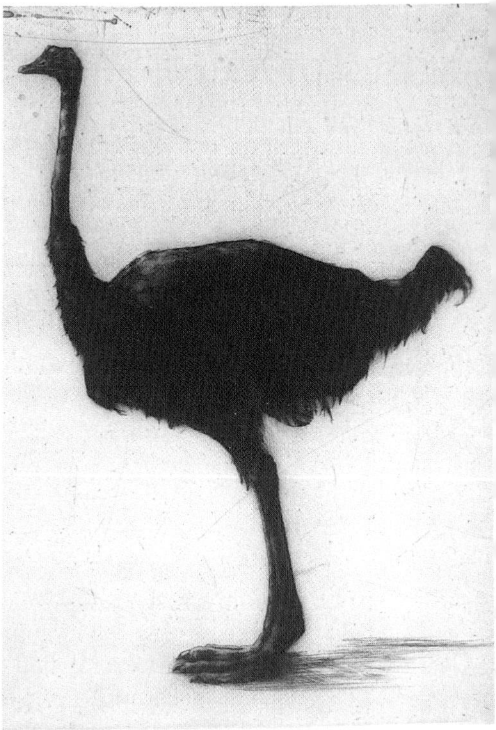

Helen Fay – *Ostrich*. Drypoint, 39 × 34 cm ($15\frac{1}{2}$ × $13\frac{1}{2}$ in.)

they become much more about the material than about solely a method of reproduction.

Helen's drawings are transferred freehand onto the plates using Chinagraph pencils, felt marking pens or even oil paint. She does not tend to do life drawing directly onto the plates as she finds the limitations of the drawing process on metal to be detrimental to capturing the subject. She then roughs in the drawing tonally using carbide paper, which is torn into small pieces and pointed with a fingertip. She then begins to build up the tonal areas with a tungsten carbide point. She has tried a diamond point tool but finds the marks too shallow. The tool that she uses allows her to put some real weight behind some of the lines with the darkest lines being gouged into the plate by holding the point in a closed fist. She does not like the harshness of the isolated drawn line and uses it only in instances where the subject matter dictates, such as when drawing feathers. She prefers large areas of tone and gradually builds these using varying line weight and cross hatching, with the lighter areas worked less rather than burnished. Once the drawing is complete, she inks the plate up with ink that is mixed with quite a bit of extender. She wipes with scrim only, and leaves a lot of ink on the plate but the extender allows you to still see the detail on the drawing beneath.

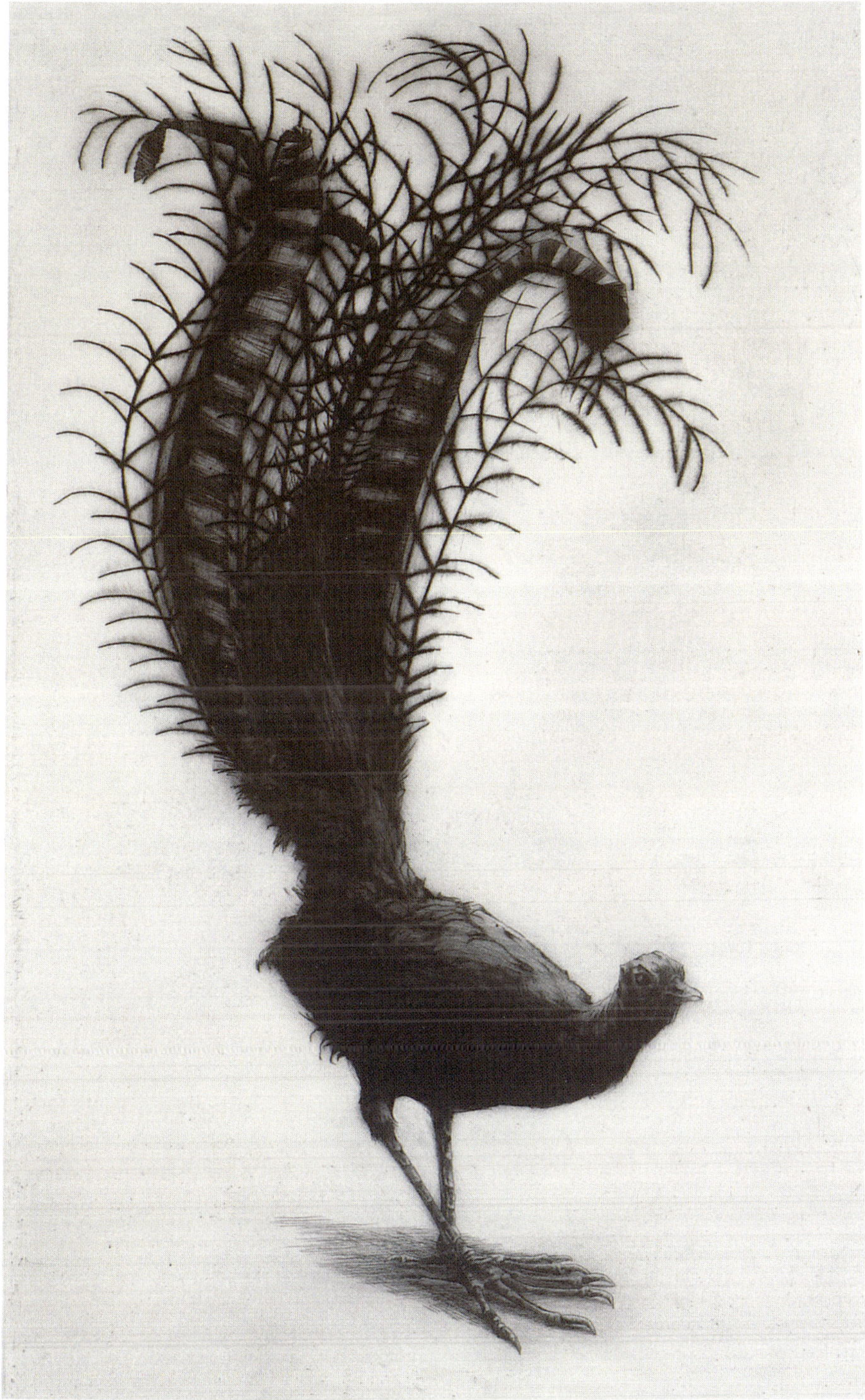

Helen Fay – *Lyrebird II*. Drypoint, 50 × 32 cm (19¾ × 12½ in.)

Helen has always been an avid drawer and although she still sees drypoint as central to her work, she is mixing it up with some etching as well. She does not want her facility with the medium of drypoint to make her work too predictable. Although this is a constant anxiety for the printmaker, in Helen's case I feel that it should not be too great a concern. There is a charming intimacy in her work which makes all of her pieces feel like portraits of beloved family members.

■ BARRY COTTRELL

As a challenge more than for any other reason I decided that it was imperative that I try out every technique included in this book. Granted, I work with quite a few of the etching techniques on an almost daily basis. There were others such as sugar lift and drypoint and even mezzotint that shared tools or other practices with techniques with which I was more familiar. Then I bought myself a couple of burins and attempted engraving. Suffice it to say that a few hours and a stack of copper later it was with renewed respect that I re-examined the work of Barry Cottrell. His images are teeming with seemingly effortless arabesques that display for me an almost unimaginable level of skill. However, it is the marriage of content and technique that make his engravings so successful.

He was studying at the Ruskin School of Drawing and Fine Art in the 1970s under Jean Lodge when he was first introduced to engraving. Jean Lodge had learned engraving from Samuel William Hayter who had wanted to 'reinvigorate the medium and liberate the line', which had been used as a purely descriptive medium previously. Hayter had recognised the huge potential of engraving beyond just imitating or copying other artworks and he imparted this to his students. Barry was immediately captivated by the physicality of the process and the beautifully sculptural qualities of the line. As part of their instruction in engraving, Jean Lodge tailor-made burins that were forged to fit the hands of each of her students and then fixed wooden handles to them. Barry got one and, although he uses

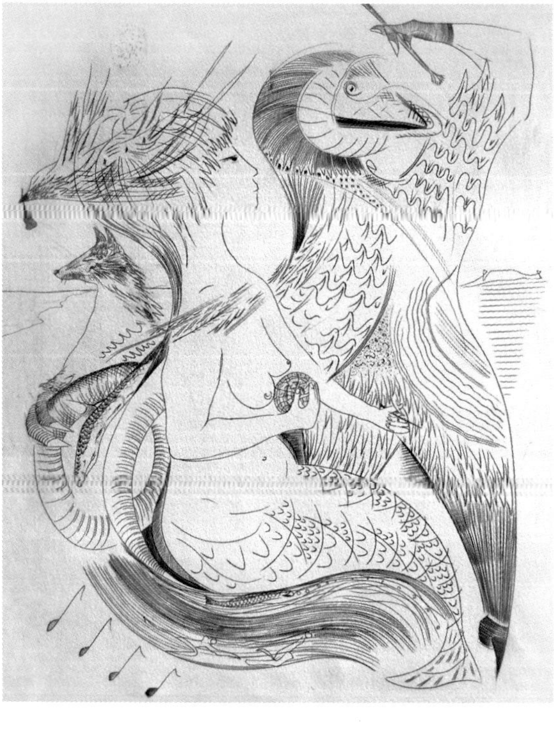

Barry Cottrell, *The Art Class*. Engraving, 49.5 x 39 cm ($19\frac{1}{2}$ x $15\frac{1}{2}$ in.)

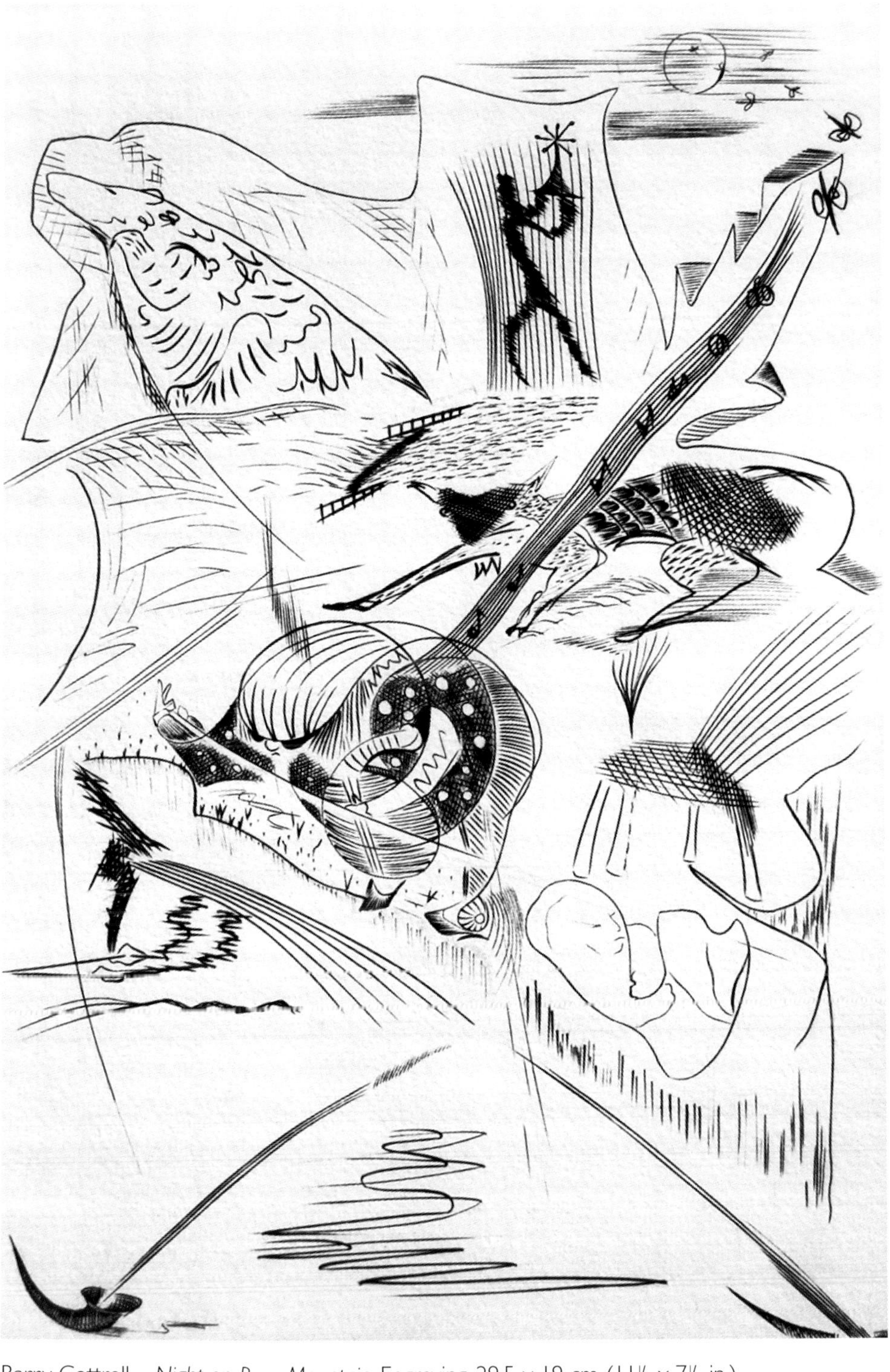

Barry Cottrell – *Night on Bear Mountain*. Engraving, 29.5 × 19 cm (11½ × 7½ in.)

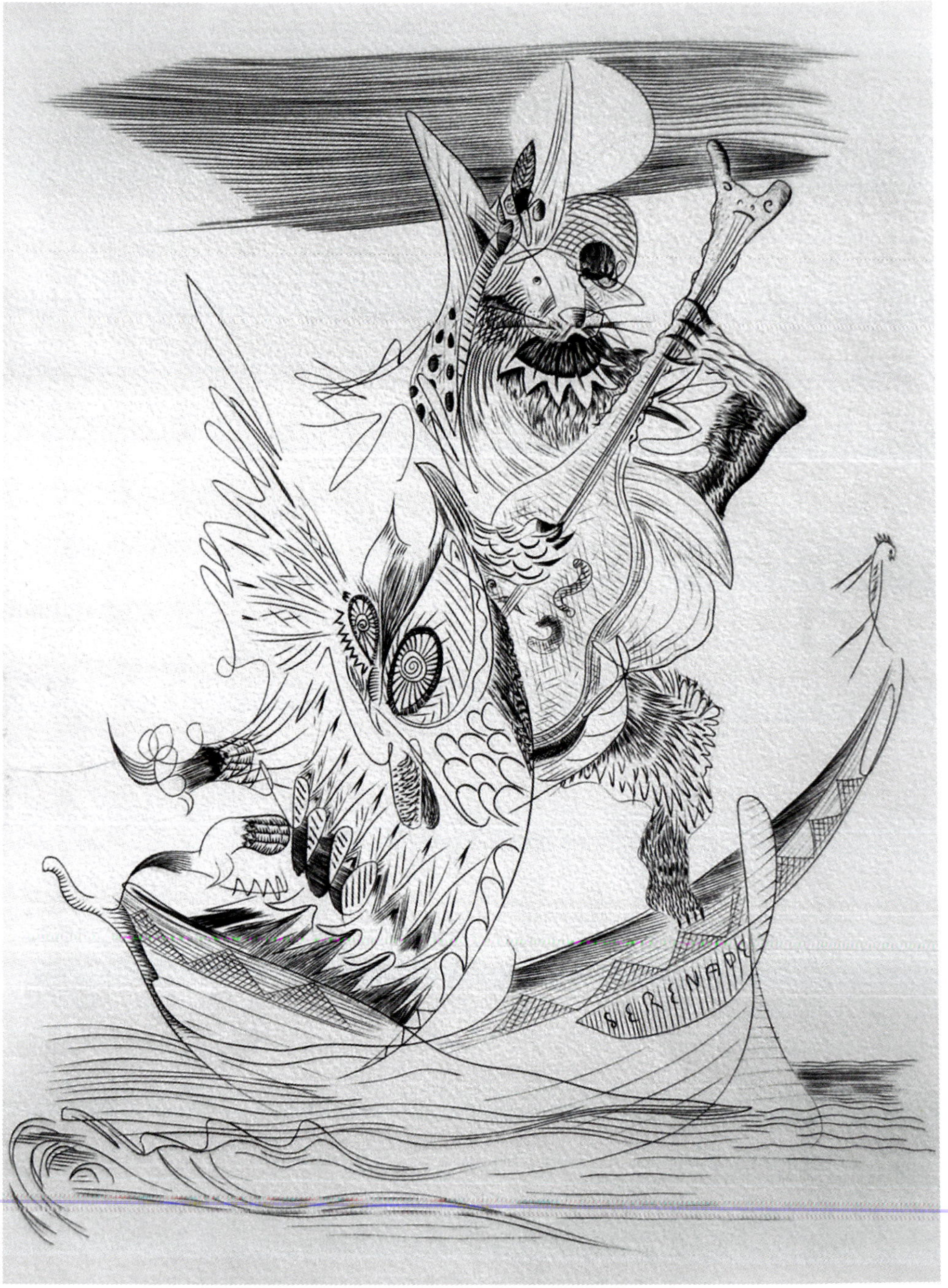

Barry Cottrell, *Serenade*. Engraving, 39 × 29 cm (15½ × 11½ in.)

three or four different burins and does not tend to vary them much within a single image, he still uses this burin frequently and is remarkably attached to it.

He loves the physicality of engraving, as for the very deep lines you have to use the weight of your entire body. He once drove such a deep line into an image that he cut right through the plate. Every time he went to print this image he had to contend with ink oozing out the back of the plate.

His work displays a natural, lovely sense of curvature, which is achieved by moving the plate with his free hand and firmly driving and pushing with the burin with his drawing hand. He refers to the perfect relationship of artist, burin and plate as the *inner secret geometry*.

When he first began engraving, his work was quite traditional and then after a break shifted to being quite abstract. The pieces he has produced since 2002 have straddled these two focuses, resulting in work that is lyrical and semi-figurative. There is a freedom and flow in his work and he keeps the images uncluttered; the more you obscure the line, the less point there is in using engraving.

Despite the undeniable challenges posed, Barry champions the only intaglio method where the line is driven outwards rather than pulled in towards you. He says that he is 'searching to find the essence of engraving' but I would argue that this driven artist with his driven line has already found it.

■ ANITA KLEIN

In the world of intaglio printmaking few artists have managed to create such an autographic mark as Anita Klein. Her rich, black, velvety drypoint lines are immediately recognisable whether you see then on the walls of a gallery or in print in a book or magazine. The ease of recognition is of course complemented by her subject matter, which almost invariably reflects the fabric of her life and depicts anecdotal remembrances of her day-to-day experiences.

Her choice of both subject matter and medium were set very early in her artistic life when she was studying at the Slade School of Art (1979-83). Her earliest drypoints were editions of five done on the back of lithographic plates and were interpretations of classical imagery such as *The Three Graces* and *The Expulsion from the Garden of Eden*. Even in these earliest pieces, drawing was the driving force behind her work and the human body in particular held a distinct fascination. A drawing holiday in Italy where she did little else but sit on the floors of major galleries copying Corregios, Giorgiones and Caravaggios gave her a firm foundation in figure drawing and she credits this with enabling her over the years to draw without reference to models. She loves Picasso and the weight and solidity of her figures owes much to his influence.

She married her partner Nigel and became pregnant while still at art school and it was at this point that her work became a visual diary depicting the domestic minutiae of her life. Focusing on drypoint allowed her to work compulsively at home during snatched spare moments and everything from her studio practice to her subject matter has developed in harmony with her

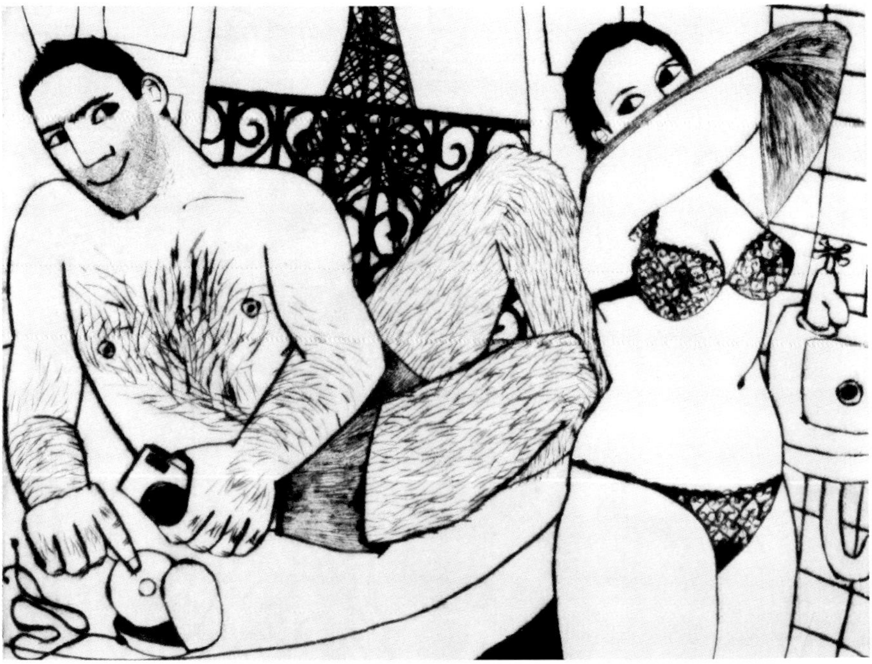

ABOVE Anita Klein, *New underwear in Paris.* Drypoint on aluminium, 30 x 41 cm (11⅘ x 16⅙ in.)

domestic environment. Her earliest pieces are charmingly self-deprecating scenes of pregnancy and motherhood. Every aspect of her life is liable to be viewed as fair game for subject matter; nothing is too mundane or trivial. For most people, the sight of their partner scouring the depths of a new box of Frosties to find the free toy would produce an ironic shake of the head at best but for Anita this is like a moment of epiphany.

Drypoint as a technique has now become second nature to Anita, and she is able to draw automatically with the drypoint scribe onto aluminium with seemingly little more resistance than using a pencil on paper. The images are drawn directly onto the plate in pencil and are only reversed in advance when the subject matter crucially dictates, for example to avoid Nigel and Anita ending up on the wrong sides of the bed.

Her style of strong, linear drypoint is not conducive to finely detailed work. This has made Anita extremely selective about which details to include. This process of editing has meant that the figures have become all-important and often virtually fill the whole image. The borders of the image often force the figures to duck their heads or tuck in their legs, and are so crucial that she never begins to draw without being aware of the limits of the composition.

Anita's increasing facility with the medium of drypoint has only added to the gestural appearance of the images, and her ability to create perfectly balanced compositions is unrivalled. There is such a refreshing lack of pretension in her work that it is easy to underestimate both its power and its

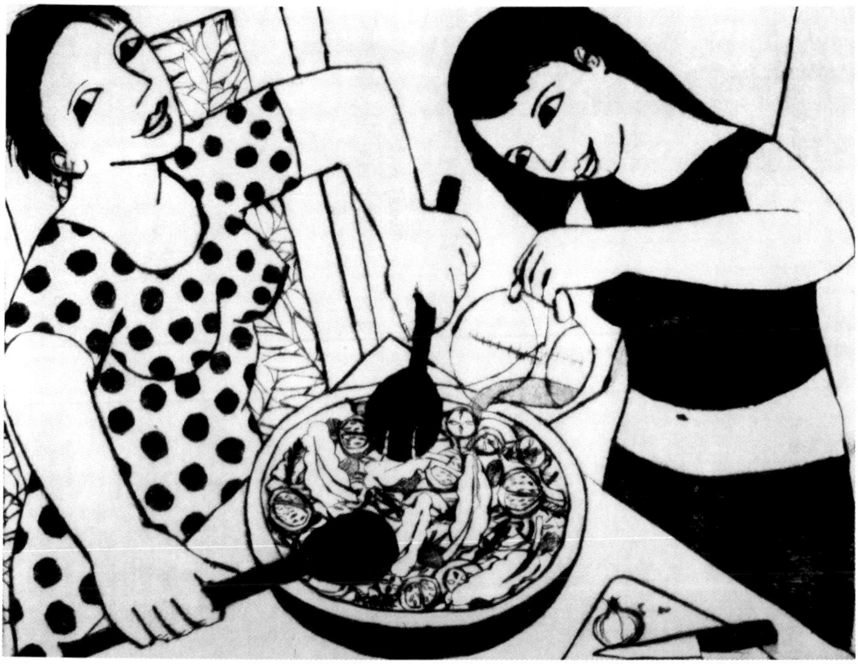

ABOVE Anita Klein, *The salad*. Drypoint on aluminium, 29 × 39 cm ($11^{2}/_{5} \times 15^{1}/_{3}$ in.)

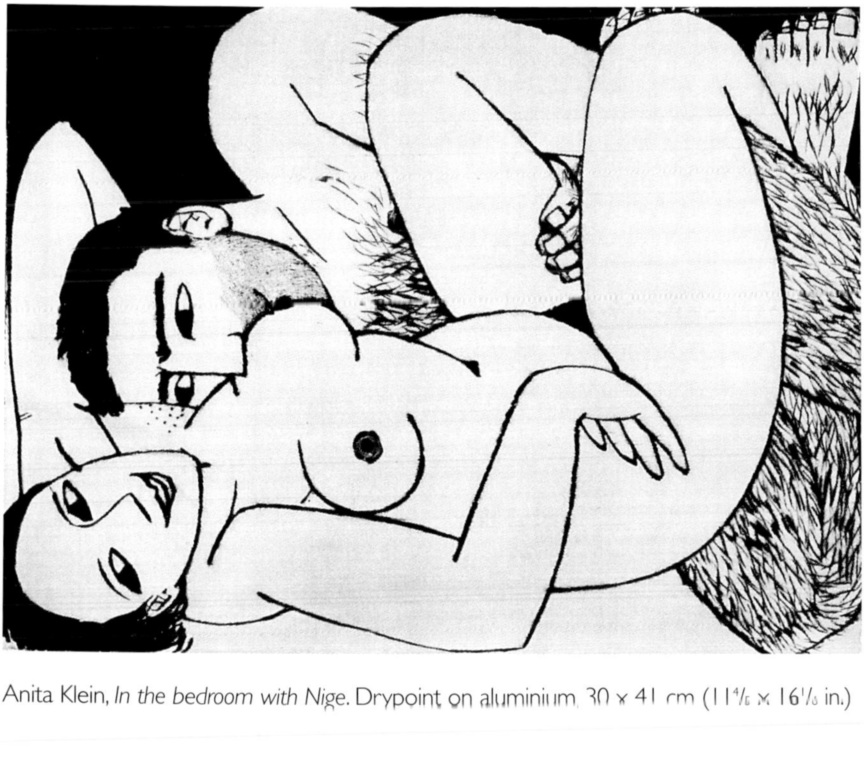

Anita Klein, *In the bedroom with Nige*. Drypoint on aluminium, 30 × 41 cm ($11^{4}/_{5} \times 16^{1}/_{6}$ in.)

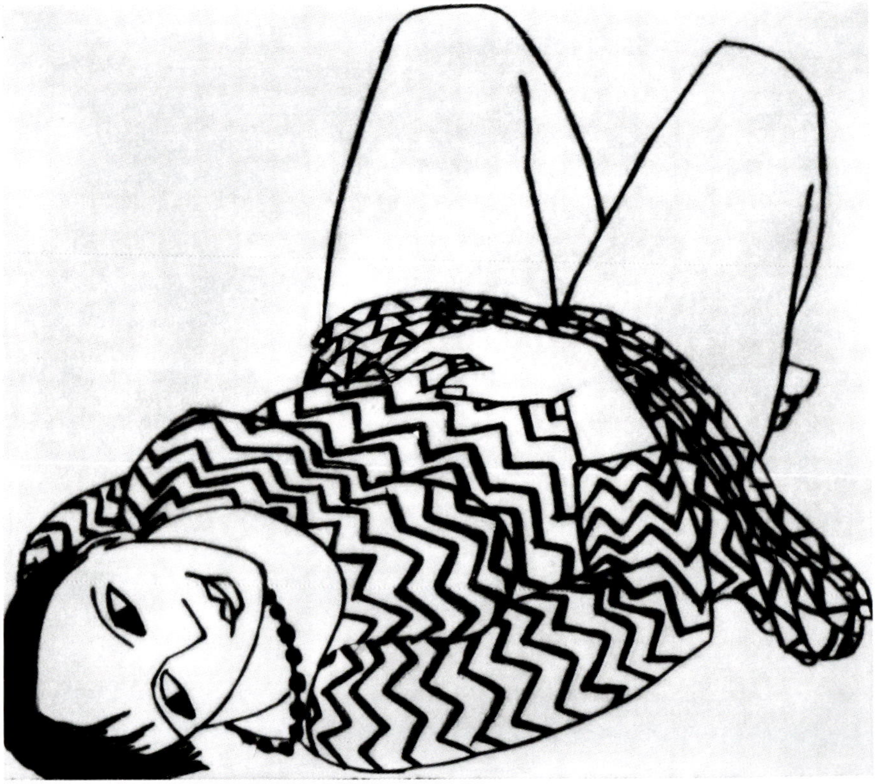

Anita Klein, *The zigzag dress*. Drypoint on aluminium, 30 x 34.5 cm (11⅘ x 13½ in.)

innovation. Anita does not deliberately eschew artistic elitism, she is merely drawing upon her personal experience and recording what she knows best, in the style of a good novelist. Her images are composed exactly as they are remembered, as the stuff of the perfect photo album.

■ MARTIN LANGFORD

Martin primarily uses the intaglio technique of *mezzotint* but steers clear of the traditional subject matter of bottles, fruit and eggs to create work with mind-boggling complexity and intricate levels of detail. His distinctive narrative images interweave people, buildings and landscapes with shifting prominence to create pieces that are clever, idiosyncratic and often laugh-out loud funny.

His creative process is 100 per cent imaginative with no reference material whatsoever being used. The moment of inspiration often comes during periods of subconscious doodling. He then labours throughout a number of stages with the finished drawing taking anything from an hour to a week to complete. He is very dubious about elaborate explanations of artistic intent, believing them to have often been conceived after the completion of the piece, and he is disarmingly unpretentious about his own motivation. 'I get ideas for prints and do them,' he wrote in a recent artist's statement.

His response about the inspiration for *It Lives*, his portrait of an anthropomorphic skyscraper, was typical: 'Our brains are like video recorders, set permanently on record. Every time we turn a corner, everything we ever do and experience, gets indiscriminately stored and comes out later. This was a strong image I couldn't get out of my head – I think it was inspired by the credits of *The Six-Million Dollar Man*'.

Although seemingly light-hearted, there are serious underlying themes in Martin's work. A genuine concern for the environment and man's encroachment on natural habitats crops up in many of his pieces. An etching entitled *Tree* is a humorous sequence of narrative panels depicting the manner in which green spaces are retained almost as souvenirs amid the inexorable advance of urban development. The alienation of the individual within society is another recurrent theme, as is the inherent danger of technological advancement.

As often happens in printmaking, the medium chooses the artist and from a very early age Martin Langford was a mezzotint artist in waiting. He has unlimited patience and loves puzzles and scrabble. He has an amazing aptitude for mathematics and as a young boy had a number of party tricks at his disposal. He could hear nine or ten digit numbers and immediately recite them backwards. Whilst out shopping he could add up the 30 or 40 items in the trolley in his head and would prove to be alarmingly accurate at the

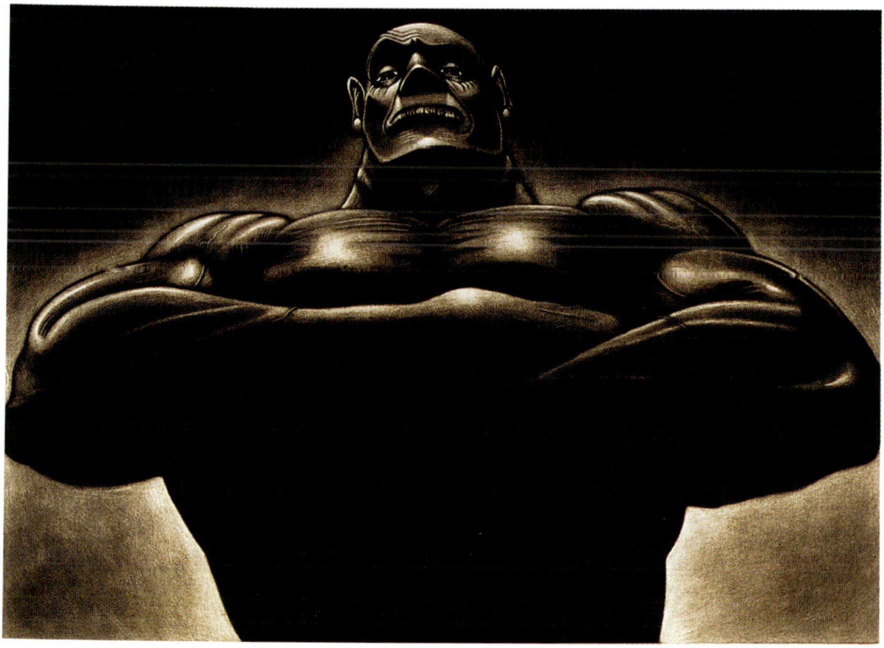

Martin Langford, *Nails*. Mezzotint, 12.5 x 59 cm (16¾ x 23¼ in.)

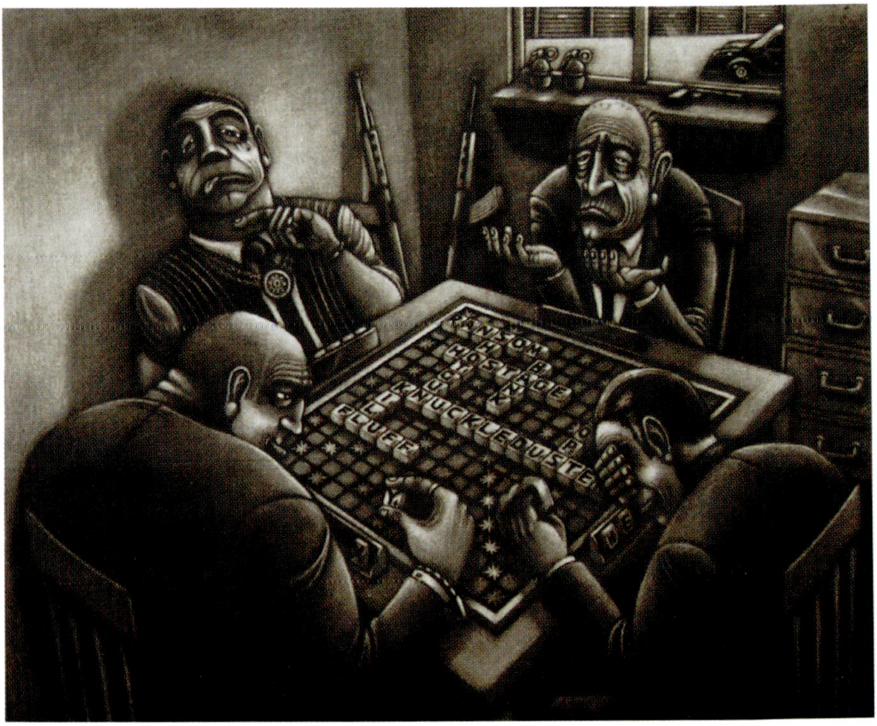

Martin Langford, *Fluffy*. Mezzotint, 22 × 26 cm (8¾ × 10¼ in.)

checkout. He cites his earliest artistic influences as comic books, non-verbal cartoons and computer games, although at 13 he became obsessed with Seurat and began creating his own monochromatic versions of pointillism. He would work for months on elaborate, meticulous, Escher-like compositions comprised solely of pen and ink dots.

He was kicked out of school for being 'disruptive' and a much-hated two-year course in interior design did little to change his view on education. However, this course did introduce him to 3D design, architecture, perspective drawing and installations, all of which still hugely inform his work.

While Martin was doing a foundation course in art at St Martins his instructor David Gluck saw him obsessively burnishing an etching plate and suggested that he explore mezzotinting. Martin felt an immediate affinity for this rarely used, labour-intensive technique. The level of effort required just to get the plate to a point where it is ready to be worked on is truly awe-inspiring but he distrusts anything that comes too easily.

'I expect things to go wrong sometimes, but nothing is really a problem in the end.' He doesn't care how long it takes to make a plate and frequently abandons of pieces if he feels that they are not working.

As a person, Martin is as witty and surprising as his work. He has an extraordinary talent for acting and can carry on complicated routines of

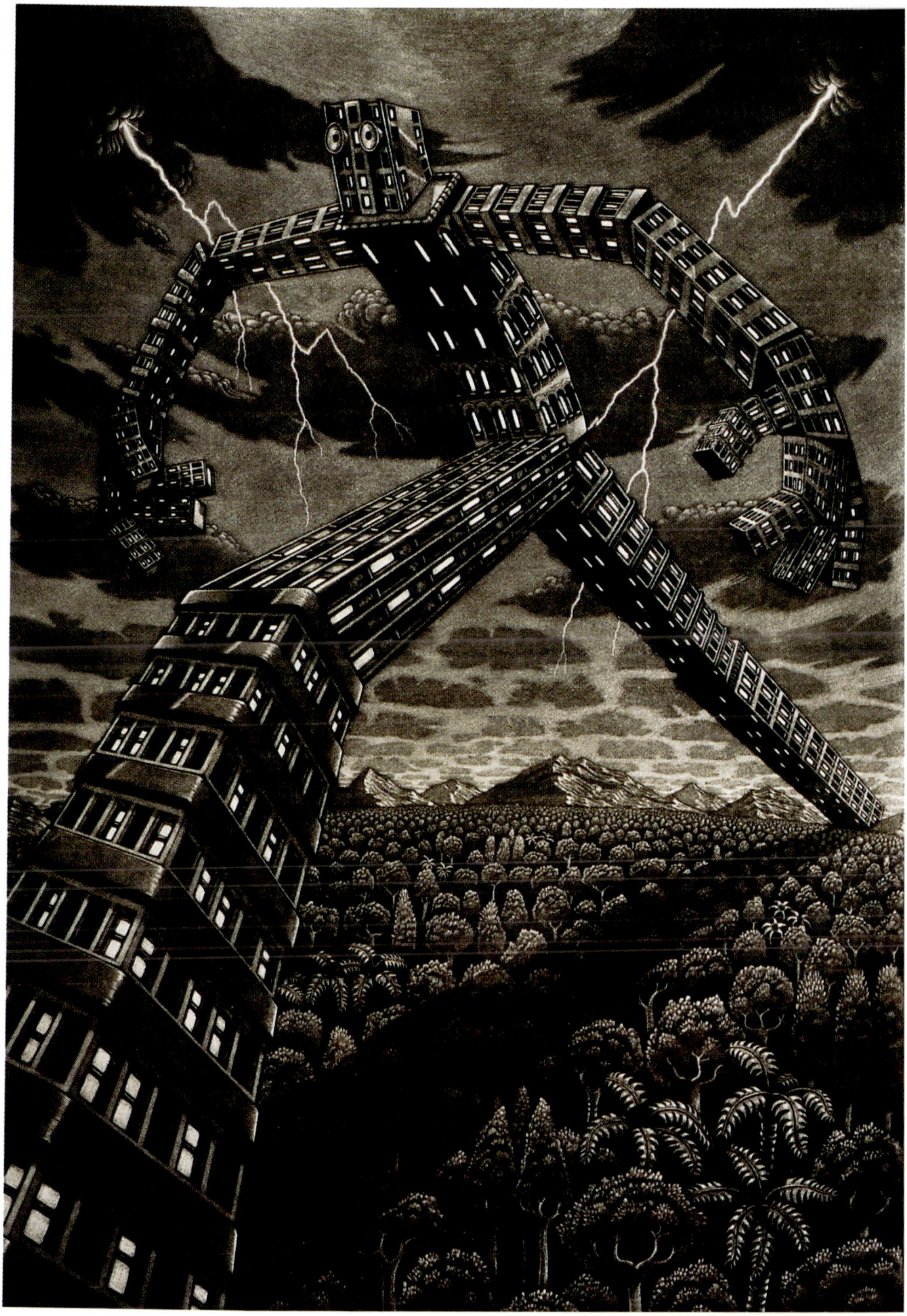

Martin Langford, *It Lives*. Mezzotint, 56.5 x 40 cm (22¼ x 15¾ in.)

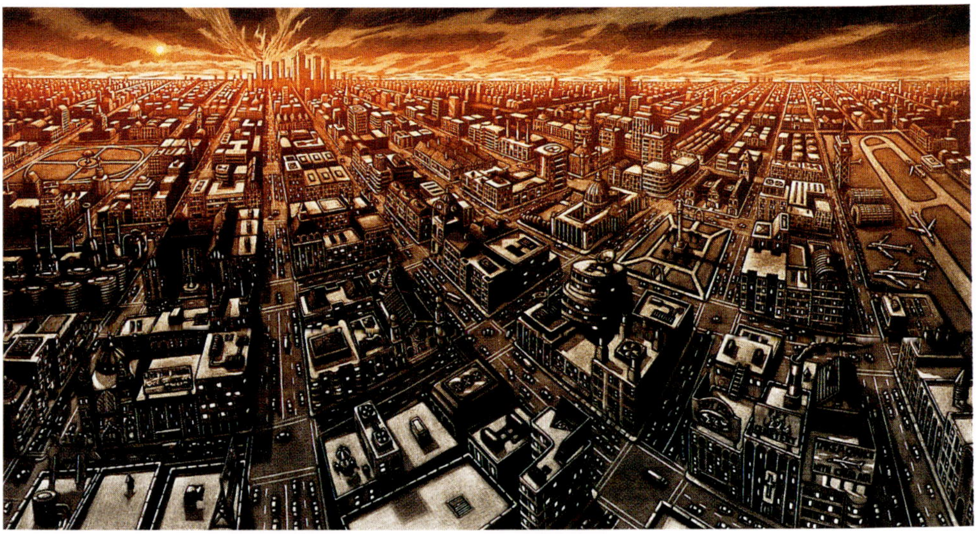

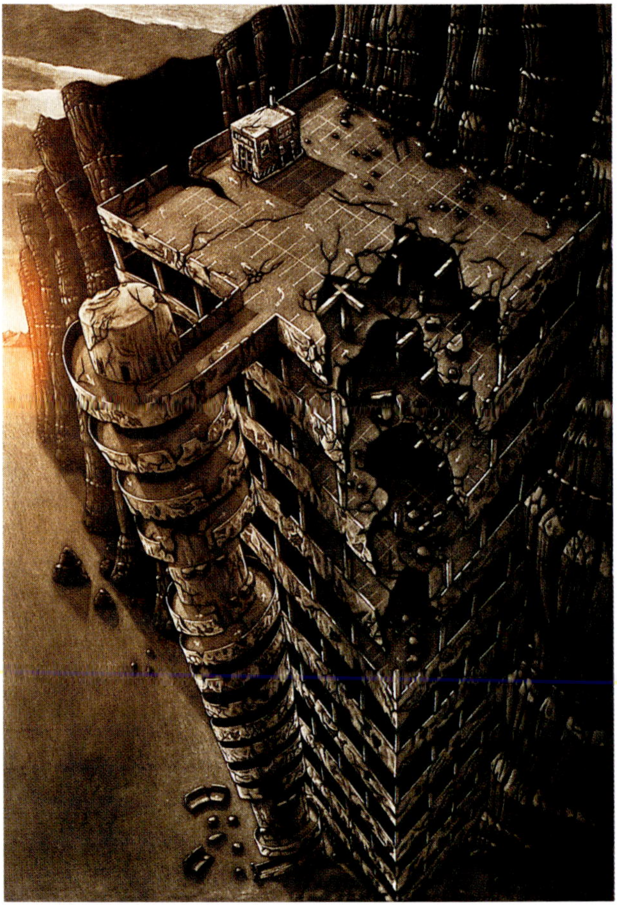

ABOVE Martin Langford, *Thriving*. Mezzotint, 35.5 × 67.5 cm (14 × 26½ in.)

LEFT Martin Langford, *Temple*. Mezzotint, 49 × 34 cm (19¼ × 13½ in.)

mistaking people's identity for inordinately long periods of time. All those looking on collapse into covert fits of laughter while Martin just keeps amiably chatting to the person whom he has convincingly mistaken for a renowned cartoonist or his long-lost auntie. The other day, upon spying a pile of balls, he broke into an impromptu and truly impressive display of four-ball juggling. You never know what Martin is going to do next.

He is now dividing his creative time between mezzotints and etchings but his etchings are as elaborate and painstaking as his mezzotints.

■ FREYA PAYNE

Freya Payne is at the forefront of altering the notion that printmaking should be regarded as a secondary pursuit. In exhibitions of her work, prints are given equal prominence with sculptures and paintings and the relationship is tangible and crucial.

It was as a printmaker that she was first offered a show by Flowers Graphics gallery, after they had seen her degree show at the Royal College of Art in London. She has had regular shows with their sister galleries in central London and Los Angeles, which have made a great feature of the interplay between her paintings and sculptures and her printmaking. These other mediums hugely inform her printmaking and there is a large cross-fertilisation, which is anecdotally evident when details from her sculptures crop up in her prints almost as stage props. This is especially true in her recent works where isolated, apostolic figures are bathed in spotlight imbuing the prints with a sense of theatricality. They resemble Christian icons but without the religious narrative. They are about the process of making art, however, a topic about which Freya is very passionate. She works obsessively, often putting in ten or eleven-hour days with few breaks. As she addresses some of her most deeply-felt concerns, such as her fears over man's 'short-termist' attitudes towards the environment, the work requires a huge level of emotional involvement and often leaves her feeling drained. The time leading up to a major show can be quite torturous.

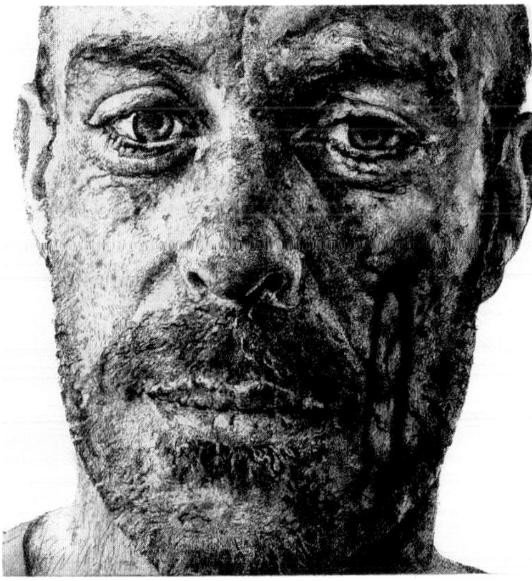

Freya Payne – *King of carrion (T.H.).* Hard ground, drypoint, roulette and spit bite aquatint, 29.5 x 29 cm (11⅗ x 11⅖ in.)

Her pieces often start life as very quick ink drawings. The plate work usually begins with a hard ground etching from which she will take a

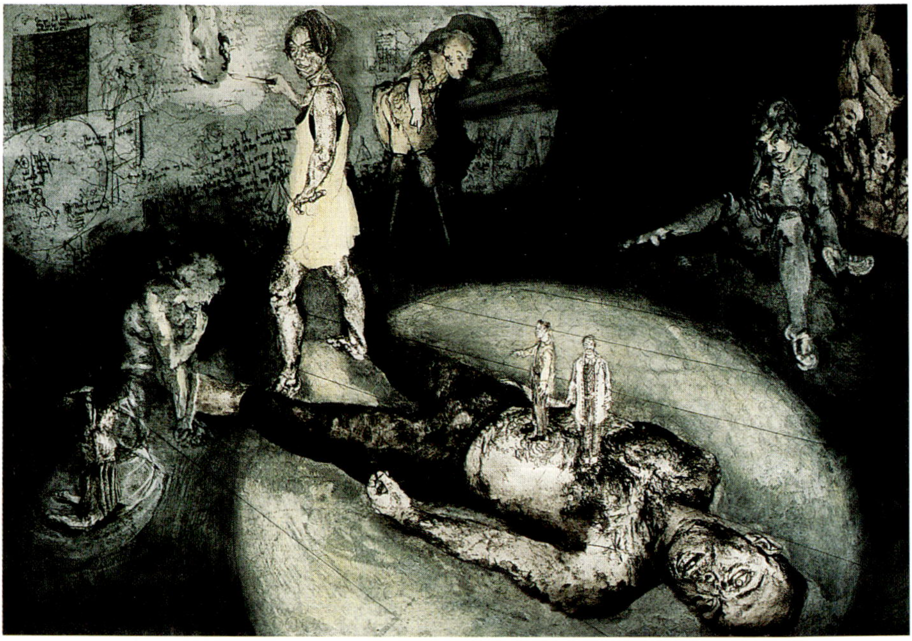

Freya Payne, *Looking for exits II*. Hard ground, drypoint, roulette, aquatint, spit bite and *chine collé*, 40 × 60 cm (15¾ × 23½ in.)

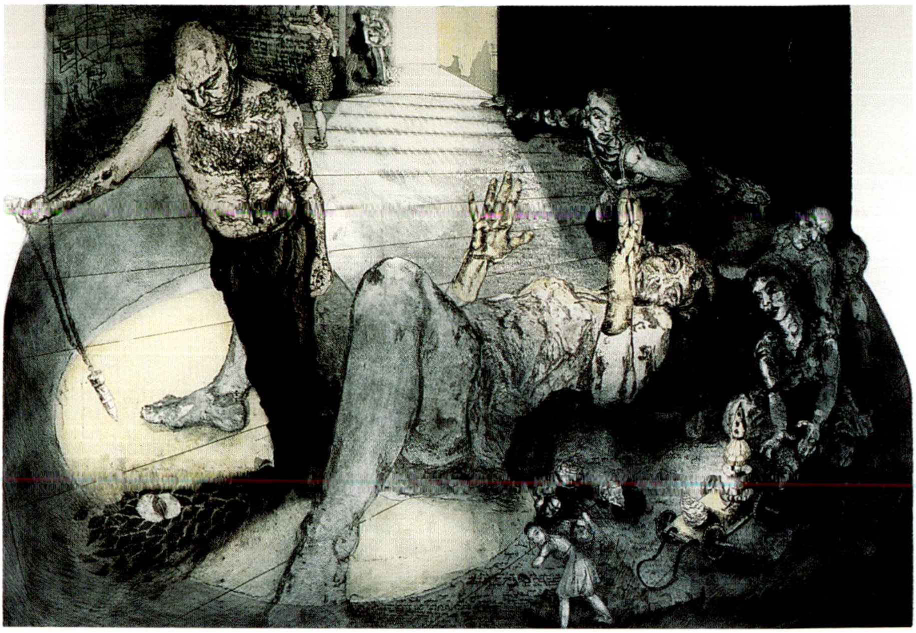

Freya Payne, *Looking for exits IV*. Hard ground, drypoint, roulette, aquatint, spit bite and *chine collé*, 40 × 60 cm (15¾ × 23½ in.)

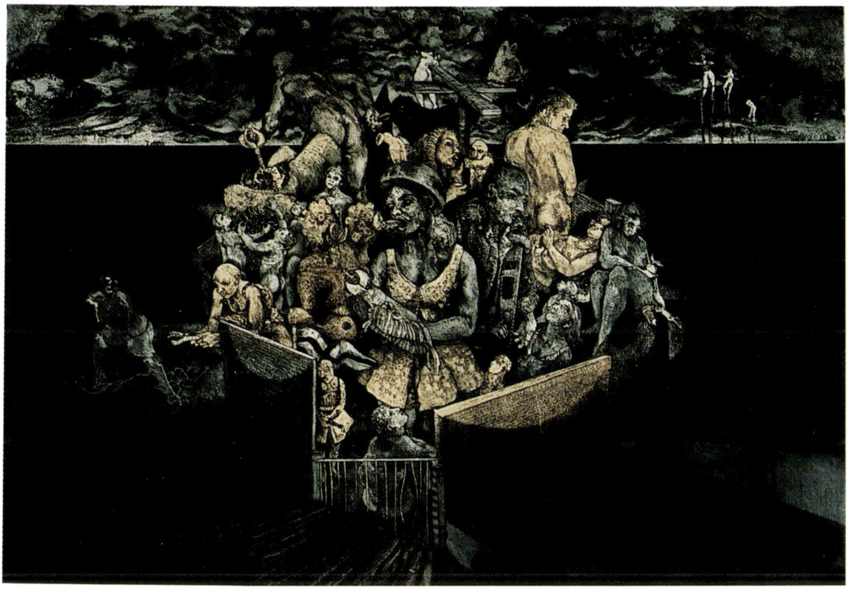

Freya Payne, *The fear of getting lost IX*. Hard ground, drypoint, roulette, aquatint, spit bite and *chine collé*, 40 x 60 cm (15¾ x 23½ in.). Freya has dropped Rhind's stopping-out varnish onto a wet plate and, in some cases, mixed washing-up liquid into the stop out so that it disperses differently.

proof that she augments with brush and ink to plan the next step. She will then build up the image layer by layer, employing a catalogue of techniques. She is not precious about her plates and is fearless about the reworking process even if it necessitates huge and radical alterations using power sanders on pieces that she has worked on extensively. The finished image is enhanced by the journey the plate has taken and it is for this reason that I have used her work to demonstrate plate reworking in a separate section of this book (see pp.67-9).

Freya often employs figurative elements for the focal point for her prints and will work from either photos or drawings. Her models are often recognisable as friends and family members although they are not necessarily intended to be portraits. Other details will come straight from her imagination, sometimes via her own sculptures or paintings. She uses a lot of text in her work, either legibly or solely as texture. She has an incredible facility for writing backwards and will quote lengthy passages either from her sketchbook or random sources or will write stream of consciousness as if drawing.

Her positive character is seemingly so at odds with the intense, haunting qualities in her work that I can only assume that she is able to comprehensively exorcise her demons onto the plate. Freya's work is hugely admired by other artists and is so accomplished that it is hard to believe the levels of creative uncertainty that she suffers. However, if a level of self-doubt is crucial for her to continue to make her etchings then long may she be unaware of the quality of her work.

■ TREVOR PRICE

Trevor did something upon graduating from art school that is surprisingly uncommon these days. He placed the prints of which he was most proud into a portfolio, packed a bag and headed to London to knock on some studio doors offering his services as an apprentice. He worked for two years editioning prints for Brenda Hartill where he learned the printmaking studio practices that he felt were severely lacking from his previous education. Her work is exacting and labour intensive to print and before long he became a very accomplished printer. In addition to this, Brenda's peripatetic style and broad range of techniques inspired him to be an experimental printmaker.

This experimentation has led him, among other things, to two techniques which appear elsewhere in this book: offsetting drypoints onto thick plaster tiles and melting drypoint lines into Perspex sheets with a soldering iron. These discoveries were very much the product of an insatiable desire to find different methods of mark making. It was during an afternoon spent with Anita Klein trying out her technique of making woodcuts with an electric router that Trevor had the moment of revelation that led him to try melting drypoints

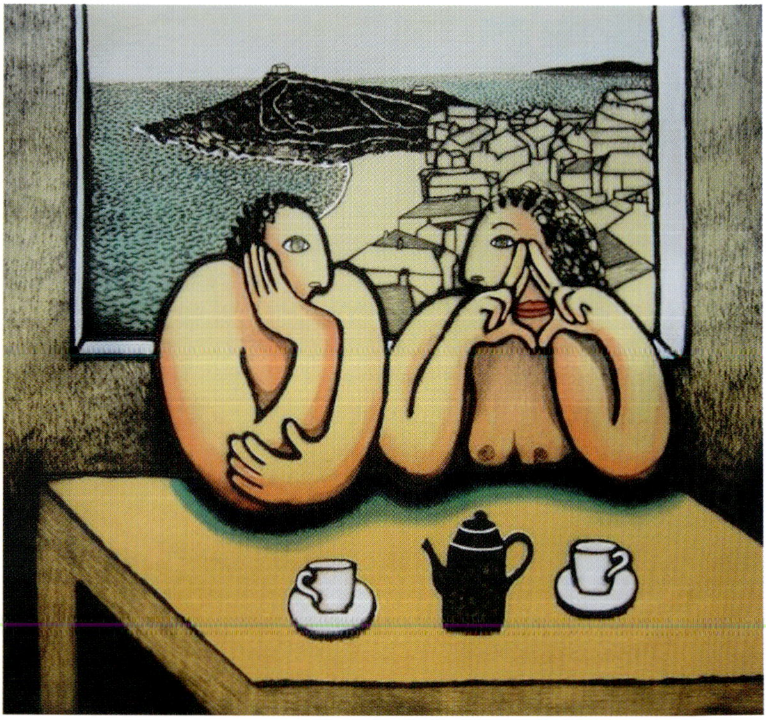

Trevor Price – *Comfortable Silence II.* Drypoint on polycarbonate sheet, 39 x 43 cm (15¼ x 17 in.). Drypoint is done using soldering iron and scribe on plastic sheet. Intaglio lines are inked up in black and then the plate is rolled over the surface using a blended ochre roll with large amounts of extender.

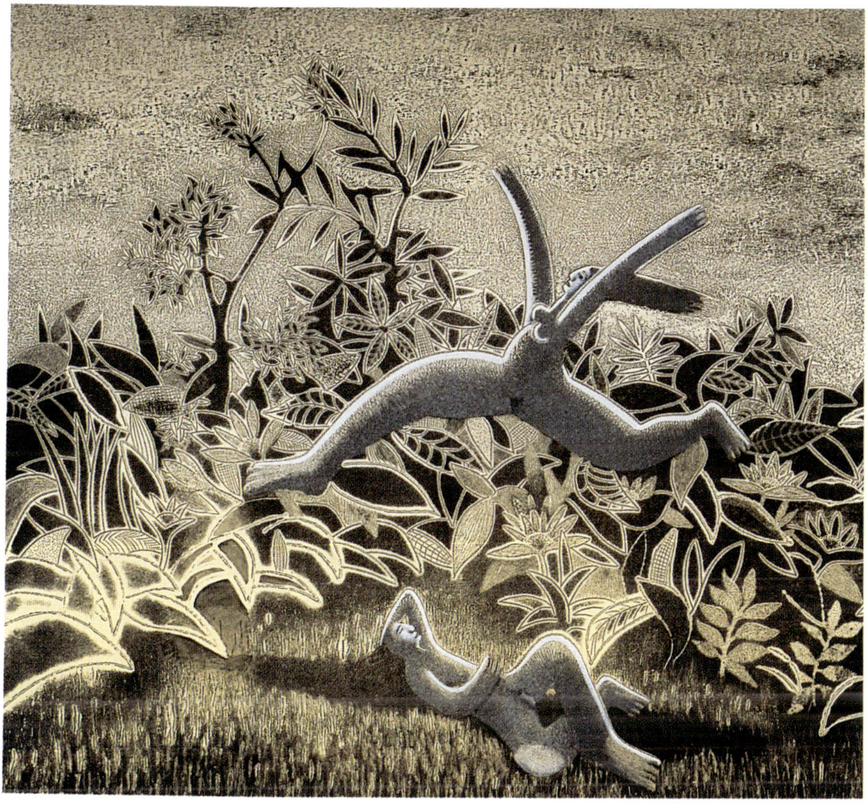

Trevor Price – *While the man sleeps, the woman leaps.* Drypoint on polycarbonate sheet, 39 x 43 cm (15¼ x 17 in.). This plate has been made using Trevor's technique of soldering iron on polycarbonate sheet but the intaglio has then been rolled up in black like a relief print. A second plate is a blank plate with a blended ochre roll once again mixed with large amounts of extender.

into Perspex. Even Trevor cannot identify whether it was the notion of making art with a power tool or something about the quality of the woodcut line that was the exact source of the inspiration but when he returned to his studio he set to work trying out different tools and surfaces.

This technique allows for a very fluid drawing style and he tends to use the soldering iron for the heavier, more dramatic lines and a drypoint scribe for the lighter lines such as the details of the background landscape. As he has perfected the use of the soldering iron he has tried to explore new ways of using this technique to make prints. The purchase of ever-larger rollers, some bordering on completely unwieldy, has enabled him to create large images that combine roll-ups with Perspex drypoint plates. In *While the man sleeps, the woman leaps* (above) he has made the marks with a soldering iron as usual, but has then rolled black ink over the surface of the intaglio lines like a relief print so that all of the marks print in reverse.

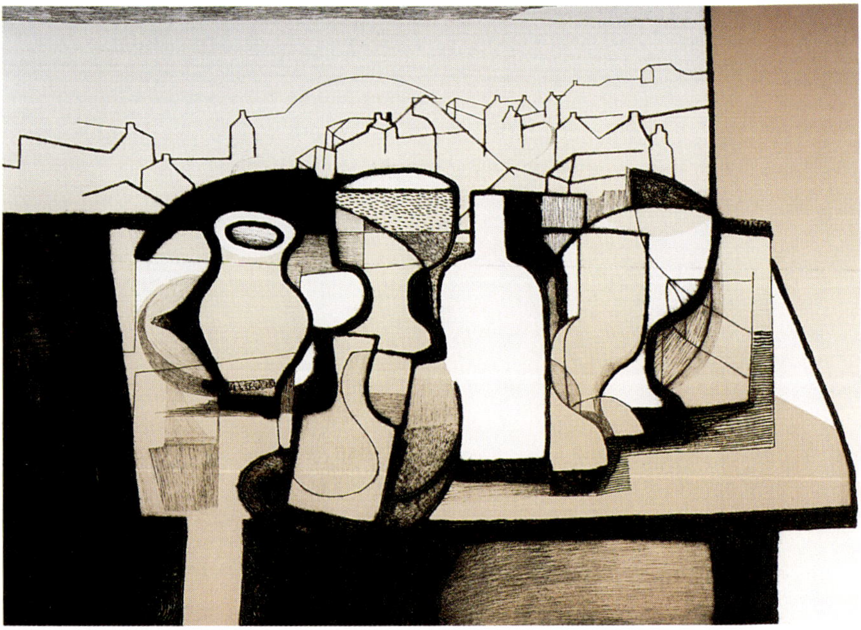

Trevor Price – *Bottles, pots and the ocean II*. Drypoint on polycarbonate sheet, 45 x 69 cm (17¾ x 27 in.). This is a two-plate print. The first is an aluminium plate that has holes cut in it so that some areas will print white. That plate is rolled up with a blended mushroom colour to which is added a great deal of extender. The second plate is a drypoint intaglio plate made using a soldering iron and scribe on Perspex or polycarbonate sheet. This plate is inked up in black.

His imagery typically features landscapes from his childhood in Cornwall, complete with playful references to Ben Nicholson and peopled with stylized figures inspired by Picasso and Rousseau. There is a strong erotic element in many of his pieces as well as a great sense of humour and sometimes the two combine with very amusing consequences.

Trevor is increasingly devoting his time to painting but is always ultimately drawn back to printmaking. Like an adventurer constantly motivated by a map promising as yet undiscovered lands, his inspiration is firmly rooted in the printed image.

■ MARCELLE HANSELAAR

The large studio room where Marcelle Hanselaar works and sleeps is the ideal artistic environment. Infused with natural light from an enormous skylight high above that makes the room glow it opens on to a secluded, urban courtyard filled with greenery and Chinese bonsais. Larger and less constrained than their Japanese cousins, Marcelle prefers her trees more liberated. 'There's something unsettling about those ancient trees forced into unnatural shapes – it's like an 80-year-old with a boob job'. Paintings in progress grace a number of easels in the middle of the room while others lean in groups against the walls awaiting more attention or the decision that they are complete. However, to depict this as the quintessentially bohemian artist's residence is to belie part of Marcelle's nature, as there is a tangible sense of order. Everything has its place and she can immediately lay her hand on anything she requires in a way that is both laudable and enviable.

She left her native Holland when she was in her early twenties and travelled extensively before settling in London in 1979. She not only enjoys being a foreigner, she feels that it is essential to her life and work as it affords her both freedom and privacy. She feels that the baggage of prejudice and cultural stereotyping that one carries about in their native country is as restrictive as a corset. In a social and cultural sense this *otherness* makes her harder to predict or pigeonhole; the only drawback to this is that you end up not truly belonging in either your native or adopted land.

Marcelle has been painting for years but took up printmaking relatively recently. This was in response to a period of personal crisis where she rediscovered drawing, which she had not done with such intensity since she was a child. She worked compulsively in an unconscious and unpremeditated manner on reams of drawings that were to form the backbone of her *Petite Mort*

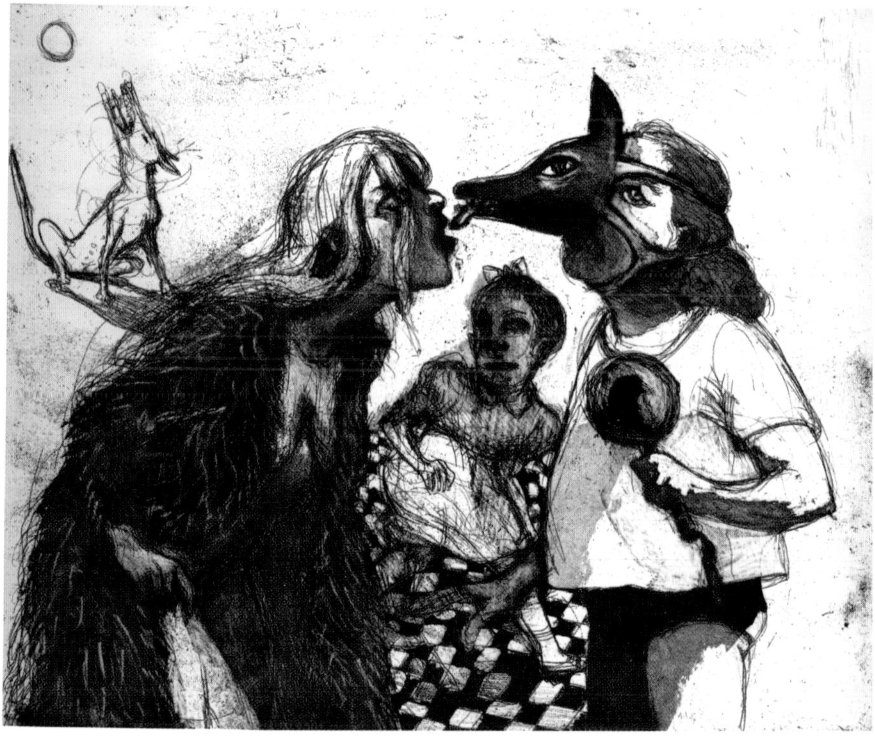

Marcelle Hanselaar – *Lot's Wife*. Hard ground, aquatint and spit bite, 21 × 26 cm (8¼ × 10¼ in.) There is a beautiful use of burnishing in the aquatint on the fur coat.

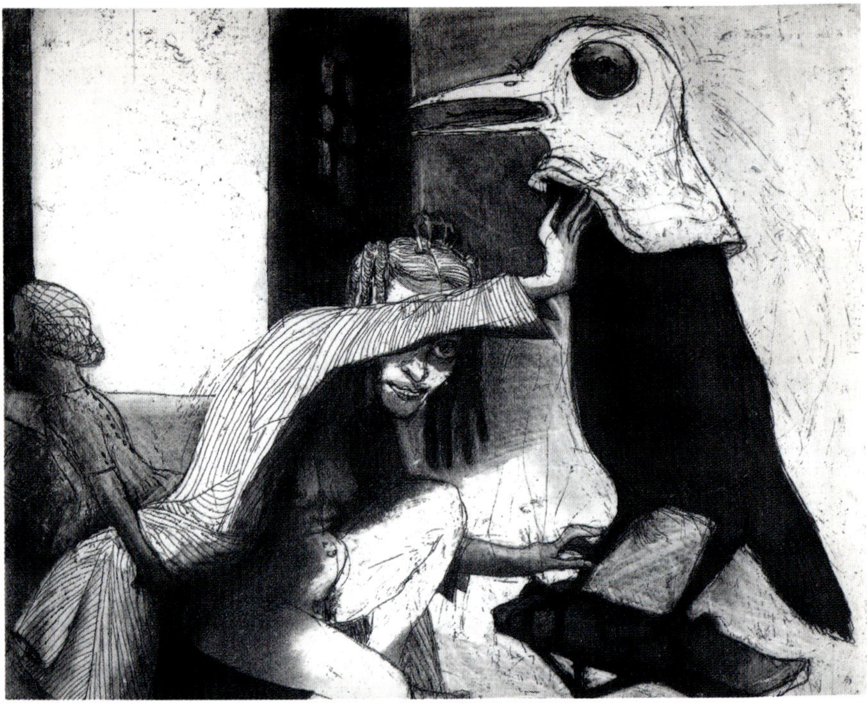

Marcelle Hanselaar – *Petite Mort 10*. Hard ground, aquatint and spit bite, 20 x 25 cm (7⁵⁄₁₆ x 9⁵⁄₁₆ in.). Marcelle uses nitric acid for her spit biting but does not use a surface tension breaker.

series of etchings. These cathartic images examine her observations about the female psyche and sexuality coupled with reflections upon her childhood but with dark and haunting overtones. All 19 prints in this series were created in an intense three-month period and to this day she still works in attacks between painting and printmaking.

She always starts with a hard ground and works directly onto the plate with no preparatory drawings and often not even a notion of what she intends to draw. She works in layers and will sometimes do as many as five overlapping hard ground stages. She will then apply aquatint, also often in three or more stages. 'Aquatint can cover a host of sins on a plate – everything but bad drawing.' She works on four or five plates simultaneously and some of the results she achieves are the product of one plate being forgotten in the acid while she is working on another. She works completely from her imagination referring only occasionally to her own body for anatomical guidance. Where her work appears carefully observed it is solely because she is an avid voyeur with a very acute visual memory. Random elements from her everyday life find their way into her imagery sometimes just as props. Her work often depicts skewed scenes of bourgeois life where everything is not quite what it seems. Her etchings always centre on figures as she thinks of the body as a 'dramatic tool of theatre' and finds figures intensely moving.

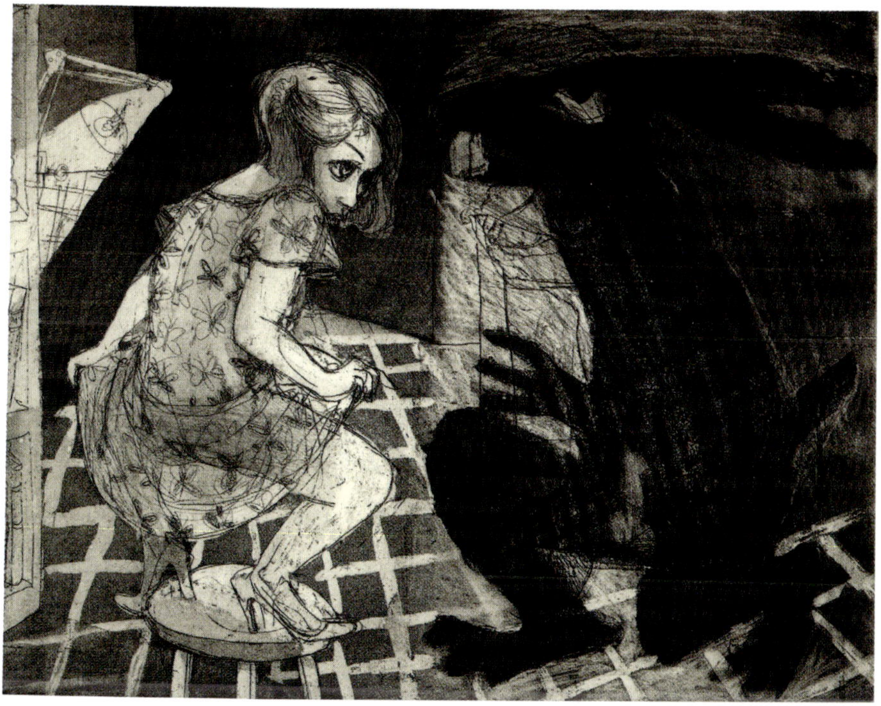

Marcelle Hanselaar – *Petite Mort 19*. Hard ground, aquatint and spit bite, 20 × 25 cm (7⁵⁄₁₆ × 9⁵⁄₁₆ in.). There was extensive reworking of this plate and the previous hard ground drawing of the rabbit is still visible.

In her art as in her life Marcelle is inspired and moved by conflict and is constantly looking towards the next hurdle. 'With every new thing I do have to raise the bar, even if it is only by a millimetre. I need to be constantly challenged.'

■ Mychael Barratt

I was painting and working as a freelance illustrator when I happened upon an exhibition of Chris Orr's etchings that was completely revelatory. The unique nature of the raised intaglio marks and the potential for intense chiaroscuro were inspirational. Storytelling is hugely important to my work and the fact that the process in every intaglio piece can be read in a narrative manner may also have been one of the things that motivated me to take up this medium. I enrolled in an etching course at a London art college.

London is the ideal location for the narrative artist. From Milton and Shakespeare to Dickens and Wilde there is scarcely a great storyteller in the English language who did not live and work there at some point. Every building is permeated with a sense of history whether or not its façade is adorned by one of English Heritage's ubiquitous blue plaques signifying some long-departed, remarkable inhabitant. I have had that immigrant's zeal for London ever since I

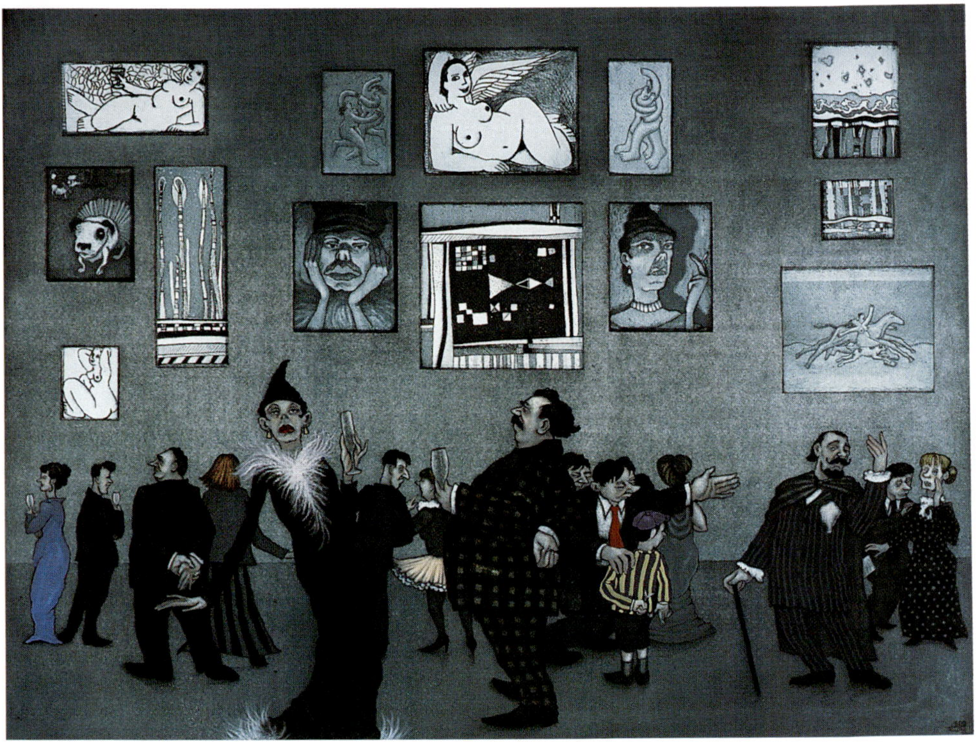

Mychael Barratt – *Private View*. Soft ground, hard ground and aquatint, 50 × 66 cm (19⅔ × 26 in.). This is actually a 14-plate etching as all of the pictures on the wall at the exhibition are separate plates. The small plates are printed the first time through the press and the large plate the second. The small plates were done by Brenda Hartill, Anita Klein, Trevor Price and myself.

decided to indefinitely extend my residency during what was meant to be a two week visit from Canada. The beauty and variety of the buildings and the constantly surprising vistas have provided more than merely a backdrop to the drama depicted in the foreground of my prints; they have become equal players.

Anecdotal incidents from my day-to-day life are at the heart of my work and I gather, hoard and use random overheard phrases and scenes like a magpie. I jokingly claim to have 'Media Tourette's Syndrome', as references to films, books and paintings almost involuntarily spill into my work. This was the origin of the *Life Imitating Art* series of etchings, in which figures unabashedly lifted from art historical sources inhabit London scenes that all have some personal resonance. Although these allusions are made in a light-hearted spirit, they almost invariably relate to my favourite artists' work and as such are meant as acts of homage.

Before I started to work on this book, I primarily used soft ground drawn lines combined with aquatint to create my images. Partly as a challenge and partly to better enable me to understand and explain them, I decided to try out every one of the techniques that I was writing about. Some of them, such as

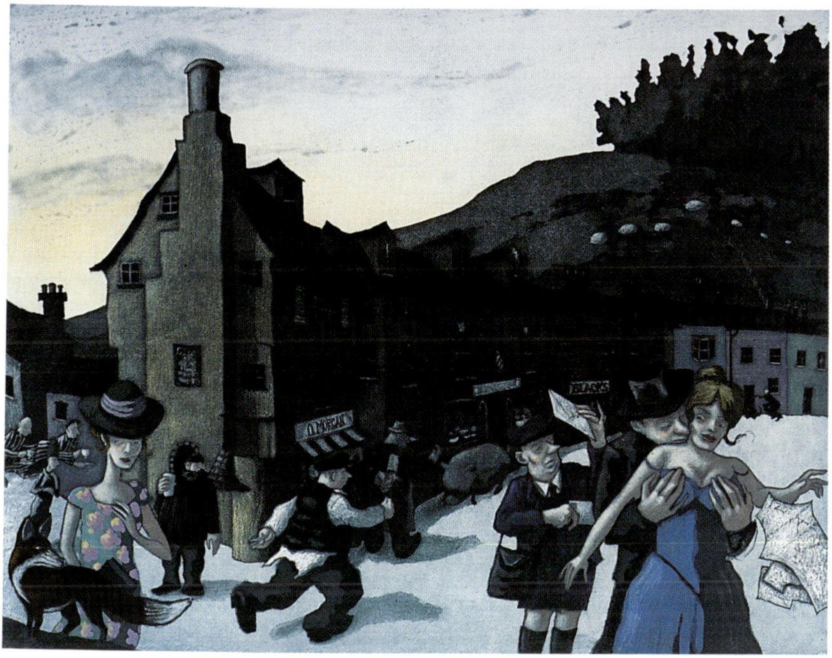

Mychael Barratt – *Under Milk Wood I*. Soft ground, aquatint and spit bite, 38 × 50 cm (15 × 19⅔ in.)

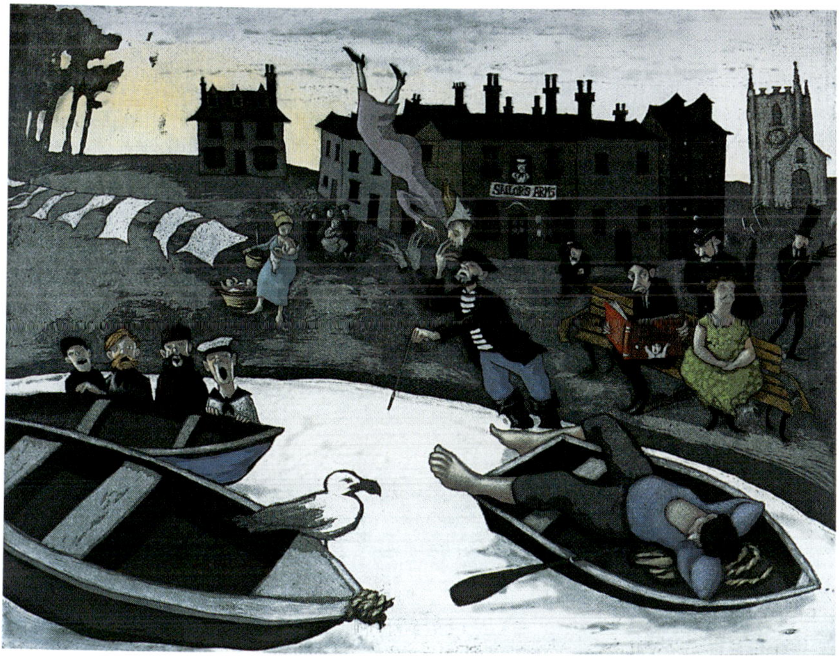

Mychael Barratt – *Under Milk Wood II*. Soft ground, aquatint and spit bite, 38 × 50 cm (15 × 19⅔ in.)

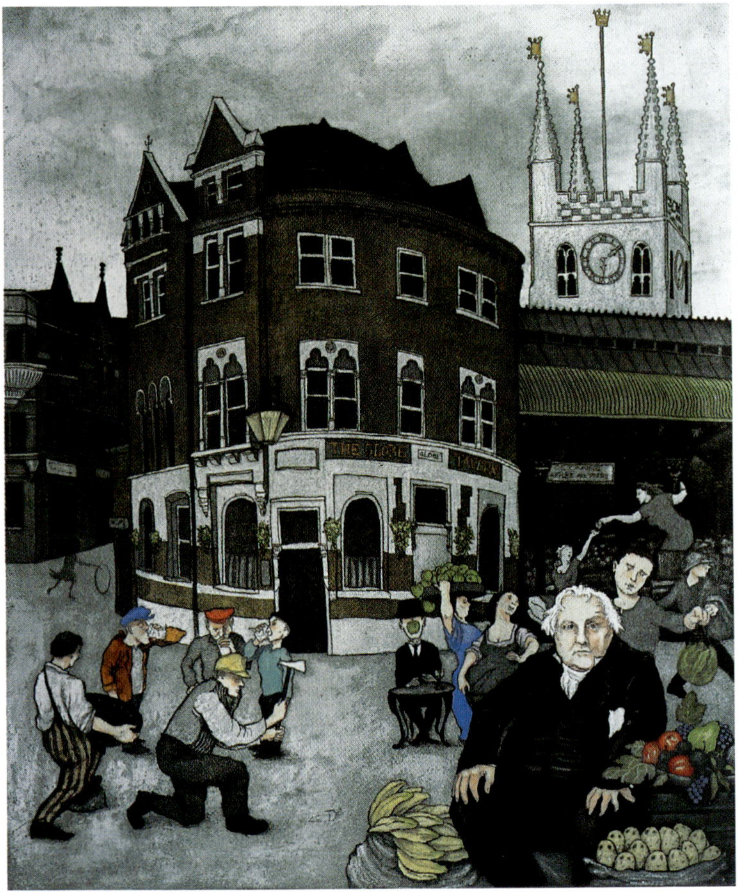

Mychael Barratt – *Life Imitating Art I*. Soft ground, aquatint and spit bite, 50 x 40 cm (19⅔ x 15¾ in.)

drypoint, sugar lift and mezzotint I feel certain I will be using more extensively in the future. In other cases, I have gained enough respect for the techniques that I will persevere with them even though they have not yet hooked me.

I constantly have many projects on the go and in the case of the more complicated images I will sometimes work on the preliminary drawings for a year or more. *All the World's a Stage* is an example of this long process of gathering and assembling vignettes. Shakespeare is depicted on his way to work at the Globe Theatre and pauses to quickly make some notes as he passes a number of people and scenes that have inspired him. This is not surprising as in every corner on the street he is surrounded by people and other paraphernalia that refer to all 37 of his plays.

This is very much in the nature of self-portraiture as this is how I view my own life and work: meandering through surroundings quite literally teeming with potential inspiration.

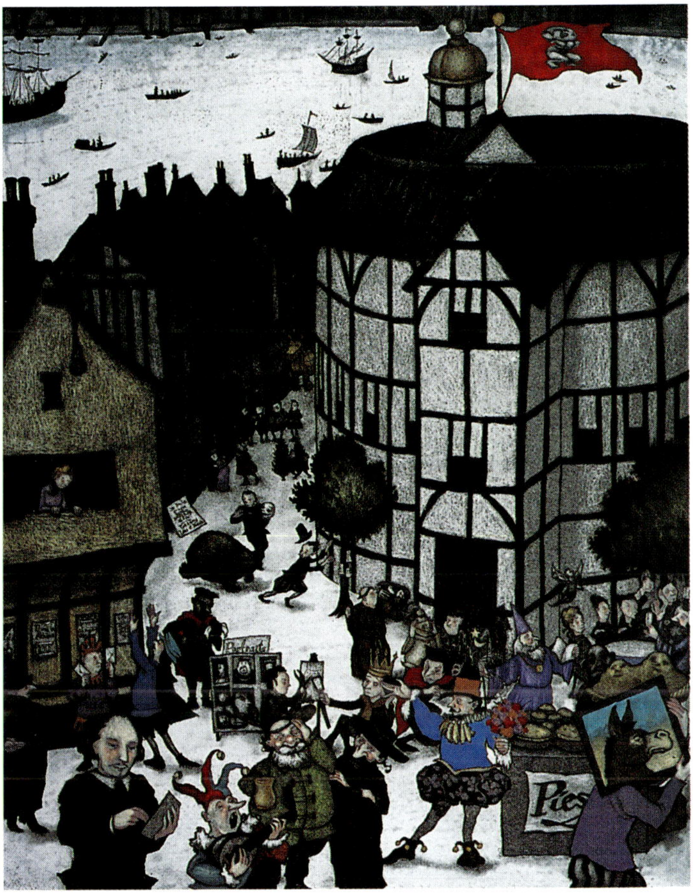

Mychael Barratt – *All the World's a Stage*. Soft ground, aquatint and spit bite, 50 × 40 cm ($19^{2}/_{3}$ × $15^{3}/_{4}$ in.). The majority of my work featured in this book has some elements of hand colouring. I use Schminke watercolours, which allow for both opaque and translucent application. Providing the print is completely dry you can even paint washes on very dense aquatints.

■ CONCLUSION

My major goal in writing this book was to impart printmaking techniques with which I was reasonably familiar and to introduce others that were new to me. I hoped that other artists would be inspired to try out some of the techniques described. What I had not counted on was how inspired I would be by the skill, craftsmanship and dedication that I was to find in the artists I encountered. Pick up a burin and give engraving a try and you will see what I am talking about.

Although we all settle into comfortable working practices, there is no artist like the printmaker where improvisation and assimilation are concerned. I believe that with patience and perseverance all of the techniques in this book can be learned if not necessarily mastered. Above all else, accept the direction that the medium dictates: great prints include everything from happy accident to pure invention.

GLOSSARY

A la poupée Using a small balled up piece of scrim or a 'dolly' to selectively ink up specific areas of a plate in different colours
Aquatint Etching on a metal plate to create tonal areas
Arkansas stone Tool used to sharpen engraving burins and mezzotint rockers
Brasso Liquid used to polish metal plates
Burin Engraving tool with angled, square or lozenge shaped end
Burnisher Steel tool used to selectively polish plates, especially mezzotints and aquatints
Chine-collé A print is transferred to a delicate piece of paper which is glued at the time of printing to a heavier piece of paper
Counterproofing Printing directly from a second print rather than a plate
Dabber Tool with a leather covered pad attached to a handle used for inking plates
Degreasing Removing grease from metal plates – essential for etching processes
Dolly A piece of scrim rolled and taped into a pencil shape is used to apply ink to specific areas of a plate in the technique '*a la poupée*'
Drypoint Direct intaglio technique where lines are incised on metal plates
Drypoint scribe Tool used for making drypoints – also called a Hayden's Point
Embossing Printing from an uninked plate
Engraving Intaglio technique where lines are incised using a burin
Etch Process where a mordant such as acid or ferric chloride is used to chemically alter the metal plate
Fablon® Trade name for a adhesive plastic covering ideal for protecting the back of metal plates before etching
Feathering A long feather is used to clear air bubbles from the surface of a plate as it is being etched
Ferrario® Trade name for a fixitive spray used for transferring photocopies onto metal plates
Ferric chloride Chemical used to etch metal plates – see mordant
Ground Wax-based acid resist which covers the front of plates in etching
Hand colouring Tinting or painting applied to dried prints
Hand wiping Technique used in printing to remove final traces of ink and plate tone
Hard ground Wax-based acid resist which dries hard and brittle
Hayden point Tool used for making drypoints – see 'drypoint scribe'
India stone Tool used to sharpen engraving burins and mezzotint rockers
Intaglio Print where the ink is held in marks or lines cut or etched into metal plates
Lavender oil Applied to hard ground to expose metal to acid – also called 'Oil of spike lavender'

Lithographic crayon Waxy substance drawn on as stop-out on aquatints or as a sugar lift tool
Methylated spirits Solvent used for removing aquatint rosin and straw hat varnish
Mezzotint Prints where drawings are burnished into plates that have been uniformly roughened to print black
Mordant Liquid that chemically alters metal plates – types include ferric chloride and nitric acid
Neoprene foam Foam blanket used for offsetting onto plaster tiles
Nitric acid Chemical used to etch metal plates – see mordant
Offset Printing from a print rather than a plate – see counterproofing
Oil of spike lavender Strong solvent , also called 'Lavender oil'
Open bite Areas on a metal plate exposed to very strong acid
Perspex® Trade name for plastic sheets used for drypoints
Polycarboate sheet Plastic sheet used for drypoints – see 'Perspex'
Registration Term for consistent placement of the printed image on printing paper and also for correct alignment of plates in multi-plate etchings
Registration blocks Heavy pieces of metal used to align plates for multi-plate etching
Relief print In intaglio terms, when an etched or engraved plate is rolled up with ink so that the ink sits on the surface
Rocker Tool used to roughen up plates for mezzotints
Rocking pattern Drawn, systematic pattern to aid rocking of mezzotints
Roller Rubber or leather cylinder attached to a handle used for rolling ink or grounds onto plates
Rosin Powder baked onto plates to create aquatints
Roulette Wheel covered with raised teeth, used to draw on plates
Scraper Tool with straight sharp edges used to scrape the surface of plates
Scrim Starched muslin used to remove excess ink from intaglio plates
Soft ground Wax-based acid resist that stays soft and pliable
Soldering iron Electric tool used to melt intaglio lines into Perspex
Spit bite Technique where mordant is painted directly onto aquatinted metal plate
Stipple engraving Technique where burin is used to create dots rather than lines
Stopping-out varnish Turps-based acid-resist used to selectively prevent plates from etching
Straw hat varnish Methylated spirit-based acid-resist used to selectively prevent plates from etching
Sugar lift Sugar-based liquid painted onto metal plate and removed once the surrounding areas have been protected
Tarlatan See 'scrim'
Tissue-wiping Plate wiping technique used to remove final excess traces of ink and plate tone

BIBLIOGRAPHY

Leaf, Ruth; *Etching, Engraving and Other Intaglio Printmaking Techniques*, Watson-Guptill Publications, New York,1976.

Smith, Alan; *Etching, A Guide to Traditional Techniques*, Crowood Press, Rambsury, Marlborough, 2004

Wax, Carol; *The Mezzotint, History and Technique*, Harry N. Abrams, Inc; New York 1990

SUPPLIERS

■ UK

W&S Allely Ltd
PO Box 58
Alma Street
Smethwick
West Midlands B66 2RP
Tel: 0121 558 3301
Copper and aluminium sheet

Art Equipment
3 Craven Street
Northampton NN1 3EZ
+44 (0) 1604 632 447
Etching presses

Artichoke Print Workshop
Unit S1, Bizspace
245a Coldharbour Lane
London SW9 8RR
Tel: 020 7924 0600
www.printbin.co.uk
Suppliers of etching blankets and the KB etching press.
Editoning services and open access workshop

Mati Basis
13 Cranbourne Road
London N10 2BT
(0) 20 8444 7833
Steel-facing copper plates

Bay Plastics Ltd
Unit H1, High Flatworth
Tyne Tunnel Trading Estate
North Shields
Tyne & Wear
(0) 191 258 0777
enquiries@bayplastics.co.uk
Polycarbonate sheets for drypoint with soldering iron

R.K. Burt & Company Ltd
57 Union Street
London SE1 1SG
rkburt.co.uk
+44 (0) 207 407 6474
Paper suppliers

Cornelissen
105 Great Russell Street
London WC1V 3RY
cornelissen.com
Printmaking supplies

Chris Holladay
Modbury Engineering
1, The Tanneries
East Street
Titchfield
Hampshire PO14 4AR
Tel: 01329 841000
Press engineer

Hunter Penrose
32 Southwark Street
London SE1 1TU
hunterpenrose.co.uk
+44 (0) 207 407 5051
Supplies and presses

Intaglio Printmakers
62 Southwark Bridge Road,
London SE1 0AS
intaglioprintmaker.com
+44 (0) 207 928 2633
Printmaking supplies

Sean Kelly
21 London Road
London SE1 6JX
(0) 20 7928 9722
Art supplies including Ferrario Fixitive Spray

Paupers Press & Publications
45 Coronet Street
London N1 6HD
(0) 20 7729 5272
pauper@talk21.com
Print editioning

John Pears
5 Witton DRive
Spennymoor
County Durham DL16 6LU
Tel: 01388 818004
Press engineer and manufacturer

John Purcell Paper
15 Rumsey Road
London SW9 0TR
johnpurcell.net
+44 (0) 207 737 5199
Paper supplies

Richards of Hull
Unit 1, Acorn Estate
Bontoft Avenue
Hull HU5 4HF
Tel: 01482 442422
www.richards.co.uk
Tailor made acid baths, sinks, ventilation and extraction units

Harry F. Rochat Ltd
15a Moxon Street
Barnet
Hertfordshire EN5 5TS
harryrochat.com
+44 (0) 208 449 0023
Etching presses

Rollaco Engineering
72 Thornfield Road
Middlesborough
Cleveland TS5 5BY
Tel: 01642 813785
www.rollaco.co.uk
Press manufacturers. Suppliers of rollers, tools and inks

Smiths Metal Centres
42-56 Tottenham Road
London N1 4BZ
(0) 20 7241 2430
london@smithmetal.com
Metal sheets including aluminium, copper and steel

T.N. Lawrence and Son Ltd
(mail order)
208 Portland Road
Hove BN3 5QT
lawrence.co.uk
+44 (0) 1273 260 260
or 0845 644 3232
Printmaking supplies

■ Finland

Hale Press
T:mi Hannu Lepannen F:a
Kaarlontie 35
46800 Anjalankoski
halepress.com
+358 (0) 5365 6570
Etching presses

■ France

Boutique Charbonnel
13 Quai de Montebello
75005 Paris
Printmaking supplies

Joop Stoop
12 Rue le Brun
75013 Paris
joopstoop.com
+33 (1) 5543 8996
Ink and paper

Netherlands

Polymetaal
Evertsenstraat 69C
Leiden 2315 SK
polymetaal.nl
+31 (7) 1522 2681
Printmaking equipment

Australia

Melbourne Etching Supplies
33a St. David Street
Fitzroy
Melbourne, Vic 3065
mes.net.au
+61 (3) 9419 5666
Etching supplies

Future Engineering
Unit 4/93 Kew Street
Welshpool
Perth, WA 6106
futureeng.com.au
+61 (8) 9470 3540
Etching presses

Art Equipment
33 Jarrah Drive
Braeside, Vic 3195
Etching presses

Blue Lake Papermill
5 Pollard Close
Mount Gambier, SA 5290
wilsonme@dodo.com.au
+61 (8) 8725 2393
Handmade paper

Mitomel International
PO Box 475
Torrensville Plaza, SA 5031
mitomel.com
+61 (8) 8234 9400
Printmaking supplies

Canada

Praga
50 Coronation Drive Unit 17
Toronto
Ontario MIE 4X6
praga.com
1 800 844 9421 or 416 281 0511
Printmaking supplies

USA

The Graphic Chemical & Ink Company
PO Box 278
Villa Park
Illinois, 60181
graphicchemical.com
1 800 465 7382
Printmaking supplies

Z* Acryl
PO Box 464
Deerfield
Illinois 60015
1 800 651 7975
Progressive etching supplies

Daniel Smith Inc.
4150 1st Avenue South
Seattle

Washington, 98134
danielsmith.com
(206) 223 9599
Printmaking supplies

Rembrandt Graphic Arts
PO Box 130
Rosemont
New Jersey 08556
rembrandtgraphicarts.com
1 800 622 1887

Edward Lyons
3646 White Plains Road
Bronx
New York 10467
eclyons.com
(718) 881 7270
Printmaking engraving tools

Renaissance Graphic Arts Inc.
69 Steamwhistle Drive
Ivyland
Pennsylvania 18974
printmaking-materials.com
1 888 833 3398

McClain's Printmaking Supplies
15685 SW 116th Avenue PMB202
King City
Oregon 97224
imcclains.com
1 503 641 3555

Gale Force Graphics
PO Box 667
Chouteau
Oklahoma 74337
galeforcegraphics.com
(918) 479 2502
Printmaking supplies

Takach Press
3207 Morningside NE
Albuquerque
New Mexico 87100
takachpress.com
1 800 248 3460
Etching presses

Griffin Printing Presses
1745 International Boulevard
Oakland
California 94606
(510) 533 0600

Ethan Etching Presses
La Jolla
California 92037

Printmakers Machine
724 N. Yale Avenue
PO Box 7191
Villa Park
Illinois 6018
printmakersmachine.com
800 992 5970
(630) 832 4888
Etching presses

INDEX